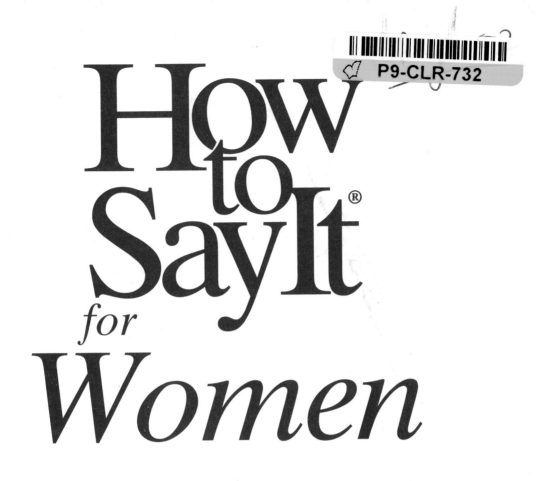

How to Say It for Women

Phyllis Mindell, Ed.D.

Prentice Hall Press

A member of Penguin Putnam Inc.
375 Hudson Street
New York, New York 10014

www.penguinputnam.com

Previously published as *A Woman's Guide to the Language of Success, Revised and Expanded*

Library of Congress Cataloging-in-Publication Data

Mindell, Phyllis.
    How to say it for women / Phyllis Mindell.
        p.   cm.
    Rev. ed. of: A woman's guide to the language of success.
    Includes bibliographical references and index.
    ISBN 0-7352-0222-2 (pbk.)
    1. Business communication.   2. Business presentations.   3. Businesswomen.   4. Self-
esteem.   5. Language and languages—Sex differences.   I. Mindell, Phyllis. Woman's guide
to the language of success.   II. Title.

HF5718.M553   2001
650.1—dc21   00-046517

Printed in the United States of America

10

To Arye

Acknowledgments

If I'm the mother of my book, it has many midwives: Marvin I. Mindell, who nurtures even my wildest ideas; Joe Mindell and Ossie Borosh, whose marriage spurred my creativity; David Mindell, who sharpens my thinking on all issues; Ruth Mills, who envisioned a structure that would work; B. K. Nelson, who bridges the gap between author and publisher; Ellen Schneid Coleman, who has ably edited two of my books; Kathleen Barry Albertini and Roberta Schwartz, who read and suggested improvements to this edition; and the thousands of women who so generously told their stories of language and power at work.

Dr. Virginia Phelan has been Charlotte to my Wilbur as I wrote this book. She's both a true friend and a good writer.

Preface

This book began in 1989 at a forum titled "Power." A speaker announced that, at his workplace, "Nobody listens to women." I bristled and thought, That's not true. People listen to some women. Then I asked, "Why do people listen to some women and not to others? What is different about women who are listened to? Can other women model themselves after those whose voices are heard? Do women have to act like men to command respect and attention?"

The answer began to unfold the next weekend when a young friend visited with her copy of *Charlotte's Web*. As I reread this beloved classic, I realized that Charlotte was a female to whom people listened; furthermore, she used the language of power in a fully feminine way. No warrior she, no master of machismo, Charlotte chose to use her power to do good in the world: to save the life of Wilbur, the runt of the litter. Could working women do the same?

Just as Charlotte sent Templeton to seek words for her webs, so I sent myself to the research library to learn about the language of women and the language of weakness. I also listened and read, seeking examples of strong and weak business communications. It soon became clear that, despite the unresolved controversies that swirl around issues of language and power, we can furnish practical, usable tips that can help working women gain confidence, respect, and success by changing their language.

As I traveled around the world, listening to working women at every level, I saw that we all hunger for language tools that will empower us to work, to communicate, and to lead with confidence. So I designed a workshop titled "Woman Language, Woman Power: What Charlotte Teaches Us." Women flocked to the workshops, eager to learn and eager to tell their tales, whether they were "horror stories" or stories of triumph. I collected these stories and noted recurring patterns: whether a woman is a secretary or a CEO, she faces common language issues at work.

Experience also showed the error in the thinking that says, "You can't change your language style." You can change your language style, for the better, and you can do so more easily than you can change almost anything else in your life. What's more, when language becomes a success agent, confidence grows, and with it the courage to say and do things you would have feared before. It's brought joy to hear the stories of the small and large victories of the women with whom I've worked for over a decade. Whether in the executive suite or the clerical pool, success breeds confidence. Confidence, in turn, breeds success.

Then, in March 1993, I attended a lecture by a well-known feminist. Nearly every audience question referred to language. One woman spoke of the message of the romance novels she and friends read. Another asked what to say when she's harassed by fellow students. Another wanted to know how to appear strong without being called aggressive. Still another spoke of her lack of confidence. Their questions confirmed my resolve to write this book.

The 1995 edition won national and international recognition. Reviews in *The New York Times*, the Gannett newspapers, and other papers, magazines, and radio and television programs resulted in sales all over the world. Letters and e-mails arrived from places as far away as Pago Pago. A German edition was scheduled. And the book continues to inspire women, to provoke discussion groups, to reach out to men as well as to women.

Now it's a delight to offer the new edition, true to the original vision but revised, updated, and expanded. The new section on interviewing skills corrects an oversight; many women have requested tips on successful interviewing. The new chapter on leadership offers ideas that have emerged as a result of additional research and work with women who lead or strive to lead in the future. The accompanying Leadership Evaluation has proved its worth as the first nonjudgmental way to evaluate leaders' skills.

The Web and accompanying e-commerce advances also spurred updated discussions of on-line communications and a new section on rapid reading and search on the Web.

Julia Penelope asserted that "Language is power, in ways more literal than most people think. When we speak, we exercise the power of language to transform reality." As women, we seek to transform the realities of our workplaces so that we can gain success, confidence, and power while retaining our femininity and integrity. This book showed how in 1995 and continues to do so in this new edition. As always, I welcome your comments, ideas, and criticism.

How to Say It® for Women is not a book about politics, nor does it lay out a particular philosophy. It taps ideas and quotations by men as well as by women (good ideas are gender-free). It's a strictly practical, usable book about language that works and language that leads. It's full of true stories told by women and about women. Enjoy it as you learn from it.

What the Language of Success Will Do for You

This book shows you how to use the language of power to succeed at work. We begin with the last two sentences of the beloved classic, *Charlotte's Web*: "It is not often that someone comes along who is a true friend and a good writer. Charlotte was both." Women who work can be both true friends and good writers. We can be powerful and good at the same time . . . and we can emulate Charlotte and other heroes both real and imagined as we shed the language of weakness and weave the language of power.

Why Charlotte? Like your workplace, her barn was a difficult and not necessarily humane place, in which the profit motive prevailed. Still, she managed to grow, to lead, to nurture, to protect the weak, to gain the cooperation of unwilling workers, and to persuade those in powerful positions. Like Charlotte, you face the challenge of accomplishing what you set out to do in the workplace. And, like Charlotte, you can do so confidently by harnessing the power of language. *How to Say It® for Women* shows you how.

First, see how weak language hinders you, drains your confidence, and blocks your success. Then progress, step-by-step, toward understanding, use, and mastery of language skills that give you confidence and power. On the way, you'll read true stories about real women. In some cases, I've changed names or job titles to protect privacy. Just as the women in this book have enriched their work lives through language, so you'll enrich yours as well. As you proceed through *How to Say It® for Women*, you'll learn language skills that enable you to:

- Overcome your dread of speaking out.
- Look and feel confident.
- Make statements without hedging.
- Take credit for your accomplishments.

- Disagree politely but firmly.
- Assert yourself without seeming aggressive.
- Craft communications that work.
- Speak so you're noticed.
- Convey positive messages with gestures.
- Give clear directions that people want to follow.
- Choose a confident personal style.
- Lead and manage successfully.
- Assess and improve your leadership skills.
- Deter slurs, insults, and harassment.
- Run effective meetings.
- Advance your career with power reading.
- Listen so you always get the message.
- Influence policy decisions at the top.

How to Get the Most Out of This Book

How to Say It® *for Women* aims to be user-friendly, so it goes beyond discussions of general ideas. It gives specific examples and models to copy and even provides "crib sheets" and scripts that fit the situations you face. The Action Plans throughout the book suggest ways to follow up and apply the contents at work. At the end of each chapter, the Quick Tips review critical points. At the end of the book, you can track your progress and benefit from the Leadership Evaluation. Finally, you'll find a short Bookshelf for further reading.

Begin with Chapter 2, Throw Off Your Shackles: Break Free of the Grammar of Weakness, and Chapter 3, Assert Yourself: Use the Grammar of Power. The ideas and principles in these chapters build the foundation for the language of success and leadership. Next, surf on to Track Your Progress on pages 277–280 to locate topics of special interest. If leadership is your goal, review the Leadership Evaluation, ask associates to evaluate you, and build the skills covered in that section. If a big job interview looms, go to the tips and ideas in Chapter 6. Then feel free to graze: read each section in detail and try all the Action Plans, or just get the general principles outlined in each section. For example, if you're already an assured and confident speaker, you may prefer to skim the two chapters on speaking and body language and move directly to the chapters on leadership. Or shift attention to the skills that ensure you receive information efficiently both in person and on the Web: listening and power reading. Except for the grammar chapters, the others can be covered in any order that makes sense to you.

If you're a mother, read the book with your daughter. Young women suffer most from the language of weakness and will benefit greatly from powerful language skills. If you belong to a networking group, consider reading *How to Say It® for Women* together. Many of the Action Plans suggest that two women work together to overcome a weakness or practice a new skill, and your group may furnish partners. From time to time, check your progress from Novice to Mentor in Chapter 15, Our Heroes, Ourselves: Empower Yourself and Others, and choose your future goals.

Whatever job you do or plan to do in the future, whether you're an executive, an engineer, a manager, a secretary, a clerk, a factory worker, a doctor, a lawyer, or a student, *How to Say It® for Women* will guide you with the principles and rules of powerful language that works.

Language is not "just words." It enables us to establish our selves and ourselves, as individuals and as members of groups; it tells us how we are connected to one another, who has power and who doesn't.

ROBIN TOLMACH LAKOFF

Contents

3 *Assert Yourself: Use the Grammar of Power* 47

4 *Words That Work: Choose Them Wisely.* 67

7 *The Body Language of Power: Lead Without Words* . . . 143

1
Follow the Leaders to the Language of Success: Leave the Sad Stories Behind

As women enter the work force in growing numbers and at all levels, we have the historic opportunity to transform the business world. But, while women have succeeded in cracking traditional business culture and forging new career paths, we still lack the clout of our male counterparts. Despite all our progress, *Fortune* was recently able to run a cover story on "Why Women Still Don't Hit the Top." and a *New York Times* headline blares, "Wall Street's Embrace of Diversity Lauded Despite Its Poor Record." In tangible terms of power, promotion, and pay, women still rank second. Ironically, much of the blame rests on a phenomenon that women not only can control, but in which we are typically believed to excel: communication. In the workplace, we unwittingly use communication styles that sabotage our messages and our ability to succeed.

Our language skills convey messages about ourselves and our capabilities every time we interact with colleagues, put a pen to paper, or stand before an audience. Whether in speaking, writing, or personal presentation, weak language lessens the impact of our words, undermines our contributions, and hinders our growth and influence. But where weak language sabotages us, powerful language enables us to take control.

Many of us have hesitated to use powerful language for fear of seeming "pushy" or in the false belief that to be powerful we have to "act like men." It is wrong, however, to believe that power and empathy are mutually exclusive or that powerful language is unwomanly. We don't have to act like men to be strong—we can act like strong women. The language that leads to our success at work is not confrontational, arrogant, or belittling. It does not take power away from or exclude others. Instead, it strengthens us and our ability to transform the corporate culture into one of dignity and civility. Language is the tool with which we define ourselves, our colleagues, and our workplace. Transform language and we transform them all.

How exactly can you transform your language? Think about the things you do best. From whom did you learn them? You probably emulated role models: your mother, your favorite teachers, your best friends. The first step, then, in transforming your language is to find and copy the language of women and men who succeed. Fortunately, we have a rich and varied pantheon of mentors to look to for guidance in communicating clearly, effectively, and confidently. Our heroes stand as beacons guiding our way as we shed the language of weakness, insecurity, and fear and acquire the language of success, power, and courage. In this book the words of Amelia Earhart, Ruth Bader Ginsburg, Carla Hills, and others offer examples to emulate as you transform your language.

But perhaps the best teacher of how the power of language can transform is an unexpected one. Charlotte the spider, the beloved character in E. B. White's classic *Charlotte's Web*, stands as a perfect example of a strong female using powerful language. The wise little spider with the big heart understood the power of language to persuade, to create an image, and to change the course of events. With her web as a medium, Charlotte communicated messages that gained national attention and saved a friend's life. As a model, she combines feminine strengths of wisdom and compassion with the determination and power to make a difference.

For those who read the story long ago, here's a quick review. *Charlotte's Web* opens as Mr. Arable, a farmer, heads out to the hog house, ax in hand, to "do away with" the runt in the new pig litter. Appalled, his daughter Fern determines to save the runt's life by nurturing him back to health. She names him Wilbur, and he thrives in her care. However, Fern has only postponed Wilbur's dark fate; he is destined to be pork chops. Then Wilbur meets the heroine of the tale, Charlotte, who befriends him and becomes his champion.

Charlotte saves Wilbur's life by literally spinning a web of language. Each time he is destined for the butcher block, she spins a web praising him. In her first web, she writes *SOME PIG*. The words do more than create a sensation; they actually convince Mr. Arable that Wilbur is, indeed, some pig. Before weaving the second web, Charlotte calls a business meeting of the animals (some companies would call this an empowered work group); they brainstorm and, as a team, choose the word *TERRIFIC*, which also works. *RADIANT* follows, with equal success. Finally, though her own death is nearing, Charlotte spins her last word, *HUMBLE*, at the country fair. Wilbur wins the pig competition, and his life is saved. At the end of the story, Charlotte dies, but not before leaving behind her masterpiece, an egg sac with 514 spiders who will carry on her legacy.

Charlotte is a particularly resonant metaphor for those of us who seek to have our messages heard without resorting to overbearing tactics such as shouting down, or to ultimately ineffective tactics such as repetition, talking fast to cram ideas in before we're interrupted, or waiting for a break that never comes in the conversation. Women who find their communications ignored, undermined, or misunderstood will find in Charlotte a model for communicating with clarity, potency, and empathy. Charlotte's sentences, Charlotte's efficiency, Charlotte's skills, Charlotte's vocabulary, and even Charlotte's management style are models for our own as we learn to weave the language of power.

The Language of Weakness

This book emerged in response to seminars in which career women described their frustration at being unable to communicate effectively, to be taken seriously, or to deflect the verbal slights they encounter at work. They hadn't learned the language of power, and their stories, related in the pages that follow, tell the sad tales of how weak language fails them in the workplace. As you read these true stories, you'll recognize problems just like your own. Each story is followed by a reference to the chapters in this book that will help prevent, resolve, or confront similar issues in your workplace. Although the women's names have often been changed, each story is true and in the words of the woman who told it. Some have been edited for clarity and to ensure privacy.

WORDS THAT WEAKEN YOUR MESSAGE

When asked why she took a woman language workshop, Cheri Goldson said hesitantly, "I think the reason I came here is because I think I've heard women who I think sound right. I would like to have that skill . . ." Goldson's words and the way they were delivered offer classic examples of the weak language that plagues women's communications. Weak language that undermines your messages comes in many forms, from phrasing that deflects the issue from the subject at hand to you the speaker, to the habit of prefacing sentences with *I think* or *I feel,* which undermine your credibility. You may have encountered some of the problems of weak language described next. Indeed, the first edition of this book brought letters, phone calls, and e-mails from all over the world, from women who saw themselves in the stories told here.

Psychobabble

The setting was a professional planning meeting at a great university; the men and women were leaders in education. Here are some of the women's words: "It's my feeling that I think we want . . ."; "It feels like that's the way it should go for me"; and "That feels good."

Describing events or issues in terms of "feelings" substitutes "psychobabble" for clear thought. As one leader said, "This is a business, not a group home." If you want to learn how to focus language and attention on issues rather than on feelings, read Chapters 2 and 3.

Generous words that fail to establish authority

Francine Adams knew she'd have trouble establishing her authority. The new vice president, she was younger than any of the men she had to lead. To build their egos, she said, "I don't know as much as you do about this . . ."

Building others' confidence at the cost of your own credibility fails as a leadership technique. To find successful leadership techniques, read Chapter 13.

Mean words that fail to establish authority

A new leader called to ask if I could help. She said, "People tell me I'm intimidating." Although she didn't look intimidating, her memos included such terms as, "I expect you to . . ."

I statements fail us when we lead and when we follow. To see why and learn alternate ways to lead with language, see Chapters 2 and 3.

Orders no one follows

Renee Whitcomb was promoted to a job in which she managed six workers who rarely found time to do the work she asked them to do. One day, under pressure to get a job done by noon, she asked one of the workers, "Could you get this done by noon today?" The worker replied that she could not.

If people don't follow your orders, read Chapters 2, 3, and 9.

I'm sorry, I'm sorry

Lida Sylvester is dean at a university. A powerful communicator in all other work situations, she says, "I turn to jelly when I negotiate my own contract with the boss." She also observes that she apologizes too often. She even apologizes on the tennis court. Every time this powerful tennis player misses a shot, she says, "I'm sorry." Her male tennis partners never do.

If you apologize too often, read Chapters 2 and 3.

Write like a wimp and you're treated like a wimp

In its Spring 1993 issue, *Harvard Business Review* featured an article titled, "The Memo Every Woman Keeps in Her Desk." Although the memo raises essential issues for women executives, it's written in the language of weakness that pervades much of women's writing.

To learn how to plan and write memos, critiques, and reports that work even when they're negative read Chapters 3, 5, and 9.

WORDS THAT MAKE YOU INVISIBLE

Women often report that they're ignored when they communicate. Weak language blocks our ability to command attention and project confidence and credibility at meetings and presentations. From reluctance to "interrupt" when someone else dominates a conversation or meeting, to allowing others to take credit for our ideas, to simply resigning ourselves to being ignored, we allow weak language to dictate our work success—or lack of it.

Shouting on deaf ears

Millicent Ruth edits books for a major publisher. She reports, "When no one listens to me, I turn up the volume. That doesn't work. So I try talking faster and cram too much in. That doesn't work either." Adds Susan Whitmeier, "I find myself repeating myself—because I get no reaction."

And Cheri Blandings asks, "How can we command attention in a positive way and be listened to? A man at any level is listened to." Sarah Channing notes, "I need an ability to gain credibility, to be heard the first time."

To get people to listen and to gain credibility, read Chapters 3 and 6.

Your moment never comes

On NBC-TV's *The Today Show* on December 14, 1992, Bryant Gumbel "interviewed" two participants at the Clinton economic summit: Paul Allaire, the CEO of Xerox and Mary Kelley, a board member of the National Federation of Independent Businesses. Here's an overview of the script:

Bryant Gumbel:	Two of those who have been invited are Paul Allaire, the President of Xerox, and Mary Kelley, a board member of the National Federation of Independent Businesses. And both are in Little Rock. Good morning to both of you.
Ms. Mary Kelley:	Good morning.
Mr. Paul Allaire:	Good morning.
Gumbel:	xxx
Allaire:	xxx
Gumbel:	xxx
Allaire:	xxx
Gumbel:	xxx
Allaire:	xxx
Gumbel:	xxx
Allaire:	xxx
Gumbel:	xxx
Allaire:	xxx
Gumbel:	xxx

Allaire:	xxx
Gumbel:	Paul Allaire, Mary Kelley, you have a busy two days ahead of you, and we wish you well. Thank you very much.

To be sure you get your words in, read Chapter 6.

Overlooked . . . then copied

Marilyn McDavid manages administrative services for a midwestern computer firm. She's usually the only woman at meetings. At one, she "came up with what I thought was a viable solution. No one listened. Then one of the men said the same thing and everyone said, 'Yeah, yeah. I want to change that.'" Linda Williams, a product engineer, urged her group "to include pricing information in a presentation, but no one listened to me; when the boss came along and said the same thing, everyone agreed and included the information."

To prevent or handle the common problem of others getting credit for your ideas, read Chapters 3, 6, and 7.

Meetings that fail

Whenever Laurita Simmons starts to speak at board meetings, one of the senior managers slams his pencil on the table and crosses his arms over his chest. Sue Bell tells of a vice president who talks to his table partner when she presents. Janet Morrell is constantly interrupted by an "enemy" in her software development group.

To learn how to control meetings and run them civilly, read Chapters 6 and 13.

WORDS THAT DESTROY CONFIDENCE

Weak language makes us invisible not just to others but to ourselves. Experiencing the "invisible woman" syndrome damages self-confidence at work, creating a vicious circle that silences our voices and destroys our effectiveness. Women from reception desks to board rooms have grappled with this disabilitating aspect of weak language.

Hurt by her hedges

Diane Threlkeldt is manager of quality training at a manufacturing firm. She makes presentations to the company president and vice presidents in order to earn their commitment to her agenda. She notes, "I would like to appear more comfortable than I am. I would like for my hands not to shake. I feel I need to speak effectively and persuasively in my role as change agent. I find in general that people in my division . . . have abysmal interactive skills. They'll get up and leave the room when I'm trying to present. . . ."

If your hands shake, your anxiety shows, and your audience disappears when you speak to the hierarchy, read Chapter 6, Stand Up and Speak Like a Woman. If, like Diane, you hedge with terms such as "I would like to . . .," and "I feel I need . . .," and "I'm only a secretary, but. . .," read Chapters 2 and 3.

Low self-confidence sidetracks me

Sharon Brown has worked in a human resources department for 13 years, yet she still seeks to "gain self-confidence when I speak to people. I get real nervous and lose my train of thought."

If you lack self-confidence, get nervous, and lose your train of thought when meeting with a group, read Chapter 6.

Trouble in the corner office

Betty Spitale manages worldwide data processing for a *Fortune* 500 corporation. Even she is not immune from the language of weakness. She describes how ". . . sometimes a light shines on you—other times you feel like a babbling idiot." And Diane Peters, who manages quality for a dictatorial male-dominated organization, observes that she tends to use "apologetic language and back down when challenged" so she hopes to "regain self-confidence." Chris Tanner's experiences under a negative boss have led her to "become a tongue-tied wimp," a "total jerk."

To grow your management skills and become "She Who Must Be Obeyed," read Chapter 3.

READING AS A POWER TOOL

Mastering the power of language demands that professionals master all forms of communication, including reading. Efficient reading is more than just a way to manage information and grapple with pertinent issues: it's a vital orb in your web of communications. Effective reading skills translate into effective communication when you interact with others in any forum.

Overwhelmed by reading

Dr. Sylvia Ortiz was applying for a top-level job in a new field. She had six weeks to master the subject matter in 50 books, 300 articles, and thousands of Web references. She had to "be able to distill what's relevant and synthesize it with the requirements of the new position." Doris Kain is vice president for communications for a six-hundred-million-dollar corporation. She reports that she returned from a six-day business trip and "found three hundred e-mails as well as piles of mail waiting to be read. I must read and master two newspapers a day, six to ten magazines a week, plus a barrage of e-mail. I don't even get to read *The Wall Street Journal*." Sue McAlpin, another executive stunned by the size of her electronic reading load, complains that most of the books she read when growing up were novels in which the girl gets the guy. Now that she must tackle *Fortune* and six dozen Web sites critically, she requires different mental tools.

To acquire reading as a tool of power, read Chapter 10.

Put an End to Predatory Language

Women are sometimes the target of misused or predatory language in the workplace that damages our confidence and our ability to do our jobs. Horror stories about the misuse of language abound, from the CEO who tells dirty jokes at a business conference to employee evaluations that stress a woman's attractiveness, to being called *my gal, darling, honey,* or much worse. The examples of inappropriate and harmful workplace language that follow can be effectively addressed with the language of success.

Diminutive names

Ruth Henderson, a national sales manager says, "When will men learn that my name is Ruth, not Ruthie or Honey?"

Kathleen McGlynn is constantly called Kathy; she responds, "My name is Kathleen."

Name-calling, slurs, and put-downs

Mary Ann Duarte does high-level systems analysis in an all-male group. She's often the target of subtle slurs from her male associates. Some of the men call her a "tough broad."

Marguerite Rojas works in personnel at an engineering firm. When managers found that the company hired few women, they met to review their strategies. One of the managers said, "What you're saying is that we just need to hire more babes."

Dolores Green was about to order new equipment on which to move the work stations. One of the men said, "We don't need equipment, because she's our dolly."

If women at your company are called *babes, hags, cuties,* and other unsuitable names and you seek ways to respond to slurs, slights, insults, and inappropriate labels, read Chapters 3, 4, and 14.

Cruelty, harassment, and incivility

Veronica Bailey was receiving praise at the celebration of her fifth anniversary on the job. The speaker glowingly described the woman's "excellent set of credentials." Several audience members laughed aloud and gazed at the woman's large bust. Sally Carruthers can't bear the constant, mocking use of foul language in the office. *Publishers Weekly* prints this sidebar story: "A female editor is often 'good-naturedly' referred to by the president of her publishing company as 'the resident bitch goddess,' especially in editorial meetings where she is outnumbered by male colleagues."

For ways to combat cruelty, harassment, and incivility and foster a civil and kind workplace, read Chapters 13 and 14.

Women's work demeaned

Executive women too often stand at the edge of the "old boys' network." Vendors and customers assume that the woman is someone's underling and hint that the real deals are made by the "boss," even though she's sitting right there. Women in leadership jobs report that phone callers assume they're their own secretaries. Joann Reynolds describes her pet peeve: "When you speak to someone on the phone, they use your first name if you're a woman, even if you're in a senior position."

Another woman told this story: The company had just been bought, and the incoming president flew to town to brief managers on global strategic plans. After a professional presentation in which he suggested that the women would participate fully in an exciting venture, the boss said, "Back to the phones, girls."

Laura Smith, a corporate trainer, was delighted to receive her first invitation to a meeting of key executives. When she entered the room, the person who'd issued the invitation welcomed her and said, "I thought we needed to have somebody good-looking at our meeting."

Judy Vidala, a personnel development representative at an insurance company, attended a professional communicators' meeting in Las Vegas, at which a gift certificate winner's name was to be selected. The winner's name was drawn from a bowl by a showgirl "all dressed up in hardly anything." The president of the association, a university professor, announced the winner, saying, "Dr. Tom Nelson, do you want the gift certificate or what drew it?" The meeting went downhill from there.

Eileen Pastorella, who writes parts documentation for service manuals, is the only woman in a group of 13 men. She says, ". . . I feel inferior because of the chauvinistic attitudes of the men. I can just watch their expressions and their gestures, like they have this doubt; I can see I'm going to get challenged. They don't take me seriously. When I said something funny, one man looked at me and said, 'Eileen, you're a trip.' I think that type of description is very worthless—it doesn't belong in the workplace. It's insulting."

Advice that demeans

In my search for a good book on presentation skills, I bought a promising paperback titled *How to Sell to a Group*. Imagine my shock when I came across the following "advice" on how to dress: "A woman's outfit can seriously detract from her success. The problem is biology. If your clothes stress la difference, your message is being diluted. Stress, adrenaline, and nervousness can cause one's nipples to become hard and protrude—if for that reason only, a jacket is a best bet for any presentation. It eliminates this problem and, for women, diminishes the bustline." The writer didn't discuss portions of the male anatomy that "can become hard and protrude."

SEEING YOURSELF IN A NEW LIGHT

Some women have trouble seeing themselves as powerful people. We have a lifetime of lessons teaching us to be modest and sensitive to other people's feelings, and these ideas conflict with the image of power as arrogance and oppressiveness. However, we can rightly take pride in the valuable qualities of compassion and empathy without making ourselves weak in the process. In this book you will find examples of women being kind without being incompetent, strong without being insensitive, truthful about their accomplishments without being arrogant. Some of the women's stories that follow illustrate the conflict between "how we were raised" and how to be effective at the office.

It was nothing

Betsy Ordway is studying for certification as a purchasing agent. She described her accomplishment to date this way: "I really don't know whether I was just lucky or not, but I was the only woman and the only person who passed the preliminary test."

Women also have learned to belittle themselves in order to get along with others. One woman said, "No matter how obnoxious they are, I try to get along with people. It's part of the whole idea of niceness. I take special effort not to alienate someone, but I get taken advantage of."

If you've acquired the "modesty" to attribute your accomplishments to luck, read Chapters 3 and 13.

I'm just a girl who cain't say no

Kathy Lu was raised to be obedient and polite. She's exploited by bosses and fellow employees because she doesn't have ways of saying no without being rude or unpleasant. She aims to be "very much a lady while being strong as well." The inability to say no leads to exploitation of secretaries, support staff, and professionals. It also mutes legitimate disagreement about ideas and projects.

To remain a lady while knowing how to say no, read Chapter 3.

Praise for the wrong attributes

Instead of being judged by standards of work quality or leadership, women find themselves judged on the basis of appearance. Lydia Ackerman thought she'd earned her manager's support with the high quality of her work until he said, "You're very personable. Your clothes fit you very nicely." Sharon Bell was shocked to read these words on her employee evaluation: "Sharon always looks attractive in the office." The evaluation neglected her superb word-processing and time-management skills. For ways to respond without making enemies, read Chapter 3.

Finding a balance

"I'm too aggressive," Liz Hacker says. "My problem is that you have to prove yourself every time because you're a woman. I guess the three things that I need are to be (1) persuasive, (2) diplomatic, (3) more mature. I want to be not so aggressive, to be assertive without turning people off."

If you want to be assertive without looking too aggressive, read Chapters 3 and 6.

Acquiring the Language of Success: What You Can Learn from Successful Women

All the problems described in this chapter can be resolved or reduced through powerful language. But these stories don't represent the whole picture. Many successful women know how to use the language of power and are doing so in our businesses, our government, our media, and, very likely, in your own workplace. The following chapters contain the lessons from Charlotte along with true words of inspiration from women like Amelia Earhart and Orit Gadiesh. These women inspire for their courage, compassion, and ability; think of them as your mentors as you grow more accomplished in the language of success.

Amelia Earhart shares the mythic status of Charlotte, yet she was a real, practical woman who insisted on the right to aim for the stars. Four decades before the women's movement, she demanded education that would equip women to do technical as well as domestic work. She modeled courage and confidence in the face of enormous dangers and powerful opposition. She was more than a great aviator: she was a successful business woman, a pioneering teacher, and, like Charlotte, a good writer. *Last Flight*, the diary of her final expedition, tells the story of her ill-fated flight around the world and ends just before her plane was lost. As you progress through this book, you'll read her words and see how to model your language after hers.

Supreme Court Justice Ruth Bader Ginsburg is another real hero, one who's very much alive. She's an attorney who rose to one of the highest positions in the country, and she did so with her powerful mind and her powerful language. Her statement before the Senate prior to her confirmation models powerful spoken language. You can copy her sentences, forms, and word choices.

Two additional models inhabit our contemporary business world. Carla Hills's career took her from the world of investments to the government: she served from 1989 to 1993 as the U.S. Trade Representative and the president's principal adviser and negotiator on trade policy, the third woman in U.S. history to hold a cabinet post. Her speech before the Commonwealth Club on March 11, 1994, offers specific examples of powerful language forms. You'll come across them as you progress through this book. Another contemporary business model is Orit Gadiesh, chairman of Bain & Company, management consultants. Her language skills mesh well with her business acumen; she's been described as ". . . a voracious reader of both books and human nature. Her most notable quality, colleagues say, is her ability to listen and process what she hears." Like Charlotte, though, she cuts an unconventional figure. We'll discuss both her language and her purple hair.

THE HERO AT THE NEXT DESK

Our mentors and heroes are not limited to those found in business headlines or books. They also come from the office, the desk, the drafting table, and the shop next door. A story from one of my seminar attendees illustrates the point. Trudy Fletcher, a top financial officer, told about a hero who mentored her. Trudy had returned to graduate school after rearing her children and was having her first job interview. The personnel woman noted the 4.0 grade point average and said, "You have quite an impressive academic record." "I worked hard," Trudy replied. The interviewer said, "Never make excuses for your success. Men say 'thank you.' You do the same." Trudy got the job, progressed up the ladder, and now reminds other women to say "thank you" and not diminish their successes.

Trudy's story exemplifies what you can gain from this book: the ability to be a hero and the obligation to be a mentor. Our language heroes need not be mythic or famous or published. The solutions to many of the issues raised in this book came from "ordinary" women with whom I work every day. The "ordinary" women with whom you work can offer rich sources of support for you. Use each other. Several of the Action Plans in this book suggest that you work with an associate to unlearn a weak language habit or rehearse a strong one. As you gain sensitivity to weak and powerful language, you'll find that the women around you can teach much of value. In turn, you can fulfill your mentorship obligation to pass the best ideas on to other women.

The Next Step

To acquire the language of success, first understand the complex elements of power and the ways in which your language can hamper your career. Then shed the style of weakness and weave the language of power. As you do, your confidence will grow and you'll gain the courage to try ever more advanced skills. With the language of success, you can, like Charlotte Cavatica, Amelia Earhart, Ruth Bader Ginsburg, Carla Hills, Orit Gadiesh, and the women you meet every day, be strong, competent, and able without sacrificing the ability to be a true friend. You can do what Charlotte and the other heroes did: use your intelligence, language skills and leadership ability to do what you believe is right. You can be powerful and good.

In the next chapter, you'll learn the aspect of language that saps your strength and success, the grammar of weakness.

Action Plan

1. Think about your language heroes, both real and imagined. List them here and note how you might emulate them. Add other heroes as they occur to you.

   _____

   _____

   _____

2. Note a few stories of language successes and failures at work. If you're reading this book with a group, discuss these stories at your first meeting.

   _____

   _____

   _____

3. List the names of people you can mentor as your skills grow.

   _____

   _____

   _____

Quick Tips

Find women whose powerful language you can emulate.

Find women you'll mentor.

2

Throw Off Your Shackles: Break Free of the Grammar of Weakness

---

Language is power, in ways more literal than most people think. When we speak, we exercise the power of language to transform reality. Why don't more of us realize the connection between language and power?

JULIA PENELOPE

Language forms a complex web, woven of delicate threads that hang together in the final creation. Think about a "simple" language event. You see an associate at a meeting. You shake hands, greet each other, and sit down. What took place? For starters, you were in a place of business: that framed your greeting. You moved, gestured, looked at one another, touched each other, listened to each other, voiced words, strung them together grammatically, varied vocal intonation, and observed each other's hair, face, and clothing. More happened as well. A change in any one aspect of your meeting could have changed the meaning and the outcome of the event. For example, if you had been wearing a sequined tank top instead of a business suit, the event would have been radically different, even if all the other variables remained the same. Or, if the greeting included the words, "You look great in that dress!", the meaning of the event would change depending upon whether you're both women, how you looked and gestured, and what kind of dress you were wearing. So, if

I, as a researcher, jotted down the words only, chances are I would have missed the meaning of that encounter.

Embrace Complexity: The Janus Principles

Advice flies at us from every direction: act like a man, speak like a woman, think like a woman, speak like a man, be tough, be gentle, tell the truth, fudge the facts, play on the team, act independently, be democratic, be autocratic, follow seven rules, be polite, don't be too polite, speak out, stay quiet, and on and on. What's a woman to do?

First, we should stop seeking simple solutions to complex problems. Indeed, our success demands that we not just accept but embrace complexity. As mothers and sisters, we understand that no two children are alike, that sometimes we must be gentle and sometimes harsh. That wisdom serves us well if we bring it to the problems of language and power at work. So let's build a framework of ideas, a web of connections that link seemingly conflicting ideas with one another.

As we model our language of success after the fictional Charlotte, so can we model our language of complexity after the Roman god, Janus. Janus, always represented as two-faced or two-headed, serves two seemingly disparate ideas. Janus is the Roman god of war *and* of peace, of past *and* of future, of endings *and* of beginnings, a god linked with gates and portals. F. Scott Fitzgerald wrote, "The test of a first-rate intelligence is the ability to hold two opposed ideas in the mind at the same time, and still retain the ability to function." Consider that the problems of language and power can best achieve resolution if we view them as dualities or paradoxes that evade simple-minded solutions, that require us to hold two opposed ideas in the mind at the same time. We'll apply the Janus Principles in this chapter and return to them from time to time later in this book.

Language is so complex that we're not always sure what critical aspects shape any one language interaction. The words that represent power in one context may represent weakness in another; this is the first application of the Janus Principles. This is why research findings don't automatically lead to simple prescriptions for what to say and what not to say. Many weak expressions could be powerful in different settings, while every powerful expression could be weak in a different setting. In language, there are few easy fixes, few absolute do's and don'ts, and no perfectly simple solutions.

Given this complexity, can you drop the language of weakness and adopt the language of success? If you're like the women I've worked with all over the world, you certainly can, if you first accept the complexity and learn a variety of practical approaches. That's what you'll have to do. When groping for a word or a grammatical form, consider the variables mentioned at the start of this chapter to determine a choice that works.

Control drives the grammar of success. To the extent that you think about language choices and control your responses, you can master any complex situation. This book usually offers various approaches to a problem. Which works best depends upon your style, the person to whom you're speaking or writing, the frame, the power relationships, and other factors. Just remember to keep your wits about you and use common sense. And, on the few occasions when I promise you a quick fix or urge you *never* to say something, trust me.

Grammar is implicated in nearly every instance of what I call "puny" language. Your grammar conveys messages either of vigor, courage, and leadership or of weakness, fear, and victimization. Your grammar defines you, both in written and in spoken communications. Like a systemic illness, weak grammar tears at the threads that hold your web of language together and undermines its very structure.

If you studied grammar in school, you may see it as a set of dry and dusty rules that quibble over "correct" and "incorrect" language. But leaders know that grammar is much more than that. Grammar holds the key to persuasion, clarity, manipulation, and control of your environment. What's more, research has shown time and again that grammar is destiny: the puny grope for the grammar of weakness; the strong embrace the grammar of power.

Working through the next two chapters, you'll find both specific suggestions and principles. The specific suggestions, in "crib sheets" of exact words, guide you as you gain experience in creating responses; the principles frame all future communications (guided of course by common sense).

Eradicate the Grammar of Weakness

Before you can shed the grammar of weakness, understand what it is and how it burrows its way into and undermines your communications, pegging you as an underling. Julius Caesar said, "The fault, dear Brutus, . . . lies not in our stars but in ourselves that we are underlings." Perhaps he should have said, "The fault, dear women, lies not in our sex but in our grammar that we are underlings." If you speak the grammar of the underling, people take you for an underling even if your job title is vice president. Let's look at the grammar of underlings. Check the sentences that you speak or write.

THE INDECISIVE *I*

❑ 1. I can be pushed around, I guess.

❑ 2. I kind of relate to that. Managers never want to hear anything bad.

❑ 3. I enjoyed myself and learned more than I had expected. I would recommend this course to any woman professional.

❑ 4. I felt she's very biased.

❑ 5. I think the reason I came is because I think I've heard women who I think sound right. I would like to have that skill.

❑ 6. I have a problem with my secretary; he never gets to work on time.

❑ 7. I have a problem with my boss; she doesn't support her group.

❑ 8. I don't have enough time to complete that job.

❑ 9. I like the way you get your work done. Thank you.

❑ 10. I noticed that the door was left open too long.

❑ 11. I observed that the lab wasn't cleaned up on time.

❑ 12. I think we need. . . .

❑ 13. I love this job.

These samples, direct quotes from intelligent women who own businesses and hold responsible jobs, exhibit varied problems. But the one problem they all share is what we'll call "the indecisive *I*." Interviews with the women who take my language of success workshops reveal that most describe work problems in sentences that begin with *I*. They do so even when they aren't, or shouldn't be, talking about themselves, as in all the examples above.

To understand why it causes problems to start sentences with the word *I* when you're not talking about yourself, let's clarify the grammatical concept of subject. The subject of a sentence is what the sentence talks about. For example, the sentence, "The computer operates on real time," is about *the computer*. Starting it with the word *I* ("I know the computer operates on real time.") implies that you are the subject of the sentence, although you didn't intend to talk about yourself. In the following sentences, the speakers intended to talk about a subject outside themselves. Although I indicated a probable subject for each sentence, the lack of clarity shows their weakness: we can't be absolutely sure of the subject when you start a sentence with *I*.

Sentence	Probable Subject
1. I kind of relate to that. Managers never want to hear anything bad.	managers
2. I think the reason I came is because I think I've heard women who I think sound right. I would like to have that skill.	reason? skill?
3. I don't have enough time to complete that job.	time or job

Sentence	Probable Subject
4. I noticed that the door was left open too long.	door
5. I observed that the lab wasn't cleaned up on time.	lab
6. I think we need	what we need
7. I love this job.	this job
8. I have a problem with my secretary; he never gets to work on time.	secretary
9. I have a problem with my boss; she doesn't support her group.	boss
10. I like the way you get your work done. Thank you.	work or you?

FIVE WAYS *I* STATEMENTS WEAKEN LANGUAGE

I statements weaken you in several ways. First, some blame you for issues that aren't yours. For example, sentences 8 and 9 suggest that whatever the secretary and boss do wrong is your problem rather than their problem. And when women use sentence 3, they invariably mean that the problem results from the size of their work load rather than from themselves.

Second, *I* statements imply that you're not sure of the facts. For example, sentences 4 and 5 allow the interpretation that perhaps the door wasn't left open too long or that the lab may have been cleaned up on time after all. Because they depend on your perception, they can be dismissed as "just the way she sees it."

Third, *I* statements characterize inadequate leadership. For example, sentence 10 doesn't make the speaker appear weak, but it's poor leadership. Is it the employee's job to produce work you like? It would be far better management to talk about what work that was good. "That work came in on time, shows the relevant details, and persuades the customer. Thanks."

Fourth, *I* statements harm women profoundly by making us appear immature and childlike. If you've watched a child grow, you've seen that, in the process of growing up, she moves gradually from believing that she is the center of the universe to understanding that she is not. That understanding permits us to look objectively at life without always referring to ourselves. The mature thinker, the successful businesswoman, the productive person speaks about the world without constantly referring to herself.

Fifth, the weak, childish *I* statement metastasizes like a cancer through women's language at work, fostering extensive psychobabble. Starting sentences with *I* encourages you to choose "touchy-feely" emotional verbs instead of the action verbs that drive powerful language (more about that in the next section). Why? Psychotherapists say that the *I* statement originated to counter the accusatory *you* statement "You make me miserable." Rather than pointing the finger at someone else, people were encouraged to talk about their feelings "I feel miserable when you . . ." However, even in psychotherapy, this approach backfires, encouraging people to turn inward rather than to face the world. Therapists confide that *I* statements not only don't work well for people in therapy but that, as I've suggested, they tend to bring blame on the victim rather than on the source of the problem.

As you drop the *I* statement, don't pick up the equally ineffectual, accusatory *you*. Don't weaken yourself by saying things like, "You make me feel insignificant"; "You make me feel wonderful"; "Your decision makes me feel angry." Julia Penelope asserts that when we speak like that, "we have no integrity . . . we attribute agency for our feelings and emotions to someone else, or the weather, which we can't control . . . [and] deny our own ability to choose alternative behaviors."

In sum, if there's one characteristic of weak women's (and sometimes men's) language at work, it's the ubiquitous *I*. Cut it, except when talking about yourself.

Action Plan

Find a piece of your business writing or a videotape of yourself speaking. Count the number of times you begin sentences with the word *I*.

A QUICK FIX FOR *I* STATEMENTS

Here's an easy change in language style, a true quick fix: ***Never start a sentence with the word*** I ***unless talking about yourself.*** I call this a quick fix because it's the easiest to understand of all the suggestions in this book. However, it proves hard to apply consistently: it requires thinking about yourself and your language in a new way and breaking the habits of a life-time. Still, this simple change will radically change your life as it has changed the lives of thousands of other women. Just stop before speaking and first ask, What am I not talking about? You are not talking about yourself. Next, ask, What am I talking about? What is the subject? Start the sentence with its subject.

You've now met the first two principles of the language of success, in the form of two questions: What am I not talking about? Myself. What am I talking about, what is the subject of my sentence? Professional writers and speakers face this question every time they construct a new sentence: What is the subject? What am I about to talk about? This question crops up again and again as we talk about public speaking, job interviews, writing, even leadership. What is this sentence about? And it's almost never about you. This doesn't mean that you won't tell a story about your own experiences once in a while; that's not making yourself the subject of nearly every sentence you utter.

Action Plan

Now you'll find the sentences we looked at earlier as they might be recast. Read the way each can be restated and, on the space below it, write an alternative version. As long as you avoid the word *I*, you have many choices of subject. I've given a couple of possibilities for the first sentence. You try the others.

Original	I have a problem with my secretary; he never gets to work on time.
QUICK FIX	My secretary has a problem: he never gets to work on time.
ALTERNATIVE 1	My secretary's lateness dogs his career.
ALTERNATIVE 2	Lateness remains a consistent problem for my secretary.
Original	I have a problem with my boss; she doesn't support her group.
QUICK FIX	My boss doesn't support her group.
ALTERNATIVE	_____
Original	I don't have enough time to complete that job.
QUICK FIX	The schedule prevents that job from being completed.
ALTERNATIVE	_____
Original	I like the way you get your work done. Thank you.
QUICK FIX	Your work always arrives on time. Thank you.
ALTERNATIVE	_____
Original	I noticed that the door was left open too long.
QUICK FIX	That door was left open too long.
ALTERNATIVE	_____
Original	I observed that the lab wasn't cleaned up on time.
QUICK FIX	The lab wasn't cleaned up on time.
ALTERNATIVE	_____

Original	I think we need more time.
QUICK FIX	More time would help us complete that job.
ALTERNATIVE	_____

Original	I love this job.
QUICK FIX	This is a dream job.
ALTERNATIVE	_____

This simple change in your grammar reaps rich rewards. Talking about subjects rather than about yourself earns the perception that you're a thoughtful, intelligent, mature person worth listening to.

INTIMACIES:
GREAT FOR THE BEDROOM, POISON FOR THE BOARDROOM

Now that we've scrapped the weak *I* sentence, let's attack its cousin: the unbusinesslike touchy-feely statement. In their efforts to make workplaces more humane, well-meaning management consultants have urged people to inject emotions. Yes, people's sensitivities matter, and workplaces should be humane, but the way to make them so is not to encourage fuzzy, emotional language and the fuzzy thinking that goes with it. Fed up with emotional language at work, Betty Spitale, manager of global data management for an international corporation announced, "This is a business, not a group home." Verbs that can inject emotions into professional language include "feel," "like," "don't like," "want," "need," and others that convey emotion rather than action: just the kind of language women are accused of using. Here are examples of touchy-feely workplace language that might be effective in a group home, a psychotherapist's office, or a love letter. Check those you say.

- ❏ I feel good about this engineering program.
- ❏ How do you feel about this million-dollar investment?

❑ What are your feelings on this matter?

❑ I really like this idea for our ten-million-dollar building.

❑ Our team doesn't like the idea of ordering six new computers. We feel it would be wasteful.

Your ear is starting to adjust to the sound of weak language, so you can hear the defects in these sentences. If you don't, consider the first and second models from the shareholder's point of view. Would you want to own stock in a company that runs engineering programs or invests money on feelings? I wouldn't! When you read the antidotes to the models, the advantages of the clear-thinking as opposed to the touchy-feely workplace shine through. Notice that the alternatives not only sound better but force the speaker to use precise action verbs as opposed to vague emotional ones.

Action Plan

1. Add alternative ways of saying the following messages with action rather than with emotion.

Emotional	I feel good about this engineering program.
Powerful	This engineering program promises to cut costs.
Alternative	_____

Emotional	How do you feel about this million-dollar investment?
Powerful	How will this million-dollar investment improve our business?
Alternative	_____

Emotional	What are your feelings on this matter?
Powerful	How might we resolve this matter?
Alternative	_____

Emotional	I really like this idea for our ten-million-dollar building.
POWERFUL	This ten-million-dollar building represents a sound investment.
ALTERNATIVE	_____
Emotional	Our team doesn't like the idea of ordering six new computers. We feel it would be wasteful.
POWERFUL	Our team opposes the wasteful idea to order six new computers.
ALTERNATIVE	_____
Emotional	Jim, it was very nice to meet you this morning (or I was happy to meet you).
POWERFUL	Jim, our meeting this morning was cordial and productive.
ALTERNATIVE	_____

2. Find a piece of your business writing. Circle all the "touchy-feely" words and verbs. Note how many of them follow the word *I*. Recast the sentences with appropriate subjects and action verbs.

TRIM YOUR HEDGES: ADD AUTHORITY TO YOUR WORDS

To hedge in language is to "hide behind words, refuse to commit oneself." We all must hedge sometimes, but women's language hedges in the face of certainty Some women actually force themselves to hedge because they aim to soften their statements. This book demonstrates that you can speak softly without losing credibility with hedges. Here are hedges spoken by women like us. As you read the list, check those you speak or write:

- ❏ You shouldn't do that, really . . .
- ❏ Well . . .
- ❏ I'd like to get the promotion, sort of . . .
- ❏ In my opinion . . .
- ❏ Basically . . .
- ❏ The way I see it . . .
- ❏ I know that . . .
- ❏ Clearly . . .
- ❏ I guess . . .
- ❏ I just . . .
- ❏ The point is . . .
- ❏ I would like to . . .
- ❏ I feel . . .
- ❏ I think . . .

Everyone hedges sometimes, but women hedge more than men do, and they use the more damaging hedges. After the *I* statement, the hedge seems the most pervasive and destructive weak language form. Why? Hedges all share two defects: they sound as though you doubt your own words and they lengthen your sentences unnecessarily. One executive wisely said, "Delete any word that does not add value." In *The Elements of Style*, William Strunk and E. B. White note, "If your every sentence admits a doubt, your writing will lack authority." So will your speaking.

Although both men and women use the preceding hedges, women utter the most damaging ones, those that belittle the speaker. Check those you use.

- ❏ I'm not sure how strongly I feel about this, but . . .
- ❏ I guess my question is . . .
- ❏ I'm not an expert on that, but . . .
- ❏ I don't know anything about financial reports, but . . .

❑ In my opinion, . . .

❑ I would like to . . .

❑ I know I'm only a secretary but . . .

❑ Because I don't know much about this . . .

❑ I don't mean to, . . . but . . .

❑ This may only be how I feel, but . . .

❑ I just . . .

❑ I may not be right, but . . .

Finally, some hedges bring those "group-home" elements into business, where they don't belong. These hedges brand you as emotional, sentimental, a sob sister, all pejoratives that won't win you the job or promotion you seek. Examples of group-home hedges are: *I feel*; *I'm not happy with*; *I'm happy with* . . . .

Next time you're tempted to hedge, ask if the hedge adds useful information. If it doesn't, don't hedge.

WHAT TO SAY IF THERE'S REAL UNCERTAINTY

Sometimes we face real uncertainty or wish to soften our assertions. Our language gives us plenty of excellent hedges for those occasions. Words such as *might, may, can, should, promises, seems to,* and *appears to* enable you to talk about genuine uncertainties without making yourself a weak sister.

Here are examples of puny hedges and strong alternatives, showing no uncertainty and some uncertainty.

Puny Hedge	You shouldn't curse on the job, really . . .
ASSERTION	Cursing at work offends people.
Puny Hedge	Well, the proposal came in under budget.
ASSERTION	The proposal came in under budget.

Puny Hedge	I'd like to get the promotion, sort of . . .
ASSERTION	Please consider my promotion.
ALTERNATIVE	The promotion will benefit the whole department.
Puny Hedge	In my opinion, this project will work better if we bid on each part of the job separately.
ASSERTION	This project will work better if we bid on each part of the job separately.
ASSERTION (UNCERTAINTY)	This project should work better if we bid on each part of the job separately.
Puny Hedge	Basically, the retail shop earns more per square foot than the restaurant.
ASSERTION	The retail shop earns more per square foot than the restaurant.
ASSERTION (UNCERTAINTY)	The retail shop seems to earn more per square foot than the restaurant.

Action Plan

The following hedged statements resemble those you speak and write at work every day. Transform each to a powerful assertion. If real uncertainty exists, show it strongly.

Puny Hedge	I would like to be aware of the pilferage level in the plant.
ASSERTION	_____
Puny Hedge	I think the new health plan will cost our employees more.
ASSERTION	_____

Puny Hedge	The way I see it, the vice president's office should be larger than the financial analyst's.
ASSERTION	_____

Puny Hedge	I know that profits jumped 15 percent in the second quarter.
ASSERTION	_____

Puny Hedge	Apparently, Kendall was late four times last week.
ASSERTION	_____

Puny Hedge	Clearly, the building on lot 6 will generate more income than the building on lot 7.
ASSERTION	_____

Puny Hedge	I'm not an expert on this, but the budget plan will result in a cash shortfall.
ASSERTION	_____

Puny Hedge	I'm not happy with what Mr. Rodriguez said about the sales force.
ASSERTION	_____

Puny Hedge	The point is that, with only 16 pilots, the airline can't serve 75 airports.
ASSERTION	_____

Puny Hedge	I would like to introduce myself and describe the features of this phone system.
ASSERTION	_____

Puny Hedge	I'm not really sure how strongly I feel about this, but I don't think people want to work overtime without pay.
ASSERTION	_____

Stop Tripping on Tags: Keep the Power in Your Expression

A tag is a short question added to the end of a statement or command. Tags can take three forms: verbal, vocal, and gestural. Common verbal tags include *isn't it?, are you? doesn't she? won't you?* Researchers suggest that women use tags more than men do. Tags can weaken your statements by admitting doubt. Read the following examples of typical women's tags; then we'll explore how they usually harm you, how you can fix yours, and how they can help you, if you're in control.

This is the best proposal, isn't it?

That's a good idea, don't you think?

You want me to type this memo, right?

I called Mr. Santori this afternoon, okay?

That happens in my office too, you know what I mean?

The legal papers must be served by noon, you see what I'm saying?

What's wrong with these tags? Note that the sentence preceding each is a perfectly clear statement of fact, yet the tags turn them into questions, hinting that they may not be facts at all. That's how verbal tags undermine your statements.

A second form of tag is vocal, the lifting of the voice at the end of the statement so it sounds like a question: "My name is Sally? I work at Finance.com? I'm a vice-president?"

Finally, gestural tags such as shoulder or head shrugs undermine our statements. One senior executive introduced herself at a meeting and told that she manages a 52 million dollar budget; then she shrugged her shoulders. When you observe yourself on video, you can detect unconscious ways in which you negate your words.

Tags as power plays

Still, as with most language generalities, provocative exceptions exist (the Janus Principles in action!). For example, one study of executive language found that the company president added tags to ensure agreement. She said, "We seem to have reached consensus to build the new factory, haven't we?" Why is it powerful for the boss to add tag questions while it's weak for everyone else? The answer goes back to the complexity we talked about earlier. In any conversation, many factors surround the words spoken. If you hold power in the room, tag questions can make you more approachable and encourage people to disagree or respond in other ways. Powerful thinking precedes powerful language. If the tag serves a purpose for you, use it; if it's an unthinking habit, a sign of subservience, or a way of denying what you just said, avoid it.

Action Plan

Get a colleague or friend to join you as you empower yourself through language. Listen and observe each other carefully and note your tags; if the tags weaken (and most do), avoid them in the future.

The OTHER Four-Letter Word That Always Fails

As a little girl, you were taught never to use a four-letter verb beginning with the letter *f*, but that isn't the only one! The four-letter *f* verb that destroys credibility is *feel*. Feel proves useful when it describes smoothness, coldness, or illness. It's a useful verb when you say it at home or with friends. It's a useful verb in love letters. At work, it's wimpy, weak, and wishy-washy: feel fails. Indeed, feel is the only verb about which my earlier comments about complexity don't apply. Unlike tag questions, which can work in some circumstances, feel always fails at work.

This seems a scandalous idea, and it shocks most people when they first hear it. What would happen at work if no one discussed her feelings all day? What about the industry training programs that encourage managers to ask staff, "How do you feel about this?" If you can't imagine a day without repeatedly saying *feel*, think a bit about how and when you hear and use it. Look at these typical quotations:

"What are your feelings about . . . ?"

"I don't feel good about this expansion."

"How do you feel we ought to proceed?"

What did those people mean to say? Perhaps:

"What are the prospects for this .com stock?"

"This expansion threatens our plant."

"How should we proceed?"

I'm not suggesting that we revert to some unsympathetic, mechanistic workplace, only to one where women (and men) think, act, weigh information, and talk about these activities in a professional, powerful, civil, and kind way. Indeed, as Daniel Goleman notes, "People with high self-awareness are able to speak accurately and openly—although not necessarily effusively or confessionally—about their emotions and the impact they have on their work." Retain your passion, express your passion, but do so in the language of power.

Action Plan

Review your writing sample or videotape. Count the number of "I feel"s. Remove them. See how much clarity and strength you gain—and how many fewer words you require to get the message across.

How to Like, Stop Looking, Like, Ditzy

You're a career woman; you're not a Valley girl or a comedian. *Like* has so infected the language of young women that it's become a multipurpose filler. I've recently heard it preceding a verb: "I, like, go . . ."; replacing a verb: "So, I'm like, let's set up a meeting"; emphasizing an adjective: "It's, like, a successful product"; inserted for no apparent (to me) purpose: "Is this, like, a financial statement?" One writer, Malcolm

Gladwell, noted that ". . . the nuanced uses of . . . like . . . are now so numer-
ous and complex that they are understood only by several million junior
high school students and a handful of academics." Too many young
women have brought that junior high usage to work, and it damages their
credibility. The insertion of *like* where it doesn't belong screams "ditz."
Young women I've worked with all agree that they must eliminate *like*
from their spoken language. Yet it's hard to do. Here's a quick fix.

Action Plan

Annihilate *like* with a friend. Make a pact with an ambitious friend at work
(or at home). Ring a bell or a buzzer or make a drowning sound every time
either of you inserts "like." Ask trusted associates to help you as well.
Within a few days, you'll stop . . . and your language power will grow.

PUNY PASSIVES: A WORLD IN WHICH NO ONE ACTS

First, a quick grammar review to define passive voice and show how
we generate passive constructions. The prevailing, and sensible, way we
cast English sentences is in active voice: subject-verb-object (example:
The CEO wrote her talk.). This voice is active because the subject (the
CEO) acts out the verb (wrote) and the object (her talk) receives the
action. Some people think that active voice involves only people; that's a
misconception. The subject may be living or nonliving (example: The
speech brought the point home.).

Here's how we transform an active voice sentence into a passive. We
move the object (the talk) into the subject position, insert a "to be" verb,
and move the verb over. Thus, the active voice sentence, "The CEO wrote
her talk." changes into the passive construction, "The talk was written."
Even if we add "by the CEO," the verb remains passive (example: The talk
was written by the CEO.). Note that the passive-voice verb always requires
a version of the "to be" verb and that not every verb can be switched from
the active to the passive voice. Only transitive verbs, those that can take

objects, can be either active or passive. You don't have to be a grammarian to exploit this distinction to empower your language. These examples show the difference between active and passive voice:

Active	The team completed the project before the deadline.
Passive	The project was completed before the deadline.
Passive	The project was completed by the team before the deadline.
Active	The telephone company requires a proposal before June.
Passive	A proposal is required before June.
Passive	A proposal is required by the telephone company before June.
Active	The medicine depleted the patient's energy.
Passive	The patient's energy was depleted.
Passive	The patient's energy was depleted by the medicine.
Active	Thanks for your willingness to give me a personal tour of the facilities.
Passive	Your willingness to give me a personal tour of the facilities was very much appreciated.
Active	The diagram can fit anywhere on the sheet.
Passive	The diagram can be fitted anywhere on the sheet.

Failure to understand and control the grammatical forms lies at the heart of weak language. As Richard Mitchell says, "Either you must be the master of your language or you must be its slave." When you understand the difference between active and passive voice you can make wise decisions about which to use. When you control your grammar, you'll sometimes choose the passive as a powerful voice. More about that in the next chapter.

Action Plan

To see the murkiness and ineffectuality of the passive voice, read the following sentences and duplicate an exercise that we do in our communication seminars. We present four managers with a passive-voice sentence and ask each to recast it into active voice. Each of the four assigns a different subject to the sentence. Imagine what it's like when no one knows who does anything in a company. That happens when we drift away from the active and fall into the passive voice.

Passive	A solution should be found for this pressing personnel issue.
Active 1	Bill should find a solution for this pressing personnel issue.
Active 2	The CEO should find a solution for this pressing personnel issue.
Active 3	The vice president of personnel should find a solution for this pressing personnel issue.
Active 4	The firm should find a solution for this pressing personnel issue.

Of course, in the preceding example, you may decide that the sentence is really about the solution and not about the firm or the other possible subjects. In that case, retain "A solution" as the subject and decide what it does: A solution should emerge for this pressing problem.

Now that you've seen how it works, try it yourself. Pick up any manual, letter, or proposal and find a passive-voice construction (you'll find plenty). Then ask two or more colleagues or members of your women's network to recast the sentence in active voice. Compare your responses; you'll probably disagree on the missing subject.

The passive voice is a weak voice. It's also the voice of poor management. It reflects a world view without agents or clear responsibilities. Although passives pervade men's as well as women's writing and speaking, they especially damage women because we must be heard, and to be heard we must be clear.

Action Plan

1. Review a piece of your writing or run it through a computer grammar program to find all the passive-voice constructions. Recast them in active voice.

2. Read an article in a good professional or business magazine or book; note that well-written pieces use plenty of subject-verb-object active-voice sentences.

3. Read our heroes' superb examples of active-voice sentences. Here are a few, as written or said by one of them. After reading each sentence, read my passive-voice version. Try copying the strong form as you might use it in business writing or speaking.

Earhart	"He worried too much."
PASSIVE	Too much worrying was done.
BUSINESS	_____
Earhart	"I've weighed it all carefully."
PASSIVE	It has been weighed carefully.
BUSINESS	_____
Earhart	". . . it required concentration for the pilot to attend . . ."
PASSIVE	Concentration was required by the pilot to attend to her . . .
BUSINESS	_____
Ginsburg	"I appreciate the time the committee members took to greet me in the weeks immediately following the President's nomination."
PASSIVE	The time the committee members took to greet me in the weeks immediately following the President's nomination is appreciated.
BUSINESS	_____

Ginsburg	"But the justices do not guard constitutional rights alone; courts share that profound responsibility with Congress, the President, the States, and the people."
PASSIVE	But the constitutional rights are not guarded by the justices alone; the profound responsibility is shared by the court with Congress, the President, the States, and the people.
BUSINESS	_____
Hills	"Efforts to open world markets hit quite choppy waters in 1993."
PASSIVE	Quite choppy waters were hit in 1993 by efforts to open world markets.
BUSINESS	_____
Hills	"The new GATT accord will establish fair competition in agriculture . . ."
PASSIVE	Fair competition in agriculture will be established . . .
BUSINESS	_____

We'll return to passive voice later. For now, remember to shun the passive voice.

HYPERCORRECTNESS: A POOR CAMOUFLAGE FOR WEAK LANGUAGE

Still another language form that dogs working women and the weak in general is hypercorrectness. You are *hypercorrect* when, instead of comfortably speaking the language, you err by going beyond what's needed. As a result, you overpronounce words and make grammatical errors because they sound "fancy." A good example of this is the use of *I* when *me* would have been correct: "Please send the memo to *her and I.*" Here are other examples: "I will give the promotion to *whomever* meets the sales quota"; "Sara thinks *as* a good engineer"; "The design was created by Jim and *myself*"; "I *feel badly* about the incident." The grammar of power is a comfortable grammar that you control, while hypercorrectness suggests lack of control.

MODIFY, MODIFY, MODIFY

—till you haven't said anything at all. Modifiers such as *very, really, many*, and *certainly* work the same way hedges do, so use them only when they add vital information. We modify too much because we're searching for attention, because we lack precise words to express ourselves, because we're too insecure to make simple assertions, and, sometimes, because we just aren't thinking clearly. Observe how much you gain when you remove excess modifiers or replace them with precise ones.

Vague Modifier	We learned really very important skills at the workshop.
PRECISE	We learned how to run the new Windows™ program at the workshop.
Vague	Yours is certainly the very, very best report.
PRECISE	Yours is the most complete report.
Vague	The engineering project is extremely important to our future.
PRECISE	The engineering project is vital to our future.

Vague	Most workers arrived a little late.
PRECISE	Seventy-five percent of the workers arrived more than three minutes late.
Vague	I really, really want that job.
PRECISE	I want that job.
Vague	Many times, when I am faced with writing a memo, I don't know where to begin and I keep putting it off.
PRECISE	When faced with writing a memo, I often don't know where to begin, and I procrastinate.

It's easy to prevent excess modification. Review the text of your videotape, audiotape, or writing sample and delete or alter the modifiers.

THE WEAK LINKS:
AND, AND, AND, BUT, AND, BUT, AND, BUT

Still another grammatical weakness occurs when you string ideas together haphazardly, linking thoughts with "and" or "but" and overlooking ways to combine your thoughts. It's a childlike and primitive approach to linking ideas that women are said to use more than men do. Here's a strung-together description of a day at work.

> I arrive at Well-Read at 8 A.M. and rush to get coffee and then I start working at the word processor but the boss comes in to interrupt me so very little gets done and before you know it lunch time has come and my friends and I head out to the cafeteria and we eat together but time flies and before you know it we have to be back at work and in the grind again.

In the next chapter, you learn more interesting and nuanced ways to combine ideas.

Overkill:
Too Many Words, Cluttering Clauses, Jibber-Jabber

A damaging and untrue accusation against women states that we talk too much. Studies find that men both talk and interrupt more than women do. Still, some of us do talk too much, and most write too many words. Verbiage is another red flag of the grammar of weakness. Four essential tips in this chapter help you cut wordiness: avoid *I* statements, trim hedges, use active voice, and reduce modifiers.

In writing, wordiness also creeps in with cluttering clauses—ideas that don't contribute to the topic. Check to see whether your sentences are too long: they should average 17 words and should vary from short to long. If you write 53 or even 70-word sentences, you are probably using too many clauses, not just too many words. Cut sentences down to size by using no more than one independent and one dependent clause; that is, one main and one subordinate idea. Here's an example of an overly long sentence:

> I have carefully listened to the customers who service, manufacture, and troubleshoot the 9890 machine and I'm in full agreement that these most recent changes—elimination of round markings and the addition of casters in the bottom of the box—do not meet our customer requirements and therefore are not in the best interest of the 9890 program. (58 words)

The sentence gains clarity as well as brevity when it's cut. The cluttering clauses are left in parentheses:

> (*I have carefully listened to*) The customers who service, manufacture, and troubleshoot the 9890 machine find (*and I'm in full agreement*) that these most recent changes—elimination of round markings and the addition of casters in the bottom of the box—do not meet our customer requirements. Therefore, they are not in the best interest of the 9890 program. (37 words and 12 words)

Action Plan

First, count the words in a sample of your writing. Next, remove the *I* statements, useless hedges, and vague modifiers. Then switch all passive voice sentences into active. Count the words again and see how many words you've eliminated. You've probably reduced word count by 25 percent while increasing clarity and power.

Having discarded the puny grammatical forms, you can graduate to the grammar of power in the next chapter.

Quick Tips

Embrace complexity.

Follow the first two principles of the language of success.
Ask, What is it not about? What is it about?

Avoid the indecisive *I*.

Start with the subject.

Save intimacies for the home.

Trim hedges.

Eliminate unnecessary verbal, vocal, and gestural tags.

Shun the other *f* verb.

Stop, like, looking ditzy.

Prune puny passives.

Be correct, not hypercorrect.

Minimize modifiers.

Cut excess clauses.

3

Assert Yourself:
Use the Grammar of Power

. . . What this country needs is a woman with verbs.

THE NEW YORK TIMES

Y ou've broken the shackles of weak grammar. Now, add muscle with the grammar of power. The mentors, models, and master weavers of language beckon us to follow them.

Here you'll find the antidotes to language poison: the phrases and sentences that show you mean business, force people to pay attention, focus on issues instead of people, enable you to choose the way to communicate, and empower you to disagree and criticize without rancor or hostility.

Charlotte's Grammar

Charlotte was a grammar powerhouse. In contrast to the long, cumbersome sentences you see on the e-mail screen, Charlotte's short, crisp, active sentences inspire every business communicator.

"You have been my friend, . . . That in itself is a tremendous thing."

"Go to sleep. You'll *see* me in the morning."

"*Look* up here in the corner of the doorway! Here I am. Look, I'm waving."

"Well, I *am* pretty. There's no denying that. Almost all spiders are nice-looking."

"You will *live* secure and safe, Wilbur. Nothing can *harm* you now."

"I *drink* them—*drink* their blood."

"It's true and I have to *say* what is true."

"Way back for thousands of years, we spiders *have been laying* for flies and bugs."

Keep these in mind as you grow into the grammar of power.

Quick Review: Powerful Forms

In the last chapter, you recognized and dropped four weak grammar forms: puny hedges, tag questions, excessive modifiers, and hypercorrectness. You also replaced other weak forms with strong ones: *I* statements with focused subject statements; passive-voice verbs with active-voice verbs; and overly long sentences with crisp, short ones. Armed with these tools, you're ready to master other aspects of powerful grammar.

Verbs and the Will to Act

You don't have to be a grammarian to understand the grammar of power, but grasp the basic ideas. If your control of grammar is shaky, get a good adult grammar guide, such as *Action Grammar* (see the Bookshelf).

First, a discussion of an unlikely language mentor: General Ulysses S. Grant. In February 1999, one of my grown children called on the phone to tell me to read the current issue of *The New York Review of Books*. He said, "Read the article on Ulysses S. Grant—it looks like a Well-Read writing manual." And, sure enough, it did. The historian, James McPherson, in a tribute to the great Civil War general, lauds Grant's clarity of language. McPherson also asserts that Grant's battlefield success linked directly not only to his language in general, but to his *action verbs* in particular. McPherson cites, "The will to act, symbolized by the prominence of active verbs in Grant's writing . . ." For example, he quotes the order, "Pass all trains and move forward . . ." and says that such clarity "illustrates another aspect of generalship—what Grant himself called 'moral courage.'"

Why prefer action verbs as you seek clarity and power? Because they symbolize both *moral courage* and the *will to act*, the two key elements of the language of success. We'll return to Grant later when we discuss the language of leadership.

Let's look at verbs. Verbs do vital language jobs for us. They show action or state of being; they also help show the passage of time. For our purposes, even verbs such as "know" and "understand" count as action verbs, despite the fact that you don't actually *act* when you *know*. State-of-being verbs act as equal signs: they tell what things and people *are* rather than what they *do*. For example, when you say, "I am the leader of a team," you use *am* as a state-of-being verb, describing what you *are*. If, however, you say, "I lead a team," the verb *lead* tells what you *do*.

The *to be* or state-of-being verbs help us convey what things and people *are*. The word *am* in "I am a woman" can't be replaced by an action verb; it's just my state of being. Still, weak communicators use *to be* verbs when they should have used action verbs, saying sentences such as "It is important," rather than "It matters," or "We will be meeting next week," rather than "We meet next week." This chapter stresses action verbs because they lie at the heart of the languages of success and leadership. Consult your grammar guide for other information about verbs.

═══ *Action Plan*

To check your understanding of the difference between "to be" and action verbs, circle the following "to be" verbs and transform them into action verbs without losing the tense information. Look at the noun to see what verb it suggests. I've done the first three for you.

1. is a participant   *participates*

2. was an influence   *influenced*

3. were contributors   *contributed*

4. am the director   ~~directed~~ directing

5. is an organizer   organizing

6. is making a decision   deciding

7. is presenting an argument presents

8. will be presenting   _____

9. was successful   succeeded

10. is a leader   leading

Add Vigor with Action Verbs

Action verbs energize your language, make it lively, and bring you authority. Here are examples of women's business communications that use "to be" verbs when action verbs would have worked better. Compare them to your sentences and see which resemble yours. Then, every time you speak or write, ask whether an action verb could have replaced a "to be" verb. Note that sometimes you should recast or reorder the sentence.

To Be	The five-week product training *has been* an invaluable asset in understanding paper handling, mechanics, fusing mechanics, and operation of optics.
ACTION	The five-week product training *increased* my understanding of paper handling, mechanics, fusing mechanics, and operation of optics.
To Be	One of my biggest challenges is *to make* my writing clear, concise, and simple for my target audience.
ACTION	I *aim to write* clearly, concisely, and simply . . .
To Be	Your suggestion to continue my education *became* an important move in my business life.
ACTION	Your suggestion to continue my education *spurred* me to . . .

In sum, sharpen your thinking and language by removing or transforming unnecessary "to be" verbs. Remember Ulysses S. Grant and the will to act.

Now you know the three principles of the language of success, listed as questions:

1. What is it not about?

2. What is it about? (What is the subject?)

3. What does it do? (Prefer action verbs.)

Action Plan

Scan any well-written business piece: an article from the *Harvard Business Review, The Wall Street Journal, The New York Times*, a fine business book, a piece from a good trade journal. Circle the action verbs. The better the writing, the more action verbs you'll find. Keep a list of vigorous verbs and copy them in writing and speech.

ance Yourself for Power and Credibility

rlier about how women's use of emotional words, combined
ndency to start sentences with the word *I*, makes us seem
immature, tentative, and unbusinesslike. Now learn how to increase your
stature and credibility through distance. You'll see how to choose just how
close or how distant you want to be by adjusting the grammar of your
assertions. Let's take a sentence and see how to change positions with
regard to its subject.

Here's the first problem. Your secretarial pool has lost a member and
is overburdened with work. You must inform the manager. The choice of
subject determines how intimate or distant you wish to be.

> *About oneself:* I feel that we have too much work to get the job out
> on schedule.
>
> *About the group:* We have too much work to get the job out on
> schedule.
>
> *About the manager:* You've assigned more work than the pool can
> complete.
>
> *About the problem (active voice):* The pool cannot complete the work
> on schedule.
>
> *About the problem (passive voice):* The work load can't be completed
> on schedule.

Good example! →

Although these four grammatically correct sentences contain the
same information, they vary in persuasiveness and power, from a subjective statement that targets the victims to a factual statement that blames
the work load. Which will work best in that situation? Can you think of a
situation in which one of the other perspectives might have worked better?

Here's another example typical of problems managers face. An
employee badgers others and keeps them from their work. The manager
must stop this behavior.

About oneself: I want you to stop badgering the crew.

About the employee: You're badgering the other workers. You'll have to stop.

About the other workers: Everyone complains about your badgering.

About the problem (active voice): Badgering disturbs the entire work crew and must end.

About the problem (passive voice): Badgering will not be tolerated; it must be ended.

Notice how, by distancing (from *I,* the closest, to *you,* to the problem), you move from statements that invite dismissal as merely your emotional positions to statements that seem objective. Gain credibility and authority by controlling your distance.

Choosing your distance empowers you to handle a common, sticky woman's problem. A man interrupts your presentations, and you want him to stop. You ask him to meet you privately. Here are distances you may choose:

About oneself: I feel terrible when you keep interrupting me. Please hold your comments till the end.

About the boor: You interrupt me in the middle of my talks. Please hold your comments until the end.

About the problem (active voice): The interruptions destroy my credibility and train of thought. Please hold your comments until the end.

About the problem (passive voice): My train of thought is destroyed by the interruptions. Comments should be held until the end.

Action Plan

Describe a problem you face at work from the distances shown here. Copy the models or generate new sentences.

The Passive As the Voice of Power

In the last chapter we cited the passive voice as the voice of weakness, yet it works well in the examples just presented. That's because no grammatical form by itself is always weak or always powerful (the Janus Principles in action!). In general, wordiness and opacity make the passive a poor choice, and you should avoid it. But if you master grammar, you will sometimes choose it precisely *because* it is detached and unclear. When you have unpleasant or critical things to say, the distance of passive voice softens the blows. That puts you in control. As you progress through this book, you'll see situations in which the passive voice can work as the grammar of power.

Here are situations in which the powerful woman may choose the distanced, unclear, passive voice. If you assign subjects and turn them into active-voice sentences, you'll see why the passive may be preferable. This is the first "crib sheet" in the book. A "crib sheet" is a list of sentences or words to copy till you master the language of success.

Crib Sheet

To complain about something:

> Cursing will not be tolerated in this room.
>
> Rudeness can be taken as evidence of low self-esteem.
>
> Four latenesses were recorded on Jim's time sheet.
>
> Calling women "broads" is not accepted as business language.

To criticize:

> A price increase of that magnitude will be rejected.
>
> The design was not found to be user-friendly.
>
> Work like that will be seen as evidence of carelessness.

To avoid blame:

> The computer file was lost.
>
> Mistakes were made.

List criticisms or negative comments you should make at work. Write each in active voice. Use action verbs. Then convert them into passive-voice sentences. Decide which seem stronger.

"She Who Must Be Obeyed": Instructions That Work

Sue Bardokowski runs an engineering group. She complains that people don't listen to her or follow her directions. At every workshop I give, women managers and executives report the same problem. Why? Well, it is true that research shows that men tend not listen to women, even when the women are their bosses. Still, as clinical psychologist Dr. Ruth Haber says, "You have something to do with what happens to you." It's also true that women aren't casting their directives in the language of power. Here are four directions. Check those you use.

☑ 1. I need you to complete this report by noon.

☑ 2. Do you think you'll get a chance to complete this report by noon?

☑ 3. If you get a few minutes, I would like you to complete this report by noon.

☑ 4. I really need this job done fast. Could you do me a favor and redesign the product?

No wonder no one listens! Direction 1 is about the manager, not about the report. The manager may need her boyfriend's affection, but this direction is not about need. Direction 2 opens with a timid hedge and never gives an order. Direction 3 combines three weaknesses: it's conditional, it hedges, and it's not an order. Direction 4 reduces professional life to needs and favors. What does "She Who Must Be Obeyed" say?

1. Please complete this report by noon.

If there's some flexibility, but you don't want to leave an opening to say no, try:

1. It would be helpful if you were to complete the report by noon.
2. It would help if the report were completed by noon.
3. Sam put a crunch on us. The product must be redesigned fast.

Luckily, English gives us a gracious, polite, yet powerful way to give orders: it's the old-fashioned "please," followed by a precise action verb. Such orders are the watchword of She Who Must Be Obeyed.

Some women prefer to give indirect rather than direct orders. The linguist Deborah Tannen studied direct and indirect orders in business and military settings. She suggests that direct or indirect orders are not intrinsically weak or powerful. She also notes, however, ". . . issuing orders indirectly can be the prerogative of those in power." If your employees understand and follow your indirect orders, continue using them, noting that the distanced voices enable you to give indirect orders without resorting to the language of weakness. But if indirection hinders your ability to lead, consider the direct request. Save indirection for the times when you can wait or the person really has choices about whether and when to fulfill your directions. When you run the corporation, of course, you can give orders any way you want. The key here, as in all language, is control. You decide whether direct or indirect orders will work for you.

Which Method Works for You?

Indirect	*Direct*
That door is still closed.	Please open the door.
A way must be found to complete that job on time.	Please complete the job by noon.
This project is due by the twelfth.	Let's get the team organized to finish by the due date on the twelfth.
It would be helpful if the lunch were served at noon.	Kindly serve the lunch at noon.
Is the mail in the box?	Please check the box and bring the mail in.

―――――――――――――――――――――――――――――――― *Action Plan*

Write orders you give at work. Try them three ways: (1) weak, (2) indirect, (3) direct.

Powerful Ways to Say No

Women have learned all kinds of useful skills: we engineer, we practice law, we heal the sick, we manage offices, we run corporations. Yet, according to thousands of women with whom I've worked at every corporate level, we don't have powerful ways of saying no. On the whole, we lack the skills of resistance, and we pay a high price: in unreasonable work loads, in exploitation, in discontent. Here are women's descriptions of the problem:

1. I'll say I can do a task even though I know I don't have enough time just so I don't have to say no to someone.

2. I'm a Christian. I find myself extremely uncomfortable when the people at work curse. Anything I'd say about it would seem rude or

unpleasant. I wish I could stay very much a lady while letting people know that I'm so upset about the cursing.

3. The department head continually interrupts me while I'm trying to work; I lose the train of thought and have trouble getting back. This goes on all day, and I don't know how to stop it.

4. I have daily things I need to get done. Then, at the last minute my boss will ask me to get something done for him. That postpones my daily work to accommodate him.

5. I lead an all male purchasing group. I keep an open-door policy. One person takes advantage of this and comes into my office, sits down, and talks and talks. I want to be polite, but I don't know how to get rid of him.

6. I'm a nurturing manager. Because I'm sympathetic with the problems women face, I'm generous about time off and late arrivals. Although most of my staff use these privileges wisely, one woman takes increasing amounts of time off and doesn't get her job done. I can't be her mommy, and I don't know how to control the situation.

The grammar of power solves all these problems. Let's see how, in this "crib sheet."

Crib Sheet

PROBLEM 1	Try the language of distance: "Time won't permit that task to be completed now" (active voice) or "That task cannot be completed now" (passive voice).
PROBLEM 2	You can use the grammar of power, let them know what you think, and remain very much a lady. Try these: "That (cursing) is unacceptable behavior (it can be illegal as well, and grounds for dismissal)." Or, "Cursing makes people uncomfortable. Please don't do it when I'm around." The worst option here is the *I* statement: "I feel bad (or get angry) when people curse around me."

PROBLEM 3	You can control your own schedule with the grammar of power: "Interruptions make it very difficult to concentrate. It would be helpful if you let me know you want to see me, and I'll call you as soon as I complete this job." Or, "My efficiency improves when there are no interruptions. Please allow me to get this job completed before we discuss the next one."
PROBLEM 4	Make your words count by choosing powerful structures: "Please set the day's priorities in the morning; that'll help me do the jobs the way you want them."
PROBLEM 5	Although other managerial techniques help, you can handle this leadership problem with the grammar of power as well. "This proposal demands my attention now; let's plan 15 minutes next Thursday when we can meet." Or, "To save time, please drop me a note on the topic. That'll prepare me to discuss the matter when we meet."
PROBLEM 6	Here's where women's ways of managing run into snags. Your flexibility has earned the loyalty of the mature workers, but is exploited by the "little girl" who can't handle her responsibilities. She needs a leader, not a mommy. Distance helps you lead: "Although it's flexible, this job requires 40 hours each week. Please note your hours for the next two weeks so you can schedule yourself to meet the job commitment."

These examples, and others that follow, reveal that the grammar of power offers myriad ways for you to say no without seeming hostile, mean, or aggressive.

How to Resist Strongly . . . Yet Softly

The rules of engagement and the predominance of emotional language in the American workplace discourage active, friendly resistance and disagreement for everyone, men and women alike. Women are especially hampered by our traditions of meekness and timidity, politeness and subservience, so we find ourselves without intellectual or language tools to resist or disagree. The sentence forms in this chapter, added to your control over distance, equip you to resist, to disagree, to argue without enmity or aggression, and to take your place as a respected adult. Here are models you can easily fit to your unique work situation.

Action Plan

On the space under each model sentence, copy the form while filling in words you might actually use to resist or disagree at work. I've completed one for you.

Gentle Resistance

Model	This proposal will not fulfill the requirements for a new computer.
YOURS	This budget projection will not meet the customer specifications.
Model	But the current procedure promises to increase profits before June.
YOURS	_____
Model	It appears that mistakes were made in the engineering department.
YOURS	_____
Model	The restructuring led to the closing of this office.
YOURS	_____
Model	That view differs from the data in the financial report.
YOURS	_____

Model	The misunderstanding is regrettable.
YOURS	_____
Model	Civility will get us further than violent argument.
YOURS	_____
Model	It's unacceptable to speak for 20 minutes when the agenda allowed ten.
YOURS	_____
Model	The record shows 15 latenesses last month.
YOURS	_____

You have the idea. Control the subject and the distance; then you can remain civil, prevent personal attacks, avoid the weak *I* form, and become She Who Must Be Obeyed. Go for it.

Gain Unparalleled Power: The Parallel Form

Weak grammar strings sentences together with *and* or *but*, overuses so-called spontaneous speech, and relies on poorly constructed sentences. One cause of these problems may be absence of the most concise, powerful, and logical grammatical construction: the parallel.

What is parallelism? *The American Heritage Dictionary* defines it as "the use of identical or equivalent syntactic constructions in corresponding clauses." That's a technical way of saying that parallels match both in parts of speech and in coordinated ideas. The parallel can comprise a simple series in a list of items, an enumerated sequence in an entire piece, or a string of sentences linked by their similar forms. The examples in this section show several variations.

Strong communicators use parallels in speaking, in writing, and on visuals. That means you have plenty of superb models to copy. In *The*

Practical Stylist, Sheridan Baker writes, "Use parallels wherever you can. This is what parallel thinking brings—balance and control and an eye for sentences that seem intellectual totalities." Intellectual totalities, of course, lie at the core of the grammar of power. Parallels also discourage interruptions, compress information, and reveal your good ideas. But parallel thinking is not a quick fix: professional writers struggle to cast their ideas in parallel, and you will, too. Still, at our seminars, women get the knack of parallelism faster than they shed *I* statements: it's easier to learn new skills than it is to break the habits of a lifetime. As a beginner, you may want to copy the models in this book or those you find in your own reading and listening. Even as skilled a writer as T. S. Eliot learned from others, admitting that all writers steal, and the good ones do it well. So don't plagiarize, but do steal.

Charlotte's Web attains greatness because of its wonderful story, but also because of its wonderful language. E. B. White fills the book with exquisite parallels for you to steal. As you read them, note the clarity and efficiency; each phrase or sentence yields lots of information.

> Wilbur amused himself in the mud along the edge of the brook, where it was *warm and moist and delightfully sticky and oozy.*
>
> It smelled *of grain and of harness dressing and of axle grease and of rubber boots and of new rope.*
>
> I have to *think things out, catch what I can, take what comes.*

Parallelism serves all your language requirements. The examples that follow show the versatility and vigor of the structure.

Crib Sheet

In lists:

> Please bring the following to the meeting: pens, pencils, laptops, and lunch. (Lists can appear in sentences or with bullets.)

Jane is a superb secretary. She excels at speaking to clients, appearing professional, working well with peers, and managing the office.

In prepositional phrases:

. . . government of the people, by the people, for the people . . .

We meet at 9 A.M., in the courtyard, near the fountain.

In instructions:

Follow these procedures:

1. Gather the subjects.
2. Collect the data.
3. Repeat the experiments.
4. Analyze the results.

Action Plan

Use the models to create a parallel list, a parallel series of prepositional phrases, and a parallel set of instructions. Underline the parallels to be sure they match each other.

Read the sentences aloud and underline the parallels. On the lines below each model, copy the sentence forms as you'll use them at work.

Model	When the <u>first light comes</u> into the sky and <u>the sparrows stir</u> and <u>the cows rattle</u> their chains, when <u>the rooster crows</u> and <u>the stars fade</u>, when <u>early cars whisper</u> along the highway, you look up here and I'll show you something.
EXAMPLE	When <u>our company grows</u> and <u>our products work</u>, and <u>our employees prosper</u> and <u>the economy flourishes</u>, come to our meeting and we'll celebrate.
YOURS	_____

Model	"To misuse language is to mismanage people." (Virginia Phelan)
EXAMPLE	To engineer efficiently is to engineer profitably.
YOURS	_____
Model	The Internet demonstrates that a scientist can be physically isolated without being intellectually isolated.
EXAMPLE	Lawyers insist that a client can be demonstrably guilty without being actually guilty.
YOURS	_____
Model	"Almost without exception, these are the remedies that CEOs of troubled companies employ. Almost without exception, these remedies fail to deliver." (Andrall E. Pearson)
EXAMPLE	Almost without exception, women have internalized weak grammar forms. Almost without exception, women can change those forms.
YOURS	_____
Model	The education system is turning out a product, but it's a product that industry doesn't want.
EXAMPLE	Women are learning a language, but it's a language that business can't use.
YOURS	_____
Model	During the cold war, E-Systems eavesdropped on adversaries, gathered intelligence, analyzed data, and distributed information for the C.I.A., the N.S.A., the military, and foreign governments.
EXAMPLE	During the 1990s, women earned more degrees, got more promotions, and took more executive-level jobs than in the 1950s, 1960s, and 1970s combined.
YOURS	_____

Model	"If the metaphor for the 1980s was desk top, the metaphor for 1990 is conversation." (John Sculley)
EXAMPLE	If the language of the 1990s was locker room, the language of 2000 is power.
Yours	_____

Here are examples of parallel construction written or spoken by models and mentors. Copy them till you gain mastery over the form.

Amelia Earhart:

I have known girls who should be tinkering with mechanical things instead of making dresses, and boys who would be better at cooking than engineering.

Ruth Bader Ginsburg:

. . . courts share that profound responsibility with Congress, the President, the States, and the people.

Ruth Scott, candidate for mayor, Rochester, New York:

We must begin with a sense of what Rochester can be. We must envision a time when every city school is an exceptional school . . . when both our downtown and our neighborhoods thrive . . . when all those seeking work can find a good job . . . when young people grow up with hope, not fear, for the future . . . when no child in the city goes hungry . . . when no elderly person lives in isolation . . . when we have all learned the hard lessons and decided it is safer to live in harmony than in anger and pain. . . .

=== *Action Plan*

Keep a word-processing file for the language of success. When you find a useful model of one of the sentence types in this chapter, save it for future reference, analyze the way the words fit together, and copy it to craft sentences at work.

You've weeded out the weak and planted the seeds of powerful grammatical forms. Now turn to the words that bring the language of success to fruition.

———————————————————————————————————— *Quick Tips*

Replace weak with powerful grammar.

Prefer action verbs.

Control distance.

Know when to use the passive as the voice of power.

Become She Who Must Be Obeyed.

Say no powerfully.

Resist strongly, yet softly.

Use parallels.

Copy the masters.

4
Words That Work: Choose Them Wisely

For me, words are a form of action, capable of influencing change.

INGRID BENGIS

Words bring life to the grammar of power. This chapter opens with a review of Charlotte's vocabulary. Next, it purges you of the puny, weak words that sap energy. Just when you think you'll never speak again, you'll start building your word store, step-by-step. You'll learn how to think about words, use resources, and grow a vocabulary of power.

Word Power: How to Follow Charlotte's Example

Charlotte's power, as well as Amelia Earhart's, Justice Ginsburg's, and all the other heroes', is born in the absence of puny vocabulary and nurtured in the choice of rich nouns and verbs. She follows Churchill's dictum: "Short words are best and the old words when short are best of all." Charlotte's verbs drive her story. She "hurls," "waves," "drinks blood," "watches," "builds," "lays for flies." She never uses any of the awful jargon that infects corporate diction: *prioritizes, tangibilizes, customizes, calendarizes, bulletizes. Empowerization* and *repriorization* are unknown to her.

67

Charlotte's word power reflects a deep and broad education in vocabulary. She says "Salutations!" but admits it's a silly big word (and weak vocabulary is littered with gobbledygook far more pretentious than "salutations"). She knows how to use her big vocabulary to draw attention to key ideas: "But, my friends, if that ancient egg ever breaks, this barn will be *untenable.*"

She knows the value of connotations, those meanings that go beyond the literal definitions of words. For example, she rejects "crunchy" as a web word because she doesn't want the farmer to start thinking about crisp crunchy bacon and tasty ham. And connotation has been used as a weapon against women in business: every time you're called a *babe, a broad, a dame, a dolly,* a *trip,* someone is using connotation to diminish you.

Charlotte knows the Greek origins of English words, describing a cousin spider who is an aeronaut (*aero* = atmosphere or air; *naut* = sailor or ship). She knows Latin: the egg sac is her *magnum opus* (the greatest single work of an artist)! And she understands that words can have more than one meaning, weaving *humble* because it means "not proud" and "close to the ground," both of which are true of Wilbur. In addition, Charlotte boasts an extensive and precise technical vocabulary, listing the seven sections of each of her legs: "the coxa, the trochanter, the femur, the patella, the tibia, the metatarsus, and the tarsus." She never tags objects in the barnyard as "things."

In short, Charlotte leads by using words that count. And women who make the grade speak words that count. Even grammar strengths and organizational skills rely on a solid foundation of vocabulary. This chapter shows you how to choose precise, colorful, powerful words.

Six Steps to the Vocabulary of Power

STEP 1. THINK BEFORE YOU SPEAK

Mark Twain said, "The right word is to the almost right word as lightning is to the lightning bug." Which modern businesswomen's words would Twain have called lightning bugs? All words serve us if we use them well; they turn into lightning bugs only when we misuse them or, worse, use them mindlessly. For example, one meaning of the word *nice* works well: it's the engineer's concept of "showing or requiring great precision or sensitive discernment; subtle," as in *a nice distinction*. If you describe a fine engineering distinction as *nice*, you're using lightning; if (as many women do) you describe anything you happen to like as *nice*, you're uttering a lightning bug. Our lightning bug words fall into partially overlapping categories: hedges silly big words, jargon, vague words, nonwords, and itty-bitty weaklings. In this section, we review each and suggest lightning alternatives.

Hedges

The chapter on the grammar of weakness includes plenty of words that can hedge (*think, feel, believe, basically, frankly, to be perfectly honest,* and so on). Add your lightning bug hedges to the lists here. The correction is easy: if the hedge adds no meaning, omit it. If, however, real uncertainty forces you to hedge, try the strong hedges I've listed on the chart. As you grow more precise, add other strong ways to hedge.

Crib Sheet

Hedge	Strong Alternative
I think it will be a good quarter.	It should be a good quarter.
I feel this product will work.	This product promises to work.
We usually have bonuses every year.	We have bonuses most years.
I would like to . . .	I aim to . . .
I hope . . .	I plan . . .
I feel that this job isn't working out.	This job doesn't seem to be working out.
I'm not sure how I feel about this . . .	This may . . .

Hedge	Strong Alternative
I think this is about . . .	This is about . . .
I estimate this to be . . .	It's approximately . . .
In my opinion, the new hire . . .	It appears that the new hire . . .
The way I see it,	Apparently,

Action Plan

Review your tape transcript or a piece of writing. Substitute a strong hedge each time you find one that expresses real uncertainty.

Silly big words

Do big words impress people? No, despite Barbara Walters' quip, ". . . many people think polysyllables are a sign of intelligence." Big words aren't inherently either silly or impressive. They enrich language when they say precisely what no other word can say. Words such as *egregious*, *paradigm*, and *exegesis* add panache and exactitude when you use them appropriately. Learn and use the big words when they fit. Steer clear of "silly" big words; they drain your power. Follow Churchill's dictum that short words are best. Choose the shortest word that says exactly what you mean.

Silly Big Word	Smart Short Alternative
facilitate	ease, enable
tangibilize	make
calendarize	schedule
dollarize	price
endpoint, environmental direction	goal, aim
conceptualization	idea
proactive	prepared, foresighted, active
customize	fit, tailor

Jargon

Now chief medical writer for an international pharmaceutical company, Jan Minton started her career as a lab research assistant. On her first day at work, she received a batch of newly stained slides and was told, "Wash these slides." Conscientious and careful woman that she is, she proceeded to do just that, with soap, producing clear and shiny slides. What she didn't know was that, in a research lab, so simple a word as *wash* doesn't mean what it does at home. Jan had yet to learn the jargon of her field.

Just what is jargon, and how does it help or hinder your success? The second edition of the *Random House Dictionary* defines *jargon* in two ways: it's "vocabulary peculiar to a particular trade, profession, or group" and it's also "unintelligible or meaningless talk or writing." When your jargon fits the first description, it's powerful and it suggests that you're on top of your field. It's that kind of jargon that Jan Minton had to learn.

If, however, your jargon deteriorates into "unintelligible or meaningless talk or writing," then it hacks away at your language and your credibility. Use jargon only when it increases your credibility with a particular audience, never when it deteriorates into meaningless talk or writing.

The two-pronged definition of jargon reminds you to tune in to the audience. A word or acronym that's crystal clear in the "skunk works" may sound like mumbo-jumbo to the financial manager.

Action Plan

Check recent e-mails or other pieces of writing that traveled beyond your technical group at work. Underline words that meet the first definition of jargon. Circle those that would prove meaningless or unintelligible to outsiders. Change them to plain English.

Vague words and anemic modifiers

Researchers and linguists suggest that women modify too much and too loosely. The author Tom Robbins lumps these vague modifiers with "sponge" words, from which "you can wring meanings by the bucketful—and never know which one is right." Sometimes our sponge words are vague to begin with, but we also use precise words vaguely because we haven't thought about what we want to express. *Important* is one example: it's a fine word with a particular meaning. It shrinks into a lightning bug when we use it to mean everything from "noticeable" to "central."

Once we bog down in the swamp of lightning-bug words, we flail about for ways to modify them (it's hard to modify something vague!). So, when we want to stress an idea, we add anemic modifiers. *Important* becomes *very important; really, really important; really very important; extremely important;* and so on. Here are a few examples of words women use imprecisely when we mean something else or something stronger. If you start with the right word, your points will flash like lightning bolts.

Vague and Puny	Precise and Powerful
provide	furnish, give
impact (negatively, positively)	shrink, drop, grow, gain, hurt, impede, influence, impair, heal
share	tell, give, explain, present, report, detail, show, inform, discuss, exchange, trade
chat	meet, discuss, examine, explore, confer
develop	design, generate, create, produce, innovate
allow	enable
spend (time)	invest, use
very, very important	critical, essential, vital, central
enormously tall building	skyscraper
absolutely false	false
inadvertently forgot	forgot
as soon as possible	by September 14

Any overused word weakens your expression. Check your sample. Your favorite words may not be on my list, but you know them. Avoid them unless they say precisely what you mean.

Itty-bitty weaklings

We've been taught that women should be small, cute, or childlike, so we often use small, cute, childlike words—just when we want to be seen as strong, sensible, and adult. I call these words *itty-bitty weaklings*. You may have a few itty-bitty weaklings of your own. Scrap those on my list, and scrap yours as well.

Weakling	Notes and Alternatives
 *share*	You've succeeded in getting five critical male decision makers to listen to you propose that they buy your $40,000 product. You open by saying, "I'm going to share the benefits of my product." Ouch! *Share* (like *need*) is a touchy-feely word that works around the sandbox, but fails at work. Prefer any of the strong alternatives: discuss, examine, propose, describe, explain, detail, outline, and so on.
 *just*	Revisit the previous scene. This time you compound the crime by saying, "I'm just going to share . . ." or, "I'll share just a little bit about . . ." What does *just* do to you? It stammers, "Don't listen to little me." Avoid *just* and its puny companions.
need	The inappropriate use of *need* has grown so much that it deserves a special note. Don't place *need* on your "never" list with *feel*, but heed its problems. If you say *need* when you mean *require* or *demand* or as part of a hedge or if it appears often in your spoken or written presentations, you depend on it instead of finding the right word. Purge *need* if you say, "You need to get this job done," "We need to finish the meeting on time," "The customer needs on-time delivery."

Weakling	Notes and Alternatives
spend (time)	*Spend* is a financial metaphor. When we spend money, we no longer have it—so what does it mean to spend time? Aren't there better ways to work with people's time? Consider *invest*; it's businesslike, and it'll invest your language with vigor.
lovely, cute, divine, sweet, adorable	These typically female words add little information and make you seem weak. They don't belong at work.

STEP 2. ENERGIZE WITH ACTION VERBS

Nouns matter, but action verbs drive the language of success. We discussed action verbs in the last chapter, and will revisit them later as well.

Generating a verb tests whether you know what you're talking about. The good news about verbs: most of them already reside in your memory. Just learn to retrieve them. Here's a tip professionals use when seeking the perfect verb: after you've chosen the subject, make a list of all the possible actions it could take. Then try combining each with the subject until you find the verb that says precisely what the subject does. For example, you're proposing that the firm acquire a costly piece of equipment. You've decided that the subject is the ABC gadget. What verb should follow? *Works, improves, enhances, helps, gains, demonstrates, produces, monitors, eases, speeds*? Gadgets can do any of these actions: one of them will earn favorable consideration for your proposal . . . and success for you.

To ease the task of finding verbs that work, jot down good ones when you see them and keep lists handy on your bulletin board. After you've used a new verb a couple of times, it'll remain to enrich your trove of words.

The idea of synthesis lies at the heart of my consulting work. Since writing and speaking well require synthesizing a variety of skills and information, I collect verbs that describe synthesis in business. Here are a few that appear on my bulletin board: *absorb, match, blend, meld, overlap, meet, mix, melt, synthesize, weave, integrate, combine, collaborate, know, harmonize, graft, weld, glue.* Of course, each of these words has a unique meaning not interchangeable with the others. Richard Mitchell notes, "It is a special richness of English that it provides its speakers with many long lists of words that mean *nearly* the same thing." And it is the special obligation of the successful woman to choose the verb that means *precisely* what she aims to say.

=== *Action Plan*

Do you enjoy the work of a particular writer? If so, read a page of her or his work, circling the action verbs. You'll find plenty, and most of them will have only one syllable. Then check your script or writing sample and circle only the action verbs. Do you have plenty? Or are you still relying on those "to be" verbs? If so, copy the action verbs used by your favorite writer.

STEP 3. EMULATE CHARLOTTE: BE SAVVY ABOUT BUSINESS WORDS

Savvy women are savvy about words and ways words engage and persuade. Lois Niland, a marketing manager with Xerox prepared a talk on the unusual subject of ink jet "wet printing." Since her company name is rooted in *xer-*, which means dry (for dry copying), her group's work with "wet printing" is somewhat of an oddity. She cast about for an engaging lead and decided to investigate the prefix *xer-*. A Greek-reading friend looked up *xer-* in *The Greek-English Lexicon* and found that *xer-* also introduced a verb meaning "to wash one's hands with holy water . . . sprinkle with holy water, purify." Lois earned attention and credibility for her talk and herself by opening with this interesting tidbit about mixed "wet" and "dry" linguistic history.

Like *xerography*, business and professional words often originate in Greek or Latin sources. Many of the new words used in business also come from Greek or Latin sources. For example, a recent issue of the edgy *Business 2.0* magazine features invented words such as *pre-IPO* and *mediaplex;* these are easy to understand: people know that the prefix *pre* means before and that *plex* means interweaving. A scan of any computer manual reveals other invented words that rely on old-word origins: *subdocuments, repaginating, resizing,* and so on. If you know something about word sources, you'll also stand ready to create new words for new products, ideas, and Web sites. You'll also avoid traps of small usage errors. For example, anyone who uses the term *very unique* marks herself as one who's not sharp: the prefix *uni-* means one. There's only one of anything that's unique. A product can be very efficient or very inexpensive, but it can't be very unique. Here are business and professional words that you'll understand precisely and use powerfully when you know more about their sources.

Business and Professional Words Rooted in Greek or Latin

LATIN ROOTS		
Root	*Meaning*	*Examples*
arma	*n.* pl. arms	arm, arms, armory, disarm
brevis	*a.* short	brief, brevity, abbreviate
caput, capitis	*n.* head	capital, captain
civis	*n.* citizen	civic, civil, civilize
clarus	*a.* clear	clarity
communis	*a.* common	community, uncommon
cor, cordis	*n.* heart	cordial, discord
corpus	*n.* body	corporal, corpse
cura	*n.* care	accurate, curator
dominus	*n.* master, lord	dominant, dominion
fides	*n.* trust, confidence	fidelity, infidel
firmus	*a.* strong, stable	firm, affirm, confirm
fortis	*a.* brave, strong	discomfort, effort

Root	Meaning	Examples
genus	*n.* clan, sort, race	gender, general
gratus	*a.* pleasing, thankful	congratulate, grateful
lex, legis	*n.* law, rule	legal, legitimate
littera	*n.* letter of the alphabet	literal, obliterate
locus	*n.* place	local, locomotive
manus	*n.* hand	manacle, manual
memoria	*n.* memory	memorial, memorize
mons, montis	*n.* mountain	amount, mountain, paramount
natura	*n.* nature	denatured, natural
officium	*n.* duty, office, function	office, officer
ordo	*n.* rank, order	disorder, ordinary
pax, pacis	*n.* peace	pacific, pacifier
planus	*a.* flat, level	explanation, plane
plenus	*a.* full	plenteous, plenty
populus	*n.* nation, people	population, popular
proprius	*a.* one's own	property, appropriate
senex	*a.* old	senate, senior, senile
solus	*a.* alone, lonely	sole, desolate, solitary
verus	*a.* true	veracity, verify, veritable

GREEK ELEMENTS

Greek Element	Meaning	Examples
amphi-	both, around	amphitheater
ana-	up, back	analysis
anti-	opposite	antitrust
biblio-	book	bibliography, bibliomania
cata-	down, away	catapult, catastrophe
chromo-	color	chromatic, Kodachrome
chrono-	time	chronicle, chronology
cosmo-	world	cosmic, cosmopolitan

GREEK ELEMENTS, *cont'd*

Greek Element	Meaning	Examples
-cracy	rule by	autocracy, democracy
-crat	supporter of rule by	autocrat, democrat
crypto-	hidden, secret	cryptic, cryptogram
cyclo-	circle	cycle
demo-	people	democrat, endemic
dia-	through, across, between	diagram, dialogue
dyna-	power	dynamo, dynasty
dys-	ill, difficult	dysfunctional
ec-	out of, from	eclectic, eccentric
en-	in, into	ensemble, engrave
epi-	upon, at	epitome, epigraph
eu-	well, good	euphemism, euphoria
geo-	earth	geography, geopolitics
-gon	having angles, angled	octagon, hexagon, pentagon
-gram	thing written	epigram, monogram, telegram
-graph	thing that writes, written	monograph, telegraph
hemi-	half	hemisphere
hypo-	under, below	hypothesis
iso-	equal, alike	isosceles, isothermal
litho-	stone	lithography, monolith
-logy	study of, science of	psychology, theology
mega-	great, mighty	megalomania
meta-	with, beyond	metabolism, metamorphosis
-meter	measure	barometer, kilometer
-metry	art of measure	geometry, trigonometry
mono-	single, alone	monologue, monotonous
morpho-	shape, structure	morphology
neo-	new	neolithic

Greek Element	Meaning	Examples
-nomy	law	astronomy, economy
-oid	like, resembling	anthropoid, celluloid
-onym or -nym	name	pseudonym, synonym
ortho-	right, straight	orthodox, orthography
parap-	beside, beyond	paralysis, parenthesis
-pathy	feeling, suffering	antipathy, telepathy
peri-	around, about	perimeter
philo-	loving	philanthropist, philosophy
-phone	sound, voice	megaphone, saxophone
pro-	before, in front of	program, prologue
pros-	to, toward	proselyte, prosthetic
pseudo-	false	pseudoclassic, pseudonym
psycho-	mind	psychic, psychology
-scope	instrument for examining	microscope, telescope
syn-	with, along with	system, syndicate
type-	image, model	type, typography

Action Plan

Invest in words. Now that the great *Oxford English Dictionary* is available on-line, either ask your company to order it or invest your own hard-earned capital to get a copy. Learn how to use it and make it "your best friend in the word." The book versions are too hard to read and handle, but the electronic version gives you everything you'll ever want to know about words—their meanings, their histories, and their uses. Take the time to check words you use often and those you're not sure about.

Play with words. Create a .com fantasy company. Check the Greek and Latin pages to invent its title.

STEP 4. MILK METAPHORS: MAKE WORK A TAPESTRY, A GARDEN, A BIRTHPLACE

In metaphor, "a figure of speech that ordinarily designates one thing is used to designate another." A project design *is* a journey, a business competition *is* a war, a group of people working together *is* a team. Men think in male metaphors, so these monopolize business communications. For example, business words tap war metaphors—*logistics, spearhead, victory, sink (blast) the enemy, battle lines, strategy, tactics, set our sights, under the gun, take aim, target*—and sports metaphors—*Team Xerox, coach, warm-up, slam dunk, strike out, home run, win, teamwork, smash hit, grand slam, scoring*. Women attend business conferences that sound like war strategy or locker-room sessions. Executives make comments like "Soften up the beach," "Run it up the flagpole to see if anyone salutes," "Get on the bus because the grenades are going to go off." If you've had military training or know sports, such metaphors can help you fit in with the men and increase your chance of communicating.

War and sports metaphors may be useful, but beware. If our language suggests that business is a war or sports competition, it might *become* one of those. Too many businesses are warlike, hostile places where winning is all-important and where good workers are jettisoned.

For a while, we were encouraged to adopt warlike stances and metaphors to prove our worth in a hostile business climate. It didn't work. Women who did so are now called "bully broads" and find that war metaphors don't make for successful leadership.

Look to other, more fruitful metaphors to enrich your business language. Can you tap other metaphors that will not only enliven your speech but suggest that work is neither a war nor a competitive sport, but something else, perhaps something more humane?

Metaphors also help convey complex and sometimes scary ideas. In the April 2000 issue of *Business 2.0*, the editor writes, "Sometimes new ways of doing business are so jarring to traditional mindsets that they are called a bubble. But don't be soft-soaped into believing it." And e-tailers are called "brick and mortarless stores," an expert prods you to "have a seamless set of applications," and a discussion of the poultry industry Web site is titled, "Point and Cluck."

Amelia Earhart preferred peaceable metaphors. She was a woman in a "man's" job, and she wrote as the world was poised to enter a great war. Yet, the reader of her diary is struck by her use of typically "female" metaphors. Here are examples:

> "Not that my faithful Wasp [her airplane, not her husband] ever had failed me or, indeed, ever protested mildly. But, at that, the very finest machinery *could* develop indigestion."

> "So, on that sunny morning out of sight of land, I promised my lovely red Vega I'd fly her across no more water."

> "What with all that lovely world to look at, it required concentration for a pilot to attend to her knitting, which is to say, her horizon and her instruments."

> "The fields and valleys were upholstered with a deep-piled green jungle in an unbelievably continuous covering made by separate trees."

And Justice Ginsburg speaks eloquently without reference to war:

> "Yes, there are miles in front . . .,"

> ". . . he buoyed up my spirits . . . he served as the kindest, wisest counselor a nominee could have."

Dr. Caroline Sperry used birth and journeys in her application for a technical leadership position in a start-up firm. Here are samples:

"As xxx embarks on the journey from xxx to xxx, we must map new methods. . . . If you're the admiral of this fleet, I'll be the captain of its flagship. I look forward to a happy journey."

She got the job.

At a difficult moment, Orit Gadiesh inspired the people at her firm with a speech. Her voyager metaphor used the navigational term *true north* to mean the idea that defines an organization and its core values. These excerpts show her rich use of metaphor:

> "We've all used a compass to navigate. Most of us, out on a simple camping adventure, use an ordinary compass to find north . . . If you really need to find where true north is, you need a gyro compass that works based on its own *internal* system, rather than the external system of the very fickle magnetic field. Magnetic north is fine for an afternoon's walk. But if you're on a stormy ocean and the winds are shifting and you're running out of food and water—you had better know where true north is, or you may not survive. . . . Companies . . . that want to survive need to find their own TRUE NORTH. . . ."

The columnist Mary McGrory described herself as a "vagrant on the information superhighway—a loiterer with an attitude. . . ." She also used a gardening metaphor to criticize the "gardeners on the House Budget Committee" for overzealous "pruning" of social programs like Head Start, which "nurtures" the nation's "tender shoots."

Any hobby or interest can deliver metaphors that work. Businesswomen successfully use metaphors of travel, space, birth, life, computers, boats, and so on. Metaphors yield an almost unlimited source of words that meet all the standards of power: brevity, precision, ease of understanding, and fun.

What metaphors both reflect your view of the world and enliven your business presentations? Here are lists of metaphors generated by women in my workshops. Sample business sentences illustrate the first list.

Crib Sheet

Metaphors

Fabrics and Sewing

weave	Let's weave that idea right into the project.
spin	He spins a great sales story, but is it true?
thread	Our profits hang by a thread.
yarn	Carla Hills opened with a good yarn.
knit	Can we knit this sales force together?
tapestry	Diversity creates a rich tapestry in our work force.
web	See whether you can catch that prospect in your web.
hem	Well-placed sales offices can hem in the competition.

Gardening, Farming

plant	reap	seed
sow	feed	till
toil	grow	nurture
fertilize	plow	harvest
weed	uproot	winnow

Childbirth

conceive	incubate	foster
nurture	birth	groom

The Kitchen

percolate	stew	stir
simmer	recipe for success	blend
melt	spice	sift
ice	chop	dice

Action Plan

1. Choose useful terms from the metaphors listed here; incorporate them into sentences about your work.

2. List action verbs and other words linked to your hobby. Check those that promise to nurture your business vocabulary.

STEP 5. FOLLOW THE MENTORS

The language of success urges you to copy good ideas. You'll also do well to copy good words, especially verbs, as you find them. We've already listed some of Charlotte's words (although you won't have much business use for "drinks blood" or "lays for flies"). Our real heroes also prefer simple, clear, short verbs. In reviewing their work, one is struck by how totally free of jargon it is. Whether they're pilots, entrepreneurs, lawyers, doctors, secretaries, executives, or engineers, successful women communicate clearly and briefly. Here are verbs you can lift from the heroes to add to your power vocabulary. They're all in present tense here; vary them to suit your requirements.

Earhart: *fly, toy, fail, protest, promise, set, down, see, plant, watch*

Ginsburg: *appreciate, take, greet, thank, accompany, gave, buoy, serve, volunteer*

Hills: *hit, hang, persuade, mire, go, remain, project, steam, continue, announce, compensate*

Action Plan

Whenever you read or hear a powerful communicator, note the verbs you can lift into your own business language.

Step 6. Keep Your Word Store Up-to-Date and Ready-to-Use

You don't wear clothes you bought 25 years ago. Why do you still use the dictionary you got when you graduated from high school? When Wilbur failed to spin a web, Charlotte told him, "You lack two things needed for spinning a web . . . you lack a set of spinnerets and you lack knowledge." Consider the dictionary as part of your set of spinnerets and as a vital source of knowledge. Here are pointers on how to get the most out of your dictionary, on-line and in print.

How to get the most out of your dictionary

1. Check the publication date: Language changes fast these days, so you want a timely source.

2. Read the introduction. Dictionaries are self-teaching devices. The introduction tells you how the dictionary is structured and how to read the entries.

3. Learn how to read etymologies. The story about the prefix *xer-* shows that the etymologies, the histories, and the structural elements of words offer rich sources for talks, product names, and precise definitions. A word's etymology is always found with the definition of the base form. For example, the etymology of *readability* will be found in the entry for *read*.

4. Use it often. The dictionary offers much more than spellings. If you learn three or four new words every time you use the dictionary, you'll harvest bushels of new words to bring to market.

=== *Action Plan*

Follow the six steps. Also keep a list of strong words you come across on the Web, in magazines and books, and at business conferences. Check their definitions and make it a point to use them once or twice at work. After one or two uses, they'll enter your word store.

Now that you have met both the grammar and vocabulary of power, you're ready to get organized.

Quick Tips

Avoid silly big words.

Use precise big words.

Be wary of connotation.

Drop lightning-bug words.

Hedge powerfully, if at all.

Use jargon judiciously.

Avoid unintelligible or meaningless jargon.

Shy away from vague words and anemic modifiers.

Lose itty-bitty weaklings.

Energize with action verbs.

Learn Greek and Latin origins.

Harvest fertile metaphors.

Copy words from mentors and models.

Acquire and use current dictionaries.

5

Get Organized: A Recipe for Confident Communication

Don't agonize. Organize.

Florynce Kennedy

It was a celebratory luncheon for a corporate award. The vice president, one of the best and most experienced in the business, was the invited speaker. Although she expressed some discomfort at the idea, she accepted the invitation. Yet this woman, who plans, organizes, and executes multimillion-dollar projects with supreme ease and confidence, fell apart at the podium. Speaking spontaneously and without notes, she started talking about the award, then gradually took on all the weak phrases and hesitations of the grammar of weakness: "and we . . . um expect this award to . . . uh to be a great success, and . . . I guess you'll all enjoy it . . . uh . . . ." And she rambled endlessly, repeating herself and taking the audience nowhere till she limped to a puny conclusion.

What went wrong? The secret to this failure lies in the words *spontaneously* and *without notes*. Except for an exceptionally gifted few, no one can give a strong talk or write a clear piece without planning and structure. In this chapter, you'll learn how to avoid the unpleasant and demeaning situation of the vice president's luncheon talk. You'll learn a recipe for planning just about any piece you'll ever speak or write. It's also a recipe for rising above the stereotype of the disorganized, "spontaneous," emotional woman. This approach won't help you speak like a man: it'll help you speak like a powerful, confident woman. Let's start with our mythic hero, Charlotte. Was she spontaneous?

Planning Is Power:
Learn from Charlotte's Organization System

Charlotte's brilliant success with the web of language was no accident: she not only planned carefully, but understood her own thought processes. "I have to think things out, catch what I can, take what comes." When Wilbur asks how she'll save his life, she says, "I don't really know. But I'm working on a plan. The plan is still in its early stages and hasn't completely shaped up yet, but I'm working on it." Because she planned so well, Charlotte was efficient: she pointed out that people took eight years to build the Queensborough Bridge while she could make a web in a single evening. No hours of staring at blank barn corners for Charlotte—or for you, after you master my system.

Contrast Charlotte's approach to the language of weakness, the language without plan, the "spontaneous" language women traditionally are said to utter. John Kennedy quipped, "Spontaneous speeches aren't worth the paper they're printed on."

Planning separates the women from the girls, the strong from the weak, the confident from the fearful. The organization system in this chapter shows you how to do as Charlotte did: invest time to consider your audience and think through ideas. The organization system enables you to work quickly and save hours of staring at a blank screen. You can even speak strongly at informal meetings by taking a moment to use the rudiments of the system to plan before you speak. You'll walk through the steps twice in this book: in this chapter through Linda Rubin's talk, and in Chapter 9 through Elizabeth Ames's letter.

Make a Million? Yes. Speak to an Audience? No!

Linda Rubin is director of development for a community home for the elderly. She was invited to give a one-hour presentation at a national conference of her peers. Because she lacks formal training (she came to her job from years as a volunteer), and because she's a woman, Linda, who thinks nothing of requesting a million-dollar grant, came to me in terror. Although she had built an annual giving program from $30,000 to $400,000, she feared she'd speak like a "blithering idiot." Dread paralyzed her so that she hadn't done anything about her presentation but worry. But in her case—and, perhaps, in yours—her lack of self-confidence was linked to a lack of skill. She knew how to raise millions but she didn't know how to plan a one-hour talk. Of course, men may not know how to organize either, but their listeners are more forgiving. Studies show that when a man and a woman give the same talk and all other things are equal, the audience finds the man more credible. Women are *expected* to be "spontaneous"—a euphemism for disorganized.

Determined to overcome her fear, Linda learned the organization system and followed each step, much as she'd followed recipes for years. Her efforts added up to a fine presentation from a confident woman.

A No-Fail Recipe for Successful Communications

Structures

First, let's frame the organization system with the idea of structures. Think of the communication as a building. A building has a series of required structures: walls, a roof, floors, doors, and so on. It also has a series of optional structures: windows, stairways, chimneys, water heaters, and others. Then it may have decorative structures such as paint, wall-paper, and moldings. Like buildings, communications also have required optional, and decorative structures. Once you understand the notion of structures, you can apply it to every talk, speech, presentation, letter, e-mail, meeting, and phone call you compose. The "Power Reading" system you'll read about later is also based on the structures of written material.

No builder ever laid a brick without planning the building's structures; no speaker should say a word without planning the talk's structures. That's why E. B. White wrote, "The first principle of composition . . . is to foresee or determine the shape of what is to come and pursue that shape." So before we organize, let's foresee the shape of what is to come in Linda's presentation (and yours too).

The overview

The overview shapes the overall structure of the presentation.

The lead

The lead opens the piece. It engages the audience, suggesting that what is to come will repay their attention. If barriers separate you, the lead must breach them. The barriers may be physical: distance, equipment, or room layout; or psychological: lack of familiarity, bias against your gender, race, or age; or may result from vast differences in educational or professional level. Awareness of the barriers helps you to figure out how to breach them in the lead. Leads can consist of vignettes, quotations, generous words about the audience, even dictionary definitions.

The thesis statement

The thesis statement is one or more complete sentences that gives the overview of the argument and predicts what is to come. Think of it as an umbrella that covers the entire talk but doesn't tell all the details.

The internal structures: reminders, transitions, topic sentences, and details

The internal structures are the building blocks of the communication. Sets of details blend to form the topics, which are covered by their own little thesis statements, the topic sentences. The reminders and transitions then form the mortar that hold the blocks together.

The end structures

Strong speakers know how (and when) their talks will end. Although the end is a required structure, it may be composed of one or more of the optional ending structures: the summing up, the review, the conclusion, the call to action, and the strong ending.

Now that you've met the structures, you'll learn how to craft them through the organization system.

THIRTEEN STEPS TO ORGANIZED PRESENTATIONS

You wouldn't think of baking a cake without a recipe. The organization system is a recipe for cooking up clear, concise business presentations. But this recipe does more: it fosters clear, concise thinking and lends itself perfectly to on-screen organizing. Systems consultant Stephanie Rathe notes, "... when I started using the system on-screen for writing, I was able not just to write better but to envision relationships as I manipulated the ideas." You may choose to apply the system on-screen; however, as of this writing, most find it easier and faster to use the sticky-note system. As with any recipe, once you master the basics, vary it to suit your own goals.

The system works in 13 steps. To show it in practice, I'll give each step in detail first and raise issues for you to consider when you apply it. Next, I'll describe exactly how Linda applied each step to create her talk.

1. Think about the audience.
2. Determine the purpose(s).

3. List the details.
4. Group the details.
5. Order the details.
6. Name the topics.
7. Sequence the topics.
8. Write the thesis statement.
9. Write the lead and end structures.
10. Plan the paragraphs, topic sentences, transitions, and reminders.
11. Write the piece.
12. Plan the visuals.
13. Practice, tape, edit.

Before you begin, assemble a set of small sticky notes and cards along the lines of the models that follow. Later, revise the size and layout of the cards to suit your unique situation.

OVERVIEW

Form: Letter Memo Proposal Report Talk Other

Step 1: For whom? _____

Step 2: Purpose(s)   a. _____
                verb
             b. _____
                verb
             c. _____
Step 3-10: On cards   *verb*

Step 11: Write   Step 12: Edit
                                        Step 13: Proof

LEAD

The lead must overcome the barriers that separate you from the audience, relax their defenses and indicate that you're about to say something worthwhile:

Good words about audience, location, group
Recognition of individuals in audience or group
Recognition of previous and coming speakers
Short apt story
Dictionary definition
Quotation

TRANSITION to thesis statement (if required) _____

Organization System

THESIS

Think of the thesis statement as an umbrella covering both the purpose and the topics, in their proper sequence.

Organization System

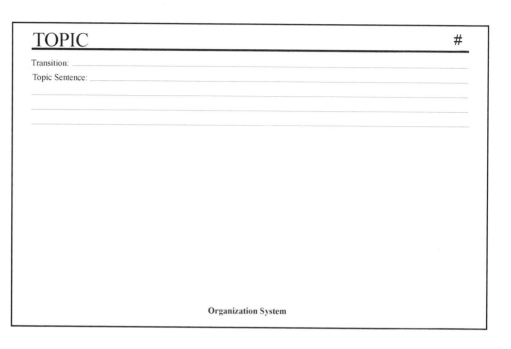

TOPIC #

Transition: _____

Topic Sentence: _____

_____

_____

_____

Organization System

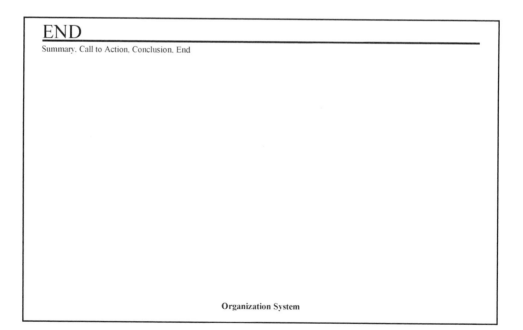

END

Summary, Call to Action, Conclusion, End

Organization System

Step 1: Think about the audience.

Before she spun a single thread, Charlotte followed step 1. She analyzed the audience: "If I can fool a bug . . . I can surely fool a man. People are not as smart as bugs." Just as Charlotte's writing reflected her understanding of the audience, so should yours. For whom are you writing? To whom are you speaking? If you answer this before organizing ideas, before setting a word on paper, you'll plan faster and more logically. Later, we'll highlight differences between spoken and written language, but at this early stage, the planning is the same whether it's for a talk or a written piece.

The decisions at this stage shape not only the forms of words and sentences but the way to edit and organize the material. Are your listeners all men, all women, or mixed? Are they your age, younger, or older? Are they used to hearing from women, or are you the first woman ever to do this presentation? You know how you feel when a writer or speaker assumes all readers are men; don't make the same mistake. Indeed, the most egregious failures in my files grew from male speakers assuming that all audience members were other men who liked to demean women. Think of a business meeting at which key speakers open with dirty jokes or sexist comments. It's hard to believe they still occur in the twenty-first century. In one such meeting, an executive told a mixed audience of a news story about male earthworms dying early because they used up their sperm; he then likened himself to those male earthworms.

Also consider your power relationship with the audience. Can you tell them what to do? Are you the buyer or the seller, the satisfied or the discontented? Are they more educated than you are, or less educated? Likely to agree with you, or to see you as a threat? If they do, you must counter that threat and win them over at the start, or it won't matter how well organized you are. One woman, the artistic director of a summer chamber-music camp, had to write a letter enlisting the aid of music teachers in finding suitable students. It was essential that they not see the camp as a potential usurper of their students. She countered the possible threat by using such phrases as "When they return to you in the fall . . ."

This first step is central: if you get it right, chances are you'll succeed even if you err on later steps. The better you understand the audience, the better your chance of success.

Here is Linda's audience analysis. A phone call to the conference organizer unearthed the information that the audience would be from medium-sized cities like Linda's and that they had an average of seven years' experience. They'd seek specific, practical ideas that they could follow in their own communities, not global concepts or motivation. In response to this information, Linda included a packet of typical fund-raising letters and flyers with the other handouts. She also steered away from the basics and addressed issues pertinent to experienced development directors.

Sometimes audience analysis requires either less or more than a phone call. If you're planning to speak to associates with whom you work every day, you already know the audience. In that case, jot down a few notes on how they're likely to respond to your ideas, what they look for in a talk like yours, who might prove troublesome. If, however, your audience is a mystery, you can get hold of the conference schedule (if you're addressing a conference) or call members of the group. If none of these sources yields the information you require, arrive early on the day of your talk, buttonhole people in the hallways, ask about them and their colleagues, and try to get a good story to add to the prepared text. You'll be paid handsomely for your curiosity. On step 1 of the overview card, add notes about the audience.

Step 2: Determine the purpose(s).

Remember Charlotte—she knew her purpose precisely, and it wasn't some weak-kneed (of course, she didn't have knees, being a spider) one like, "to share ways to save Wilbur's life." Ask yourself, What does this communication aim to accomplish? If Charlotte had completed an overview card, her purpose would have said, "to persuade (the humans) that Wilbur is a unique pig whose life must be preserved."

Jot down the purpose(s) on your overview card. If, for example, you wish to sell an engineering software package, list that as a purpose; but you may be more persuasive if you also ask what steps the audience has already taken to solve a related engineering problem. Elizabeth Ames's memo in Chapter 9 fails in part because she hadn't decided what that memo was to accomplish.

Women of action use action verbs. Your communication must do something. Here are some verbs you might select:

alert	implore	propose
cajole	impress	rectify
clarify	incorporate	report
compare	inform	request
complain	initiate	review
convince	inspire	sell
demand	instigate	specify
describe	instruct	stimulate
detail	integrate	suggest
enlist	intimidate	support
enumerate	introduce	synthesize
explain	motivate	teach
foster	persuade	threaten
frighten	present	train

On the line following the purpose(s), complete each phrase. For example,

inform (accounting department) of three new procedures

describe the steps to amend a contract

persuade (the committee) to use the new accounting software

train to operate the six-foot press bench

intimidate (football coaches) into accepting girls on the team

Here are Linda's purposes. At first, Linda made a common error: she thought the talk was about her and her program, of which she's justly proud. Here's how she described her purposes:

share how we grew from a small development office

tell the story of our program

describe how we organized successful annual campaigns

Then she thought more about the audience and realized that they weren't interested in her or her program: they were interested in improving their own programs. So she changed the purposes to

tell how to grow from $30,000 to $400,000 a year

detail management of an annual membership program

describe methods that have worked in a medium-sized city

Note the subtle changes in Linda's language: she went from the equivalent of *I* statements to distanced and powerful purposes geared to the audience's interests and expectations.

Step 3: List the details.

Here's where the organization system differs from other ways of planning communications. Instead of starting with general topics, start by listing the details you might want to include. Write the details, in words or phrases, one detail to a card or sticky note. Don't write much, but be specific. For example, "save 30% or more" is better than "save time." This approach enables you to add or remove particulars as you analyze the readers, the purposes, and the information to present. Evaluate each detail. Does it advance the purposes of the piece? Does it speak to your audience? If not, discard the sticky note or delete the detail. A thoughtful view of details enables you to write or say less because you include only essential data and never repeat yourself. Careful selection of details prevents those oft-heard complaints that women say too much, say too little, or say trivial things.

Linda's successful programs grew from her understanding that "God is in the details." She knew that the $400,000 she raised each year was the sum of many small gifts, the result of myriad minutiae carefully considered. But she also knew that her speech would be long and dull if she included them all. She wrote the details on the sticky notes and spread them on a large table top so she could see them all at once. Linda's original list contained these entries (only 25 percent of the details are shown):

introduce direct mail	plan first
annual giving	get database in good order
handout	hired new manager
362 beds	importance of consistent image
community of 25,000	high-quality image
moved in 1985 from old to new	suggest next gift
started in 1920	tell what to do
mission statement	P.S. (got $1,000 gift)
15 percent in one financial category	if stranger, no salutation
operating support for ongoing programs	response choices recognition
opposed to building fund	gifts
nurture and develop leadership	cards
80 volunteers	membership open house
know own community	tell names
take time to identify prospects	

Step 4: Group the details.

Grouping details involves more than putting material together, it enables you to reason at a high level. Move the sticky notes around, grouping and regrouping them to see how they fit together to support the purposes. You can group the details in unexpected ways; for example, the financial data and quarterly profits may be more impressive if presented separately. As you think about the details and assemble the groups, you're synthesizing. Synthesis is the highest level of reasoning, the kind of thinking essential for success in business and professional life.

Linda's "brain dump" of details that fell in no particular sequence began to take shape. Some ideas fit logically together. For example, Linda saw that she'd begun to craft some general principles that guided the program, so she grouped those together. Then she noted that it made sense to separate the details on the direct-mail program and annual-giving club and that clusters of ideas emerged within these groups.

Step 5: Order the details.

When you're satisfied with the logic of the groupings, think about how to order the details within each group. Ordering challenges your creativity: Will the piece be more powerful if you hit the strongest point first? Should the date rather than the place of the appointment go first? Examine the possible sequences critically and choose the most effective one for each group.

The outline for step 7 shows how Linda ordered some of the details.

Step 6: Name the topics.

Affix the detail notes to the topic cards. Name each topic just as you'd name a heading in a report. The topic names may not appear in the final piece, but they'll grow naturally into the topic sentences.

Here are Linda's topics:

Introduction
Annual-Giving Club
Direct-Mail Program
General Principles
Ongoing Activities
Conclusion

Step 7: Order the topics.

Just as you ordered the details within the groups, order the topics. For example, in a sales letter, would you place "Customer's Needs" before or after "Product Description"? As with all sequencing decisions, there is no correct way to order the topics: you decide as you reason through the planning process, keeping in mind the audience, the purposes, and the line of argument you plan to follow.

Linda selected the following order, but she could have chosen other ways of ordering the topics. For example, General Principles could have come at the end rather than near the beginning of the talk. As a matter of fact, a month after her presentation, she was asked to address the local board of directors. It was easy to reorder the topics, omit information everyone already knew (for example, the size of the institution), and introduce details that wouldn't have interested the group at the first talk. The organization system allows her maximum flexibility and efficiency. Here's a portion of Linda's final outline, showing the order of topics and the layers of detail under one.

I.   Introduction and Overview
II. General Principles
    A. Strong mission statement reflects community's goals
    B. Every gift matters: little gifts grow to big ones
    C. Annual giving
        1. Supports ongoing programs

2. Broadens database
3. Nurtures leadership
4. Increases community visibility
5. Requires consistent high-quality image
   a. Design good graphic standards
   b. Personalize where possible
   c. Spell names correctly
   d. Say thank you, thank you . . .
6. Builds on strong database
   a. Institute strong record-keeping practices
   b. Ease retrieval of names and addresses
7. Works only to extent it's tailored to community

III. Direct-Mail Program
   A. Background
   B. Pointers
   C. Tips on letter content
   D. Acknowledgment
   E. Recognition

IV. Annual-Giving Club
   A. Background
   B. Design

V. Conclusion and Call to Action

Step 8: Write the thesis statement.

Think of the thesis statement as an umbrella covering both the purpose and the topics, in their proper order. Write the thesis statement on the thesis card in one or a few *complete sentences*. Remember that the thesis is general. It clearly outlines the big picture, not the details, although it can predict the order of the topics to follow. In speaking or in writing, a clear thesis statement shows you're one to be reckoned with. Apply everything you've learned about the grammar and vocabulary of power as well as the three principles: What is it not about? What is it about? What does it do? That means, of course, that the word *I* won't appear in the thesis statement unless you've been asked to give a talk about yourself (and even then you can avoid most *I* statements).

Here's Linda's thesis: "Although it took years to develop our annual membership campaigns, our insights and approaches can help you to grow from $30,000 to $400,000, or whatever your organization aims for. After a brief introduction, this talk lays out general principles, then details how to run a direct-mail and an annual-giving program."

Step 9: Write the lead and end structures (by adding the words on the appropriate cards).

Note that, although you write the lead after you've written the thesis statement, you deliver the lead first. The lead plays three crucial roles in the language of success. First, it establishes your credibility; second, it builds a bridge to your audience; and third, it sets the tone of your presentation. Women must accomplish all three of these at the very beginning because many people expect us *not* to be credible, they envision us as outsiders (or, worse, as interlopers), and they anticipate the wrong tone. So the lead deserves great care.

Although my male clients often have difficulties in their openings, they don't seem to diminish their credibility in the ways women do (unless they tell dirty or demeaning jokes—then everybody marks them as jerks). Here are examples of failed leads written or spoken by professional women: "I've never given a talk like this before, so I'm very, very nervous"; "I don't really know much about this subject, so I'm really happy to be here today"; "Let me share my department's budget with you"; "I apologize for making you sit through this boring talk."

E-mail rarely requires a lead—simply open with the thesis statement (not I). Opening with the thesis is a good way to communicate efficiently and also a sure way to cure yourself of the "staring-at-the-empty page" blues.

As an alternative, the lead may simply thank the reader or listener for an inquiry or for meeting with you. For example: "Thank you for your inquiry" or "Our lunch last week clarified your requirements for an efficient system." Note that both of these leads talk about the audience or the business subject, *not about the writer*.

Since she's not widely known outside her city, Linda knew that she had to establish credibility about her financial and business savvy before anyone would want to learn about the particulars of her development program. She decided to be fully professional and friendly, but somewhat formal at the beginning. She opened by building a bridge to the audience:

> Welcome. I'm Linda Rubin, development director of the Foundation for the Aged in Middle City, New York. It was a great joy to meet [names] before the session and to learn of our common goals. We all seek to enrich the lives of the elderly in our communities at a time when they no longer can do so for themselves.

She then gave straightforward information about how long her program would take, how it was structured, and how she hoped people might benefit from it:

> My talk discusses how to grow an annual membership program from $30,000 to $400,000 in several easy lessons (or maybe many hard lessons!). We have one hour: the talks take about 25 minutes and then we'll have an informal discussion about how you can use these ideas to build your programs.

She held her delightful stories and anecdotes and told them after she'd established credibility.

Next, she prepared the end structures, choosing a conclusion, call to action, and strong ending (quotation). Here's her ending:

> We have built an annual-giving club, step-by-step (sometimes stepping backward to be sure!). If our experience can help you avoid any pitfalls or speed your progress, this talk will have done its job. Please use these ideas, tailor them to your community, copy any of the materials in your

folder. I wish you luck as you embark on the most honorable of call-ings, your response to the commandment, Honor thy father and thy mother. Thanks.

Write the end on the appropriate card.

Step 10: Plan the paragraphs, topic sentences, transitions, and reminders.

Each topic card and its accompanying details usually form a para-graph. Crafting a paragraph taps the logical skills women are thought to lack. Each paragraph generally presents a major idea and defends, details, or explains it. Well-constructed paragraphs can convince the audience, advance your purpose, and give a professional tone.

Linda's thesis statement revealed her logic right at the start. Then, as she spoke, she led the listeners through by reminding them of what the last paragraph was about (reminders and transitions) and what the new topic would be (topic sentences). Here's how she led the audience through the *internal* logic of the talk:

> First, meet our organization . . .

> Now that you know about us and our community, here are general princi-ples that guide our development programs and can guide yours as well . . .

> These principles result in practical tips on a direct-mail program . . .

> Thus, the direct-mail program not only raises funds, but also builds the foundation for the annual-giving club.

Step 11: Write the piece.

The job of planning a powerful communication is almost done. That blank screen no longer intimidates. Now work directly from your cards to flesh out the details and complete the piece.

Step 12: Plan the visuals.

Visuals can aid or distract, clarify or confuse, motivate or bore. My company's view of visuals found inspiration in the brilliant work of Edward Tufte at his seminars and in his book *The Visual Display of Quantitative Information*.

Step 13: Practice, tape, edit.

Linda practiced before her office staff, her boss, and her peers. She didn't ask them to be kind to her—she requested legitimate criticism. Each time she practiced, she gained confidence and fine-tuned her talk. We'll return to Linda's actual presentation in the next chapter.

=== *Action Plan*

Try the system. Plan a talk or written piece. Follow the 13 steps. When you're at ease with them, vary the system to meet your singular requirements.

THE PRICE OF "SPONTANEITY"

Both the research and my experience suggest that businesswomen often fail to follow either my organization system or any other. To see the price you pay when you neglect such careful planning, read the wimpy memo in Chapter 9. It reviews the organization system and suggests how the writer could have used it to plan a memo that worked.

Master the Recipe—Then Create

Pastry chefs master basic butter creams before they spin delicate frostings. Master the organization system; then spin your own variations.

This system saves endless hours of rewriting and enhances not only your image but your ability to think clearly. Its variations work on the phone, at informal meetings, and in planning long documents. All my seminars, books, and speeches started as sticky notes on the dining room table. Phone calls may require only a couple of sticky notes and a quick thesis; whole books require added layers of detail.

You've come a long way. After shedding the grammar of weakness, you acquired the grammar and vocabulary of power. Next, you learned 13 steps to follow as you move from confusion to structure and organization. You've cured some but not all of the dread of the presentation itself.

Quick Tips

Follow the 13-step recipe to organize presentations.

1. Think about the audience.
2. Determine the purpose(s).
3. List the details.
4. Group the details.
5. Order the details.
6. Name the topics.
7. Order the topics.
8. Write the thesis statement.
9. Write the lead and end structures.
10. Plan the paragraphs, topic sentences, transitions, and reminders.
11. Write the piece.
12. Plan the visuals.
13. Practice, edit, tape.

6

Stand Up and
Speak Like a Woman:
Perfect Your Presentations

*Somewhere in your presentation, the audience stops thinking of
you as a five-foot six-inch woman with freckles on your nose. If
people think you are immersed, are serious, have done your
homework, then they take you seriously.*

CARLA HILLS

Careers rise or fall on spoken presentations, formal and informal, stand-up and sit-down. New jobs and career moves demand interviewing skills that show you at your best. The language of weakness, with its accompanying insecurity, kills talks, meetings, and interviews no matter how much you know about the subject, no matter what you've accomplished on the job.

In the last chapter, you learned to organize both formal and informal presentations. This chapter starts with the formidable challenge of persuading yourself to speak at all. Here you pick up dozens of pointers, many never published before, on the verbal aspects of talks. You learn to apply the organization system, write scripts, choose the right words and sentences to get your points across, start on the right foot (literally!), and end powerfully. You also learn to avoid sentences and words that have traditionally hurt women as we internalized the roles of meekness, deference, and seductiveness. Finally, we explore that infrequent but all-important presentation, the job interview.

Overcome the Credibility Gap

Do women's presentations differ from men's? Yes. Study after study has confirmed what we see at work: people listen to men and give them credibility while they both blatantly and subtly (and often unconsciously) discount women. Women must earn what men are granted. Rather than offer a generic set of rules for presentations (you'll find a superb book on presentation skills in the Booklist), this chapter aims at the special problems women face and must overcome in order to be heard, respected, and obeyed. Of course, all weak presenters can benefit from the tips and ideas.

Despite the high visibility of and anxiety around the stand-up talk, most of your business is conducted less formally, sitting down. What you say informally counts, too. And informal talks dog women as well. You can't get the floor. No one listens. Men constantly interrupt. How do you prevent glitches from silencing you? The language of success comes to your aid here as well.

Invisible and Silent or Seen and Heard?

"Pretty is as pretty does," not as pretty says. Should you speak at all? Although we're accused of talking too much, women actually speak less than men do, and get interrupted more. Yet those who speak most get the most respect.

Poets explore the silences women have been taught. The poet Audre Lorde wrote, "My silences had not protected me. Your silences will not protect you." In business, your silences do not protect you; they render you more vulnerable. They deny you the opportunity to lead others. They label you as weak and wimpy. If you want to succeed in your career, delay no more: you must speak out.

Women are acutely aware that people don't listen to us. We may not be as aware that sometimes our own actions or words deter people from listening. Here are the voices of business and professional women:

What is it that makes people charismatic and display leadership in front of an audience? Some are extremely funny, they tell jokes and sports stories.... I'm not a natural stand-up comedian, I don't know sports, I can't make analogies.

A man at any level is listened to. Why not a woman?

I hope to get an ability to gain credibility, an ability to be heard the first time.

I'm starting my own consulting firm. I must speak so people remember.

I didn't feel that they understood the important message. Maybe the message wasn't clear enough.

You Have the Floor. Now What?

When you give stand-up presentations and talks, most listeners will give you the floor and at least some attention, however grudgingly. This applies to formal as well as informal talks, for audiences of one thousand as well as for audiences of three. Still, given the choice of giving a five-minute talk or being boiled in oil, many women would gladly choose the oil. You probably dread the stand-up presentation more than the sit-down, so we'll start with stand-up talks.

Action Plan

Before you read the rest of this chapter and the next, ask a friend to video-tape you twice in actual business situations. For the first tape, record yourself just before, during, and after a business talk or presentation. For the second tape, record yourself at a business meeting at which you are a participant but not the main speaker. If a job interview looms, tape a mock interview. These tapes help you get the most out of this and the next chapter. However, if it's not possible to record yourself, give a collaborator the Quick Tips at the end of these chapters and ask her to observe how you follow them.

How Not to Give a Talk

Women who give puny presentations stick to rules that most of us internalized in childhood, rules that worked for us at home, in school, on the cheerleading squad, and on the dating scene. Since laughter is a good teacher, and since the ability to laugh at ourselves eases our anxiety, please read the rules that follow, check those that you obey, and add some you've seen other women obey.

Appearance

- ❏ Hair counts. Big hair counts most. Spend more time teasing your hair than organizing your talk. And play with it while speaking.

- ❏ Wear plenty of make-up, especially deep-blue eye shadow and red rouge.

- ❏ Wear long earrings that jingle.

- ❏ Select a polyester suit in a bright color that was popular three years ago.

- ❏ Wear tube-tops that show cleavage.

- ❏ Prefer cute short skirts, especially if you're a few pounds overweight and must sit on a raised stage.

- ❏ Wear stiletto heels—they make legs look thin.

Planning

- ❏ Never plan. Charming women speak spontaneously.

- ❏ Don't worry about beginnings and endings. Just pretend you're on the phone with your friend.

- ❏ Act absolutely natural.

Language

❏ Speak the grammar of weakness; insert *like, you know, and whatever* as often as possible.

❏ Remind the audience how little you know about the topic.

❏ Apologize often.

❏ Giggle.

Structure

❏ Open with the words, "I never gave a talk before, so I'm really really scared."

❏ Don't tell the thesis; let them guess.

Gestures and Body Language

❏ While you wait to speak, wring your hands as you whisper your notes to yourself. Slouch with your legs wide apart.

❏ Keep your chin and eyes down as you read the talk.

❏ Avoid eye contact. Fix on a wall at the back of the room and don't avert your gaze.

❏ Pull your skirt up or down.

❏ Adjust bra straps and pantyhose.

❏ Hold one leg up behind you in flamingo position.

❏ Clutch the podium till your knuckles turn white.

❏ Engage in hair-related activity.

❏ Cross arms tightly across your chest.

❏ Heave a visible sigh of relief or shrug shoulders at the end of the talk.

❑ Twirl the pencil in your hand and gaze at it while speaking.

❑ Position your body between the projector and the screen.

❑ Face the slides as you speak to them.

Voice

❑ Pitch your voice as high and squeaky as possible.

❑ End every statement as if it were a question?

❑ Talk fast: aim for 200 words a minute.

Other Ways Not to Give a Talk

_____

_____

_____

If you've been to or given enough talks, you know that I didn't have to invent the rules of How Not to Give a Talk. Laughing at your speech foibles takes the first step toward eliminating them.

Action Plan

Watch the tapes as you check off the relevant How Not To's.

How to Construct a Talk That Works

The organization system works for any form of written or spoken presentation. In the last chapter, you saw, step-by-step, how Linda Rubin planned a talk for a national conference. Whatever the length of your talk, follow the system step-by-step. Now we'll highlight issues and pitfalls to consider as you plan presentations that work.

DECIDE WHAT TO SAY . . . AND WHAT NOT TO SAY

Charmaine McDaniel describes her presentation skills:

> I talk too much. I ramble from one item to another because I know so much about the technical details, I feel I must include them all, so I never finish on time. I love this work. To me every detail is important, so I put them all in. It comes out really boring.

Women are accused of talking too much, of rambling, of being "chatty." Including all the details in her talks reinforces that image and stymies Charmaine's career. Charmaine's problem probably plagues you as well. When you love every detail of your work, how can you leave any out of your presentation? Consider this: people remember about three ideas from a 20-minute talk. A day later, they may have forgotten two. Including all the details sends a strong negative message to the audience: "I can't analyze and synthesize my work; I'm too weak to determine what's essential and what's not; I can't generalize so I'll bore you with all the details."

This list guides you as you choose which details to include and which to remove as you sort and group your sticky notes. Include

- Only the details that support the thesis statement
- Clusters of details rather than individual items
- Summaries

If all the details must be included in the presentation, put them in a handout and summarize or give a couple of samples in the talk.

Write a Script

If you followed the organization system, you have the beginnings of a script to work from. You can, of course, work from an outline, but few speak as clearly and strongly from an outline as they do from a script. Scripts offer so many advantages and overcome so many problems that, after trying scripts once or twice, you'll wonder why you ever deprived yourself of their benefits.

Four Advantages of Scripts

1. Scripts imbue confidence.

The security of a script prevents common problems, such as "getting flustered and losing my train of thought," and "I forgot to mention the main point," or "I left out the thesis statement," or "The fourth item, or the third, or whatever . . . ," or "Um . . . uh . . . um . . ." Once you've bolstered your confidence, you'll feel secure enough to deviate from, add to, or ignore all or parts of your script. That's what professional speakers do.

2. Scripts reinforce new language habits.

Although some speakers do well with notes alone, a written script ensures that you speak the language of power. Remember that powerful language is relatively new for you: strong sentence forms and words don't come naturally yet. Left to your "spontaneous" language, you'll slip right back into statements like, "I'm really so excited to just take this opportunity to um . . . um . . . tell you the benefits of the 8090 computer system."

3. Scripts enable you to look professional while managing word count and timing.

It takes about one minute to deliver 100 to 120 words. If you're to deliver a five-minute talk, it should be about 500 words long, a 20-minute talk should be about 2,000 words long, and so on. To gain confidence in your timing, buy a small timer and clock each practice.

4. Scripts save time.

Your investment in careful writing pays rich dividends. Linda Rubin, for example, delivered an altered version of her talk to her organization's local board of directors. She also plans to recast it as a professional article. This book started its life in 1989 as a talk delivered to the Rochester Women's Network. Rather than starting from scratch each time I spoke to a new group, I reworked the 1989 talk, adding insights gained along the way, honing the language, and inserting stories. Although the first version of a talk takes many hours of research and preparation (my major speeches require as much as a hundred hours of research and preparation), the revisions require only a few minutes: careful preparation turns out to be an efficiency tool.

INCLUDE ALL THE INGREDIENTS

Delicious cakes contain many ingredients: oil, flour, sugar, flavoring, eggs, and so on. Tasty presentations also contain all the ingredients: an engaging lead, a thesis statement (repeated several times), paragraph topic sentences, logical transitions, necessary details, and a socko ending or call to action. In the speech that inspired her company, for example, Orit Gadiesh concluded with a powerful call to action:

> We've turned around financially, we've turned around the business—and even our competitors are beginning to acknowledge that. Now it's time to turn around what they really fear, what they've always envied us for: it's time to turn around our collective pride in what we do.

Skilled bakers vary the type and quantity of ingredients; when you're a skilled speaker, you'll vary these components as well. But first bake by the book.

WRITE FOR LISTENERS, NOT FOR READERS

She Who Must Be Obeyed understands that spoken and written language differ. Grasping the differences improves both speaking and writing. The central difference—writing stays around while speaking is, literally, ephemeral: it disappears into thin air. As women, we are often treated as though we, too, are ephemeral, so our spoken language must compensate with weight, depth, and breadth.

People can hold an average of seven unrelated letters, syllables, or words in short-term memory. This means that when the speaker gets to the eighth word in a sentence, people probably have forgotten the first. As an effective speaker, you compensate for the memory problem in a number of ways.

MAKE YOUR WORDS EASY TO REMEMBER

The highest praise is that your talk was memorable. To earn such praise, help listeners supplement their short memories. Follow a clear structure and be sure the audience knows what it is. For example, when you state the thesis, tell how many major points you'll cover and in what order. Enumerate as you proceed logically from point to point (first, the problem of overheating . . . second, the proposed solution . . . third, the cost . . . finally, the benefits to your group).

USE THE GRAMMAR OF POWER

The grammar of power delivers your message succinctly and clearly. All the strong grammatical forms work splendidly in presentations. The most perfect spoken form, the parallel, not only makes up for short memories but clarifies your thinking and makes you sound right. Every good speaker, male and female, understands and exploits the parallel form. Use the parallel as often as possible. Here are models:

Mr. President, I speak as a Republican. I speak as a woman. I speak as a United States senator. I speak as an American. —*Margaret Chase Smith*

In education, in marriage, in religion, in everything, disappointment is the lot of women. —*Lucy Stone*

Women are in the forefront of the peace movement, the civil rights and equal rights movements, the environment and consumer movements, the child care movement. —*Bella Abzug*

My faith in the Constitution is whole, it is complete, it is total. —*Barbara Jordan*

We've turned around financially, we've turned around the business. . . . Now . . . it's time to turn around our collective pride in what we do. —*Orit Gadiesh*

TELL STORIES

Muriel Rukeyser reminds us, "The universe is made of stories, not of atoms." In *Charlotte's Web*, Fern says, "Charlotte is the best storyteller I ever heard." Stories are easier to remember than abstractions: they bring ideas to life. When Hillary Rodham Clinton spoke about health care in the United States, she illustrated the impersonal numbers with stories of individuals. And President Reagan used vivid stories to illustrate every point.

If you agree that good stories enhance talks, you may wonder how to find them. As the traditional family storytellers, women already have troves of yarns they can tailor to business presentations. For example, everyone knows the story of Goldilocks and the Three Bears. With business *downsizing, rightsizing,* and otherwise changing size, the notion of a "just right" size lends itself well to all kinds of business applications. And how often does the story of the emperor's new clothes come to mind at business fiascos? Familiar stories bridge the gap between you and your listeners by tapping a common core of shared experience.

Ordinary business experience furnishes another rich source of stories. Beth Linley opened a sales presentation for her video conference center by telling the story of an old-fashioned meeting, with people traveling all over the country, getting stuck in airports, eating hotel food, and so on. The contrast between that meeting and the teleconference set a theme for the whole presentation. Another woman, a product designer, opened her talk with a story of the specific product failure that led to the innovation she proposed.

Start your own story collection. Every time you see a business link in a popular tale or an actual event, record the story for future use. Every time you hear a well-told story at a business meeting, make note of it. Keep your business stories short, relevant, simple, and tasteful. When you deliver your stories, be sure to clarify the relationship between the story and the business talk.

Carla Hills used a delightful story in her speech at The Commonwealth Club of California. After a straightforward lead and clear statement of the thesis, she illustrated the first point with this short, amusing story:

> Efforts to open world markets hit quite choppy waters in 1993. Both NAFTA and the Uruguay round negotiations were stridently attacked by those who wanted to hang on to their protections and could not be persuaded of the perils of their course.

> Indeed they reminded me of the vice admiral who was commanding a battleship in the North Atlantic on a particularly stormy night. He saw a light coming toward his vessel and he sent a radio message, "Give way and move twenty degrees south." Immediately a message came back, "Give way and *you* move twenty degrees north." The admiral was not used to having his orders disobeyed, so he thought there might be some confusion. He sent the same message again, and again immediately the message came back: "You give way and move twenty degrees north." This time he was very perturbed and he sent a very precise message, "I am a vice admiral commanding a battleship, and I order you to give way and

move twenty degrees south." And this time there was a long pause, but the message came back, "I am a seaman first class. I am manning a light-house." (pause for laughter)

And so while we can breathe a sigh of relief that we avoided the rocks and shoals in 1993, many of the underlying issues that challenged us in the last year are still with us.

This story meets all the criteria for success in business: it's short, tasteful, interesting, and directly linked to the business content of the talk.

REMIND AND REPEAT

When swinging from one topic to the next, briefly recall the preceding topic or topics. Here's an example from Linda Rubin's talk: "After we surveyed the current membership lists and scanned the photo albums, we looked at a third source of new members in the community's list of donors." Linda jogged memories of the first two sources just before she introduced the third.

Repetition also works. Repetition of words, phrases, sentences, thesis statements, even of leads, eases the memory burden. Parallels are so effective because they repeat parts of speech, words, phrases, and even whole themes. For example, the constant repetition of one sentence enhances the greatness and memorability of Martin Luther King, Jr.'s "I Have a Dream" speech.

Crib Sheet

Phrases That Remind or Repeat

The xx don't only xx (reminder): they xx as well.

In addition to xx (reminder), . . .

The product benefits go beyond (point 1), (point 2), (point 3), (point 4).

Despite the problems of (problem 1), (problem 2), the project succeeded in . . .

Just as xxxx, so xxx . . .

IT'S NOT JUST RHETORIC

It's a popular perception that someone can't be emotional and logical at the same time, and, since women are emotional, they can't be logical (an illogical and silly conclusion based on two other illogical and silly assumptions). Justice Ginsburg, Amelia Earhart, and Orit Gadiesh display their emotions and remain brilliantly logical. The strongest speakers convey passion so powerfully because they follow an inexorable logic. Reread the Gettysburg Address or one of Churchill's great speeches: they attain greatness precisely because the passion and the logic complement each another.

Perhaps one reason women are accused of being illogical is that we are largely unaware of the use and value of rhetorical devices. What is rhetoric? Nothing more than "skill in using language effectively and persuasively." We've already covered quite a few ways to improve skill in using language effectively and persuasively. Now add these devices to your bag of tools. They're easy to learn yet they win points. They include: (1) enumeration, (2) rhetorical questions, and (3) tricolon.

Enumeration

Enumeration serves you well either in the overall structure of the talk or within any section. In the overall structure (as part of the thesis statement): "The supercomputer meets your engineering requirements in three essential ways: in planning, in designing, and in analyzing prices." Within a paragraph: "The financial plan fails to meet the IRS criteria. First, it's not accurate: columns 13 and 16 are only gross estimates.

Second, it's not supported by adequate documentation: the 1099 forms are absent. Third, it's not formatted for electronic scanning."

Amelia Earhart enumerated: "There were three factors which determined me to try a flight to Mexico. One, I had a plane in perfect condition for a long distance effort. Two, I had been officially invited by the Mexican Government. Three, Wiley Post."

Here's another Earhart enumeration you can copy: "About all a pilot could do was to joy-hop. That is (1) taking a few hardy passengers for short rides; (2) teaching even hardier students to fly; and (3) giving exhibitions."

A caveat: use any form of enumeration only once within your talk; it's too hard to follow embedded numbered sequences. You can, however, use a first, second, third, and an (a), (b), and (c), just as in a written outline. Rather than saying, "The third topic is promoting women. We've tried to do so in three ways. First, . . . " try, "The third topic is promoting women. We've tried to do so by: (a) xxx."

Enumeration is easy to learn. It never bores the audience. It aids understanding. It helps organize ideas logically.

Rhetorical questions

A rhetorical question is one that you don't expect the listener to answer. Punctuating your talk with simple questions like, "How does it function?" "What went wrong?" "What's in it for you?" as a pretext for answering them helps move your talk along. Rhetorical questions show you're organized, enable you to lead the way, and open new topics in your talks.

Tricolon, the rule of three

Our ears like to hear items in threes: they sound good, they're easier to remember, and they show you've taken the trouble to plan. So, when possible, group information in threes, as Amelia Earhart did in the passages earlier, and as Justice Ginsburg does in her talk: "Neither of my parents had the means to attend college, but both taught me (1) to love learning, (2) to care about people, and (3) to work hard for whatever I wanted or believed in," and "The constant realization of a more perfect union, the Constitution's aspiration, requires the (1) widest, (2) broadest, (3) deepest participation."

To synthesize passion, logic, and persuasion, control the elements of language.

Use Precise, Concrete Words and Images

The journey from weakness to power has already relieved you of vague, abstract words and reminded you to choose those that are precise, concrete, and memorable. Abstraction weakens writing and dulls talks. But what, you may ask, if your work is abstract by nature? A software designer had to give a presentation to journalists about a futuristic project. Software is intangible: it can't be seen or touched or smelled, yet companies want people to pay real money for it. How can a group of nontechnical journalists be persuaded to buy into a grand, abstract vision, understood by only a few specialists?

Metaphor came to the rescue. It's hard to understand the notion of software that reaches out to the world; it's easy to understand the notion of the information superhighway or the electronic Concorde or the computer supermarket. The software designer warmed to the idea of metaphor and gave an engaging, accessible talk about "the entrance and exit ramps on the information superhighway." If you, too, must talk about abstractions, try spicing your talk with metaphors.

Enliven your talk with plenty of specific information: if you know how many, say "over fifty," or "26 percent," or "We made five adjustments to the design." Also, take advantage of those short, punchy action verbs we stressed in Chapter 4.

You do not have to be a man to speak strongly; you do not have to be like a man: you can be a powerful woman. And wise word choices help make you one.

SHOW VIVID VISUALS

Whether they're handouts, transparencies, or handwritten notes on an easel chart, visuals highlight key points. When your visuals look clear and strong, you look clear and strong. Ron Mix, the film director, urges common sense in designing visuals. He suggests you ask, "Is this the simplest way to get my idea or information across?" A woman brought a transparency like this one for his critique:

MOTHER BROWN'S COOKIES AND BROWNIES, INC.
1995 SALES - EASTERN DIVISION AND TOTAL CORPORATE
WITH DIVISION AND CORPORATE QUARTERLY PERCENT INCREASES
SHOWN BY MONTH AND QUARTER WITH TOTALS FOR EACH QUARTER AND YEAR

MONTH	QUARTER	SALES EASTERN DIV.	CORPORATE	EXPLANATION	DIVISION PERCENT INCREASE MONTHLY	QUARTERLY
JANUARY		$8,125,000	$ 32,500,000.00	WE GOT OFF TO A REASONABLE START WITH THE NEW SARDINE FUDGE LINE.		
FEBRUARY		$8,250,000	$ 28,875,000.00	NOT MUCH OF AN INCREASE HERE.	1.53846	
MARCH		$3,500,000	$ 17,500,000.00	CHIEF BAKER BREAKS LEG (SHE'S BETTER NOW)	-57.57576	
	FIRST	$19,875,000	$ 78,875,000.00			
APRIL		$9,500,000	$ 35,625,000.00	CANARSIE PLANT GOES ON LINE WITH VANILLA SARDINE FUDGE.	171.42857	
MAY		$10,500,000	$ 42,000,000.00	BETTER SHIPPING PROCEDURES.	10.52632	
JUNE		$7,500,000	$ 29,250,000.00	CONSUMER BACKLASH TO SARDINE FUDGE.	-28.57143	
	SECOND	$27,500,000	$ 106,875,000.00			38.364780
JULY		$12,500,000	$ 47,500,000.00	LICORICE PARSLEY COFFEE CAKE WAFERS INTRODUCED.	66.66667	
AUGUST		$13,750,000	$ 58,437,500.00	DELIVER "BARNFIRE BOYS" ORDER	10.00000	
SEPTEMBER		$15,400,000	$ 53,900,000.00	VANILLA LICORICE PARSLEY COFFEE CAKE WAFERS SHIPPING COMMENCES.	12.00000	
	THIRD	$41,650,000	$ 159,837,500.00			51.454545
OCTOBER		$6,500,000	$ 32,500,000.00	PATERSON PLANT FIRE (NOT VERY SERIOUS, THOUGH)	-57.79221	
NOVEMBER		$17,750,000	$ 66,562,500.00	NOTICE THE DIFFERENCE BETWEEN THIS MONTH AND LAST MONTH.	173.07692	
DECEMBER		$24,700,000	$ 98,800,000.00	THESE NUMBERS ARE VERY INTERESTING.	39.15493	
	FOURTH	$48,950,000	$ 197,862,500.00	A GREAT FINISH FOR THE YEAR!		17.527011
TOTAL		$ 96,325,000.00	$ 543,450,000.00			

This deadly transparency doesn't just fail to convey information. It actually hides the outstanding corporate results. With Ron's assistance, she created this transparency:

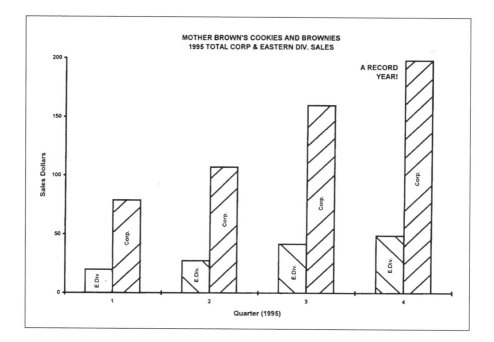

This woman didn't have to brag; the transparency shows her accomplishments.

How to Control What You Can't Control: The Question-and-Answer Session

You've seen how to organize, design, and write successful presentations. Careful planning erases most of your anxiety but doesn't address the most dreaded element: the question. No matter how well you plan, you control neither the questioners nor the questions. Still, forewarned is forearmed.

One sure way to prevent question woes is to ask the moderator or group leader to do her job. It shouldn't be the speaker's responsibility to cut off "lectures," quash rudeness, or call an end to the question period.

The section that follows offers tips and a "crib sheet" for issues that trouble women with whom I've worked.

Question   I get nervous and flustered when anyone asks a question. How can I overcome my anxiety?

ANSWERS   1. Answering questions calmly starts with listening precisely. Jot down the words of the questioner. Take a moment to think. Then repeat her words in your response—that'll focus your answer and give you thinking time. For example, if the questioner says, "Why do you think the equipment failed right in the middle of the storm?" your answer starts, "The equipment probably failed right in the middle of the storm because the generator died." If you don't know, you might say, "No one knows why the equipment failed in the middle of the storm."

2. Hand out index cards and request that people write their questions. Don't say, "I get nervous when you ask questions, so please write yours on the card." Do say, "To be sure I understand and respond appropriately, please write your questions on the index card." Keep control. The index card method works well for large audiences as well as for hostile ones. If you have a moderator, ask him or her to group the questions by topic.

Question   Some people ask questions designed to trip me, not to gain information. How can I avoid looking flustered?

ANSWER   If you anticipate trouble, ask people to hold their questions till the end of your talk. Prepare a crib sheet of responses. The following suggestions should handle everything from hard questions to downright ugly ones.

Crib Sheet

Ways to Respond to Tough Questions

I don't know.

Please leave your name and I'll call with the answer.

That's beyond my area of expertise.

That question is beyond the scope of this talk.

That question can't be answered at this time.

That question would take too long to answer now.

The research doesn't give answers to that.

Thank you for asking that question. Can anyone in the group answer?

That question is inappropriate.

Would you want to answer a question like that?

How Not to Ask Questions

It was a professional conference. The speaker encouraged questions from the literate, educated women in the audience. Here are the opening words of the first six questions:

I only wanted to ask about . . .

I just wanted to know . . .

I wondered if you could talk about . . .

I want to ask a question . . .

I have a question . . .

Can I ask a question?

In each case, wise and intelligent questions followed the sorry beginnings, but the damage had been done: the questioners lost credibility by talking about themselves and not the subject matter. How should the women have asked their questions?

Crib Sheet

How to Ask Questions

How . . .

What . . .

When . . .

Where . . .

Why . . .

Who . . .

Please (describe, tell, detail, defend, and so on) . . .

The tips and suggestions so far assume that you speak in more or less formal settings and that you've been allocated time in which to speak. But what about those sit-down situations in which it doesn't matter what you would have said because no one wants to listen to women? Tips work only if you have the floor.

What to Do When You Get the Floor

Studies confirm what women say at my workshops: both at home and at work, men don't listen to women. Patricia O'Brien wrote an article about it, which is excerpted here.[*]

> The Outsider must either reap the terrain of Inside or adopt guerrilla tactics that will allow her to command attention. The more successful a woman is, the more artful her strategies for being heard are likely to be. Sandra Day O'Connor, the first woman to be named to the Supreme Court, was asked shortly after her appointment what problems she had encountered on her way up the legal ladder. She replied that getting men to listen remained a continuing challenge. "I taught myself early on to speak very slowly—enunciating every word—when I wanted someone's undivided attention." In effect, she trained herself to make people lean forward and pay attention if they wanted to hear what she had to say, building authority into her persona by turning the classic male model for commanding attention inside out. It is sobering to realize that even the

[*]First appeared in *Working Woman*, February 1993. Written by Patricia O'Brien. Reprinted with permission of MacDonald Communications Corporation. Copyright ©1999 by MacDonald Communications Corporation. www.workingwoman.com. For subscriptions call 1-800-234-9675.

highest ranking female judge in the land needed a trick technique to make herself heard. But that's not as bad, perhaps, as witnessing the painful, classic mistake many women make when a man's attention appears to be flagging: they start talking faster and faster, as if they are about to be yanked off the floor at any moment.

Susan Estrich, the campaign manager for Michael Dukakis's 1988 presidential bid, found another way around the problem. . . . Estrich developed a style of commandeering the floor at meetings by laterally carving out space in the air with her hands, silencing those around, punctuating her words with gestures worthy of a symphony conductor and creating an aura of authority. By fashioning her own style to get and keep attention, she avoided using the boys' techniques that probably wouldn't have worked for her anyway and also avoided being *nice*—frequently the least useful route women use to get attention.

. . . "You have to be a player instead of waiting for the perfect moment to present the perfect idea," says Kathy Bushkin, director of editorial administration for *U.S. News & World Report*. "Men don't wait. When women do, men don't listen."

. . . "I try to get things done by addressing issues straight on," says Barbara Spollen, a senior business analyst for the Federal National Mortgage Association in Washington, D.C. "But it's easy to go above the levels of aggressiveness that are acceptable. Women aren't allowed to be angry; if we are, it's our hormones. You have to count on your perceived competence to see you through."

Columnist Ellen Goodman, commenting on her less-than-satisfying experience as a pundit on ABC-TV's *This Week with David Brinkley,* says, "I found that moving up in the system meant you got to be ignored by a much higher class of men." Frequently, even when a woman is recognized as competent, she still can't get the floor unless she has irrefutable technical skills, says Ross Webber, chair of the management department of the Wharton School. "The irony is, women have difficulty being heard in fields like advertising and communications—where they constitute a large part of the work force—because men's judgment of which ideas are good or bad are so subjective. . . . It's easy to understand, in light of all this, why women begin to wonder if it is somehow their fault that men don't hear what they are saying. . . ."

O'Brien pinpoints the problems that beset us as we strive to get the floor and the ways women gain attention. Studies of meetings in various settings tend to confirm the bad news in the piece you just read. At mixed meetings, men speak more than women do, and interrupt more. Women use a variety of devices to get and hold the floor. Some work; some don't. You can't single-handedly change the social situation in which you work. You can't do much about those who won't listen to you just because you're a woman. But you can change your ways of sitting and speaking at meetings if they operate against you. Here are techniques women use to try to get and keep the floor.

TECHNIQUES THAT FAIL

Talk loud.

Talk fast.

Wait your turn.

Sit quietly throughout.

Raise your hand and open with, "I guess I have a question . . ." or other *I* statements.

Use puny body language (next chapter).

TECHNIQUES THAT WORK

Set a formal agenda to ensure everyone has a turn.

Work with the chair to prevent damaging interruptions.

Open with comments that review or reinforce what the last speaker said.

Plan before speaking. Start with the subject, not with "I."

Listen to others when they speak.

Open with someone else's name.

Say intelligent things, and say them powerfully.

Use action verbs and parallels for compression.

Use rhetorical techniques to prevent rambling.

Never just talk. Earn a reputation for making substantive contributions every time you speak.

If your comments cover more than one topic, start by saying, "Three critical points affect our decision." Then enumerate each point.

Use the body language of success (next chapter).

Crib Sheet

Techniques to Handle Destructive Interruptions

Build a repertoire of polite ways to say "Shut up."

Please . . .

Just a moment . . .

I'm not finished . . .

Kindly hold the remarks till I'm done.

Please hold the questions till the end.

Push with open palm or sweep the arm to show that you're not finished.

These interruptions break everyone's train of thought.

If you're often singled out for oppression (a cruelty generally exercised by powerful managers against the young and vulnerable), ask for help from the person who runs the meetings or from the oppressor. Do so in private, using the grammar of power. For example, you might say, "When a younger person is interrupted by a manager all the time, she loses credibility with the others. If some of my words seem wrong to you, is there another way to let me know rather than interrupting me?"

Sit Down and Speak Like a Woman

Mostly, you speak sitting down: informal talk fills your business days. I'll make points about the verbal aspect of sit-down presentations here and return to this topic in the next chapter on nonverbal communications.

CHOOSE POWERFUL, PRECISE LANGUAGE

The story told most often at my workshops is about a woman making a suggestion or describing an idea, being ignored, and hearing a man get accolades for the same idea a few moments later. If that happens to you, consider the language in which you cast your suggestion. Did you speak the language of success or did you say the traditional, "I don't really know much about this subject, but I feel it would be a good idea if we revamp the computer system in the factory." Of course the person who says, "Hey, a revamped computer system will up efficiency 20 percent," will be heard, and get the credit.

MAKE YOUR MEETING COMMENTS MEMORABLE

Plan on a notepad, determine which sentence form will work best, and pick strong action verbs. Sitting down or standing up, language is language. One executive says that whenever she's at a difficult juncture at a meeting she asks herself, "What would Phyllis tell me to say?" She jots the sentence on her notepad and then speaks.

BLOCK THE BOORS

Boorish people who interrupt with distractions or personal remarks can cut off your message and shake your confidence. But you can protect—and project—yourself and your ideas through intonation, enumeration, deflection, and modeling. Be sure your intonation tells that you're not finished yet. Use enumeration. If you start by saying, ". . . Three critical issues.

One . . . ," you signal that you won't finish till you've done number three. Finally, if someone's rude enough to interrupt you anyway, try holding your hand up and saying, "Just a moment, please," or "Kindly wait till I've finished," or something that will work in your group. If it's really ugly, try the well-distanced but very strong, "It's rude to interrupt."

WATCH THE POWERHOUSE WOMEN BROADCASTERS

Copy women like Eleanor Clift and Cokie Roberts, who refuse to be interrupted.

The Job Interview in the Language of Success

You're up for a big promotion You're entering the work force. You've been "downsized" and are working with an outplacement firm. You're seeking a new job. The first hurdles are passed, the resumé has worked, and the coveted interview is set. Whether you've never worked before or you're up for CEO, you're pondering how to handle this infrequent but all-important sit-down presentation. This section tells how to apply what we've covered so far to the language of the job interview. Thanks go to Anne Fisher (askannie.com) of *Fortune*, Maria Reilly of Korn/Ferry, and Emily Neece, Larry Peeler, and their colleagues at The Executive Center for thoughtful tips and discussion of the issues. Not meant as a comprehensive survey of interviewing skills, this section addresses only the difficult language questions women are likely to face (the next chapters touch on the body language and style of the job interview), the experts' suggestions, and the ways to speak the language of success during interviews.

Although many research studies have explored the interview from the interviewer's point of view, few have explored it from the interviewee's. Studies do suggest that interviewers ask "closed end (yes-no)" questions more of women while asking men questions that offer the opportunity to sell themselves or build rapport. In one study, when candidates were assessed on a "feminine/masculine" scale, the less "feminine" a woman's assessment the more likely she was to be accepted as an eligible candidate. So, as in every other aspect of business, women have to climb a slightly steeper mountain, negotiate a slightly narrower road to build our careers and succeed at job interviews.

This expert Q & A offers tips and answers questions. After the answers, if appropriate, you'll find crib sheets with sentence starters that follow the Well-Read principles. Check them before your next interview, rehearse, and win the great job you deserve.

Expert Q & A

Q. What candidate behaviors are likely to make a positive impression?

A. Do your homework. One executive recruiter insists, "You can't stress preparation enough. It even matters on pre-interview screening. If I'm to meet a candidate during the screening process, it makes a big impression if the person shows the initiative to gather information before we meet."

All the experts agree: learn as much as you can about the company, group, or job before the interview. Search Web sites, read annual reports, check recent newspaper and magazine stories, or call people. Don't just research the company, research the person (for high-level jobs, you often know whom you'll meet). Don't just wing it. Your knowledge and enthusiasm mark you as a leader rather than a follower.

Crib Sheet

How to Show You've Done Your Homework

My research showed that xxxx has grown 15 percent in the last year.

According to your annual report, xxx expects to add more global partners in the future.

The departure of the CEO last June seems to . . .

According to *Fortune*, the work climate here . . .

Q.   What else should the candidate do before the interview?

A.   *Practice on video.* The career service or your colleagues can offer a mock interview on videotape. View the tape with and without sound, critique your performance, and practice any required change.

Compose intelligent questions. Anne Fisher suggests that you ask a lot of questions, perhaps 10 to 20 in a one-hour interview. She says good questions can avoid future mismatches with the company's culture.

Crib Sheet

Good Questions

What kind of culture do people here experience? Do they work together with lots of "face time" or mainly in their own enclosures?

Would someone like me fit in?

Is this a formal or casual work environment?

How might my talents serve your growth?

What educational opportunities do you offer?

What career path do you envision for me?

Does your firm offer investment opportunities?

Prepare a detailed resumé and notes about any item that might come up. It makes sense to prepare notes, as long as you don't focus on the notes rather than the interview. Carry the notes in an elegant briefcase and refer to them only as needed. Without notes, you might end up saying words like, "I'm not really sure, but I think maybe we cut the costs by 10 percent," or "I forgot why the xxx." Some experts discourage candidates from bringing notes. Without research to guide us, all the answers are opinions. The answers aren't in on this one, so try interviewing with and without notes.

Crib Sheet

Good Answers

> My education, experience, and leadership skills (fill in any other words: successes, computer skills, engineering experience, and so on) have prepared me to (fill in any other verb: sharpened my ability to ... tempered me ... taught me that ...)

Decide the level of formality. Young women tend to be more casual than older women. New firms tend to be more casual than old firms. If you don't know about the environment at a particular company, call an employee or the person who answers the phone and ask. Just remember, young or old, formal or informal, entry clerk or senior executive, remain civil and strong and never compromise your dignity. The experts say that if you err, err on the side of conservatism.

Q.   Please give tips about what to do and say during the interview.

A.   *Level the playing field.* Don't look down your nose at or try to commandeer the interviewer, but don't act subservient either (women are more likely to act subservient). Don't apologize ("I'm sorry for taking so much time" should be "Thanks for giving me so much time." "I just really want to thank you" becomes "Thanks for xxx.")

Don't let settings fool you. Some job interviews take place at restaurants or clubs. Don't give in to the temptation to get too informal. An interview is a business, not a social, encounter.

Read the interviewer. Read and respond to both the body language and the words. Candidates often are so anxious and self-conscious that all they can think about is themselves and their reactions, but if you stick with the first principle, it's not about you, you not only make a good impression but actually relax and concentrate. You can even seek to mirror the movements of the interviewer: if he or she has a strong handshake, offer your hand strongly; if he or she opens the body and looks relaxed, do the same.

Listen. "A good listener is not only popular everywhere, but after a while she even gets to know something." People who display weak listening skills—whether by trying to bully the interviewer, by averting the gaze, by failing to respond to the specific questions—raise what one expert calls "a big red flag." One possible advantage of taking notes at your interview is that it forces you to listen precisely. But, whether you take notes or not, attend closely to both the nonverbal and verbal content of the interviewer's presentation.

Crib Sheet

Good Responses

Thank you for that clear explanation of . . .

Please explain . . .

That's an important issue at work.

You've shed light on this opportunity.

Think conversation, not interrogation. Although it feels agonizing, the interview is not meant to be a form of torture; it's a conversation in which you and the firm get acquainted. One expert also urges you to be yourself, saying that some women "feel they must check their femininity at the door." You're a professional but you're also a human being, a friend, a parent, a community volunteer, a music lover, a spouse. It's not appropriate to jabber about your kids or your trips, but it's fine to mention them if the opportunity arises. My travels around the world have convinced me that two topics that link people are children and weddings.

Observe even as you participate. A part of you disengages enough to act as an observer, noting what you both say, how you react to each other, what's going well, what's not going well. Record these immediately after the interview and review your notes before the next interview.

Control your emotional expression. If you've been laid off, lost a couple of jobs, or are leaving because the company is run like a coal mine, don't flaunt your anger or say nasty things about previous employers. This never means lying; some things are best left unsaid or said in a distanced voice. Also control the expression of your passions. Avoid expressions like, "I'm so excited," "I love to work on xxx," and "I always wanted to . . ."

Crib Sheet

Models of Diplomacy and Tact

The environment didn't always generate our best work.

Morale suffers when people are treated that way.

Xxx has always been my role model.

My passion lies in improving the world.

Finance fascinates me.

Hard work never scared me.

Neither belittle or nor magnify your accomplishments. Be sure to put your best work on the table. For delivery, remember to tell just the facts. Shun terms such as *I sort of, just, only.* Integrate your personal qualities with specific behaviors and events, as in the following examples. Think in terms of the problem or situation, the task, your action, and the results, as appropriate.

═══ *Crib Sheet*

Putting Your Best Foot Forward

The situation demanded xxx (fill in your own words) and I was tasked to xxx. I called the team together, analyzed the problem, cut the costs 15 percent, and improved customer satisfaction by 50 percent (note how parallelism and tricolon enhance the presentation).

My qualities of willingness to risk, of knowing how to nurture talent, of getting the job done seem to fit the requirements of the job. For example, . . .

My greatest strength lies in my blending of leadership styles that incorporate what are seen as traditionally male and female traits: vigor, hard work, kindness, rigorous discipline (add any others). For example, xxx . . .

═══ *Action Plan*

View the tapes. Watch yourself and the others around you and note your words, their words, and the body language. Decide if failures to listen and interruptions stem from rudeness on the part of others or response to your own language style. Do your ways of getting and keeping the floor tend to fall on the list of Techniques That Fail? If so, experiment with those that work. If an idea seems promising, try to adapt it to the particulars of your own workplace and tape yourself again. Although success or failure rests on some factors outside yourself, seek to master those factors you can control.

If a job interview looms, prepare crib sheets for questions you're likely to hear. Use the models.

Your communications are more than the sum of the grammar, vocabulary, organization, and substance of your speech. In the next chapter you meet another crucial component of communication—body language. The body, too, speaks volumes.

Quick Tips

Disobey the rules of How Not to Give a Talk.

Be seen *and* heard.

Design talks that work.

Script for success.

Time yourself.

Write for listeners, not for readers.

Build strong structures.

Be memorable.

Tell stories.

Use rhetorical devices.

Pick your metaphors.

Show strong visuals.

Ask and answer questions powerfully.

Get and hold the floor.

Sit down and speak like a woman.

Interview in the language of success.

7

The Body Language of Power: Lead Without Words

When a man gets up to speak, people listen, then look.
When a woman gets up, people look; then, if they
like what they see, they listen.

PAULINE FREDERICK

In the last chapter, you learned about the verbal language of the talk, the differences between written and spoken presentations, the structures to include, and one way to organize and write scripts. You learned weaknesses to obliterate and strengths to gain. You also explored the crucial sit-down presentations, the kind you make every day at work, and picked up techniques to get and hold the floor and succeed at job interviews. However, another language plays a central role in your success: that of the body.

Research on nonverbal communications demonstrates that women (and subservient groups in general) adopt postures that suggest meekness or self-protection, that these stances are both unconsciously taken and read, and that gestures vary across cultures. As Edward Sapir noted, "We respond to gestures with an extreme alertness and . . . in accordance with an elaborate and secret code that is written nowhere, known by none and understood by all." Women often ask why, and scholars have explored the history and offered explanations (see, for example, the work of Kathleen Hall Jamieson and Nancy Henley). In this book, we take a strictly practical approach: if it works, do it; if it doesn't work, change it. Again, the practical approach never suggests that we act like men or take on their gestures, only that we act like powerful women. This chapter examines the body languages of weakness and power. As you've done for the verbal, you'll learn to avoid feeble body language signals and add strong ones to your repertoire.

Action Plan

I suggested previously that you videotape yourself giving a stand-up talk and sitting down at a meeting or interview. Turn the sound off and view those videos for each Action Plan in this chapter.

Achieve the Posture of Power

At 25, Maureen Light has a solid start on her career. She's a fine engineer who is personable and "loves her job." She aspires to move into management and knows she must compensate for her diminutive size, her age, and her high-pitched voice. When she arrived at our workshop, we didn't know anything about her except what her appearance told. And it told a sad tale: cute, but sad. Her clothing was appropriate for the casual setting: walking shorts and a tailored blouse. Yet her presence whispered, "Weak, cute, young, wimpy . . ."

Why? It was more than just her pastel pink, ingenue nail polish, though that contributed to the overall impression. Maureen's body language did her in. Her head tilted forward, so that she looked up at you whether she was your height or not. She crossed her ankles or bent one leg back. Her shoulders slouched forward slightly. She smiled deferentially. She had absorbed every lesson about the demeanor of the weak. Despite her ability and personal appeal, Maureen was not destined for the fast track.

But women run a narrow path here. You've also seen women whose body language says, "bully, mean, hostile." Influenced by the outdated view that business is a war and only hostile fighters win, these women have adopted, not the posture of wise leaders, but that of aggressive soldiers. They may fight their way into management but they engender so much resentment that their leadership is ultimately undermined, just as it is for men who bully. Jean Hollands calls them "bully broads." I've met women like this. They don't understand why they're resented. Often, their aggressive image stems from their body language rather than only from their words. So the Goldilocks principle applies: it's no good to appear hostile; it's no good to appear meek; find the gestures that are just right.

Before you despair, read the story of Kira Marchenese, whose gestures are just right. When she was a college student, Kira assisted at our workshops during vacations. Kira, a diminutive size two, was younger than the youngest working women in the program by several years. Her job originally was to help with clerical work and verify lunch orders, but she gradually become involved with the workshops, led table discussions, assisted people as they wrote, and so on. Our course critiques began to show comments such as, "Both the instructors . . ." "Kira and Phyllis . . ." "Phyllis and Kira . . ." The course participants had accepted this tiny 18-year old as their instructor.

After my 55-year-old ego recovered from the shock, I began to ask why. The research on status, age, gender, and size predicted that no one would listen to Kira, let alone see her as an instructor. Was Kira breaking the rules, or was she following rules that aren't yet understood? I suspect the latter is true. Like Charlotte, like Justice Ginsburg, like Amelia Earhart, Kira is tiny. And, like Charlotte's, Justice Ginsburg's, and Amelia Earhart's, Kira's soft voice was listened to. Why? Because, like these females, she speaks the language of power and because her demeanor says "leader." If you act like a leader and carry yourself like a leader, you'll be taken for a leader no matter what your age, sex, or dress size.

You're Seen Before You're Heard: Send a Powerful Message

When you're ready to deliver that carefully planned presentation, remember that *you're seen before you're heard.* Your presence, your demeanor, your walk, your eyes have already sent a message. It can say, "Here is She Who Must Be Obeyed," or it can say, "I'm just a ditzy, flighty, weak, insecure little girl: it's okay to overlook me."

But what people see isn't necessarily what they get. Highly intelligent, extraordinarily competent women too often get labeled incorrectly because their body language tells the wrong tale. Just as you've learned powerful words and grammatical forms, so you must learn powerful nonverbal moves that foster success.

First Impressions Count: How to Make Yours Memorable for the Right Reasons

Just because you're not standing in front of the audience yet doesn't mean that you can't be seen. At our workshops, we videotape participants while they're sitting, waiting their turn. Lori Nolan was shocked to see herself on that videotape. Tall, imposing, a real presence when standing, Lori slouched with her legs splayed in front of her as she waited her turn. Your audience glimpses your overall appearance, your straight back or slouch, your crossed or splayed legs, your nervous mannerisms, while you're still sitting. They see you stand. Then they see you as you approach the podium.

Action Plan

Turn the sound off and view the portion of the tape that precedes your presentation. Check any of the following weak mannerisms that you observe. Then try the powerful gestures that follow.

Weak Body Language

❏ Looks nervous.

❏ Plays with pencil or notes.

❏ Reads or mumbles talk.

❏ Rustles transparencies.

❏ Whispers to someone nearby.

❏ Slouches with legs apart or scrunches body.

❏ Crosses legs and keeps one moving.

❏ Grips notes with both hands.

❏ Closes fists.

❏ Crosses arms tightly over chest.

Strong Body Language

❏ Sits straight, leaning slightly forward.

❏ Attends closely to the previous speakers.

❏ Takes notes (perhaps to refer to when her turn comes).

❏ Places feet comfortably flat on the floor or crossed.

❏ Rests comfortably (if not taking notes).

❏ Surveys audience to spot potential problems with line of sight or hearing.

❏ Looks relaxed.

❏ Smiles when appropriate.

❏ Seems to enjoy herself.

Slouch, Shamble, Trip, Leap, March, or Stride

It's pathetic to see a terrified speaker shamble to the podium, shoulders stooped, feet dragging, eyes staring, hands clenched, looking as if she'd rather do anything else than give this talk. The walk to the podium is your

THE BODY LANGUAGE OF WEAKNESS

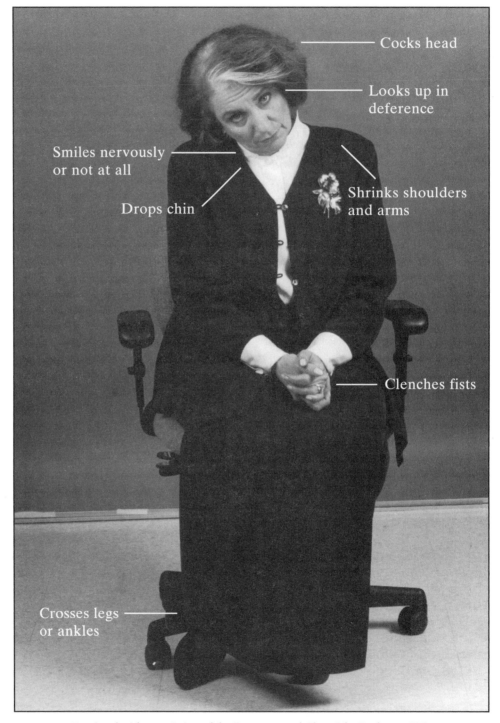

Cocks head

Looks up in deference

Smiles nervously or not at all

Drops chin

Shrinks shoulders and arms

Clenches fists

Crosses legs or ankles

Reprinted with permission of the Democrat and Chronicle, Rochester, NY.

THE BODY LANGUAGE OF POWER

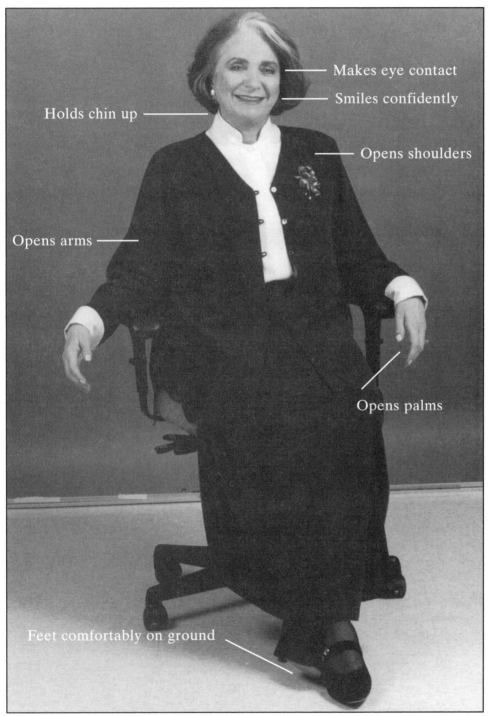

Makes eye contact

Smiles confidently

Holds chin up

Opens shoulders

Opens arms

Opens palms

Feet comfortably on ground

first action shot: make the most of it. Stride comfortably, swing your arms, smile, look proudly at the audience, nod to someone you recognize.

=== *Action Plan*

Videotape yourself walking to the podium, down the hall, up the stairs. Viewing yourself a few times on video can help you identify and change your weak habits. It hurts, but it's a great way to learn.

Body Power from Head to Toe

As I do before writing each section of a book, I reviewed the research literature on gender, gesture, and power in preparation for this chapter. I also reviewed videotapes of businesswomen and conferred with Ron Mix, the film director who consults with us on nonverbal aspects of presentations. The research describes the differences between men and women and between the weak and the powerful. These differences are significant: Judee Burgoon notes that "gender differences are far from trivial. They have the potential to create tension, conflict, and dissatisfaction . . ." But it was the videotapes and the director that revealed what we women can do to *change or enhance* our gestures. Rather than dwell on the differences between male and female that we can't readily change, I'll comment here on the gestures *that you can control*.

=== *Action Plan*

If your video reveals any of the weak gestures, try to change one at a time. Practice in front of the mirror or the video camera. Ask a friend to monitor you. If you're not sure what to do, watch a woman you admire and see if you can mirror her gestures. Children learn the body language of their parents by unconsciously mirroring them; you can consciously mirror the body language of strong women you admire.

We'll work from top to bottom.

HOLD YOUR HEAD HIGH

The head gets most attention. Change the way you hold your head and you change your image. There are several characteristically weak head positions and gestures, but the most common is chin down with eyes downcast or furtively glancing upward, the modest gesture of subservience that women, especially young women, have absorbed all too well. One of the negative outcomes of the chin-down gesture is that when you look up, your eyes take on the "scared-doe" look. The second weak head gesture is the cocked head, another characteristically female, characteristically weak position. The third is the tossing of or pushing back of the hair (works well in the bar, perhaps, but not on the podium), and all other hair-related activities. Avoid the three weak head gestures. Vicki Casarett, our drama coach, suggests that you hold the head as if suspended by a cord from the ceiling, shun extraneous movements, and use appropriate gestures, such as nods.

THE EYES HAVE IT

Here's a sad story about failed eye contact. A senior manager sent us a presentation videotape for analysis. Her words came out of the best leadership manual: she graciously recognized and welcomed new members to the work team. Had we read a transcript, we'd have lauded her leadership style. But the video told a different story: she failed to smile, and her eyes looked only at the slide. The lack of eye contact belied the leadership message.

We've all heard about *eye contact*, but what is it? Look at the structure of the word *contact*. It has two elements: the prefix *con*, which means "with" or "together," and the stem *tact* which comes from *tangere*, "to touch." So *contact* means literally "to touch with." If you consider eye contact to mean that you actually *touch* people with your eyes, you're more likely to do so. Experience shows that successful eye contact lasts long enough to "touch together." This means that when you speak, you should look at the listeners' eyes at least half the time, get and hold true eye contact with several audience members, and reach people at various locations. Because women have been taught that it's brazen or aggressive to maintain eye contact (men are taught to "look people right in the eye"), they find this skill especially daunting. Indeed, one researcher suggests that reduced eye contact may be implicated in the interruptions women endure.

Successful eye contact rewards you fast. When you touch people with your eyes, most of them offer warmth and support (through smiles, nods, and other gestures), and they give feedback about how well you're conveying the message. (If you have any doubt about that, try taping a talk without an audience.) Be sure to reach people at the sides of the room, even if it means turning the body to them once in a while. People who never see your eyes feel overlooked and won't appreciate your message. If, however, one audience member seems uninterested or hostile, give up on her or him (if the whole audience looks uninterested or hostile, you're in deep trouble). Poor or hostile listeners distract and unnerve you. You're a speaker, not a masochist.

Eye contact also holds the secret to reading the script. Simply follow this rule: never say a word without eye contact. Look at the script or slide as long as necessary; look at someone's eyes; say the words. That's all there is to it.

Action Plan

Unlike head position and other gestures, it's nearly impossible to "read" eye contact on a videotape. If you seek to master the skill of eye contact, either monitor it as you speak or ask friends to do so. In our workshops, we assign one listener to monitor eye contact for each speaker.

THE FACE TELLS ALL . . . OR NOTHING

Studies show that women have more expressive faces than men do and that we smile and laugh more as well. Some view smiling as a weakness and tell women to be like men and strip the expression from their faces. Yet we enjoy people who smile pleasantly at us, we know that smiling is relaxing and healthful, and we find no welcome as warm as a smile. Roger Axtell reminds us that smiling is the only universal gesture: it has the same meaning all over the world. Indeed, women who appear hostile do so in part because they fail to smile. Why the discrepancy? Perhaps we're using "smile" as a generic word to describe a variety of different looks and gestures. Think of your own experience with smiles. Contrast the nervous, inappropriate one to the confident smile of She Who Must Be Obeyed. Avoid the first and learn the second. Listeners find the confident smile appealing (for men as well as for women), and it's an easy gesture to learn. Still, the smile, like all other gestures, must fit the message. If you're laying off a work team, a jolly smile won't work for you at all, but if you're reporting savings of a billion dollars a year, it wouldn't do to look grim.

Think of the smile as a gesture that meshes with the rest of your message. If you want to look confident, hold your head high and smile before you speak and after you finish. Smiling gives another instance where you don't want to communicate like a man but like a strong woman. As with the grammar of power, the solution lies in control: you decide when it's appropriate to smile.

Action Plan

Turn off the sound on your video and note all the smiles. Do they look confident? Do they mesh well with the content of the message? Decide whether you smile too much, too little, or too deferentially.

THE TRUNK SHOW

Oh, if only you followed all your mom's reminders: don't slouch, stand up straight, keep your stomach in, hold your head high, carry yourself with dignity. Right on every count! Studies find that women tend to shrink into their spaces (remember the shrinking violet?) while men tend to expand. For example, women are more likely than men to clutch their arms around their trunks and slouch, while men are more likely to open their arms and hands.

One dramatic example of this came at a fast-track management training session. The division president strode into the room with his top aide. Both looked great. The first impression of the aide was, Now here's a woman of power! But when the aide rose to introduce the division president, her body betrayed her. She stood between the slide projector and the screen, so that the slide marched across her face. Then she clutched her arms over her chest and held them there while she spoke. No one remembers the words of the introduction, but no one will forget the body language of weakness.

To gain power and look confident, expand beyond rather than shrink into your physical space. For example, open your palms and your arms instead of clenching your fists and wrapping your body. If you're pointing at a slide or transparency, position yourself so that your body faces the audience and opens to point. If you're right handed, stand so the screen is at your right, vice-versa if you're left handed. Common sense helps, too. People who don't know enough to get out from in front of the slide look foolish no matter what else they do.

ARMS AND THE WOMAN

The women at an executive luncheon were introducing themselves and their jobs. Martha Hoffner, who seems to be stuck just below the glass ceiling, told of her job. In her soft voice, this executive said that she manages a fifty-million-dollar budget. As she said the word "budget," she shrugged ever so slightly. Had you watched her video without voice, you'd never have imagined that she said anything about fifty million dollars. That shrug erased the big numbers, just as your shrugs erase the powerful words you say.

Another senior woman whose arms betrayed her found out by seeing herself on tape. Her dignified head and trunk were undermined because she nervously made little circles with her hands each time she spoke. After she learned to rest her arms on the side of the chair, her dignity prevailed. My book collection includes just about every guide to gesture for speakers. They often conflict with one another. And our experience often conflicts with the guides. For example, moving the closed fist up and down is described as a hostile gesture, yet strong speakers can use it effectively to show power. Also, open-palm gestures may be described as weak or cold, yet they work well as gestures of friendliness and inclusiveness. If anything, the more open the arms, elbows, and hands, the better. Think of the famous "Evita" pose: arms high, wide, and open.

The apparent discrepancies result from the extreme context dependency of gestures: the setting of a gesture is as restrictive as the setting of a jewel. Still, we've seen enough gestures that never work (like shrugs when there's no uncertainty and pencil-twirling) and enough that work nearly all the time that we can set out some principles and suggestions for you to follow.

Before you acquire other powerful hand gestures, however, learn one indispensable, easy-to-acquire posture: the *resting position*. Ron Mix, the film director, coined this term when he observed that strong speakers don't necessarily move their arms much, but always find a comfortable, relaxed resting position. If you use a podium, simply rest your arms on it or rest one arm while holding your note cards with the other. Or you may choose to rest your hands calmly at your sides or grasp them loosely in front of you, below the waist. If you work with a pointer or note cards, holding them loosely in one hand works. Whatever your resting position, it must look relaxed and comfortable.

As you refine a repertoire of hand and arm gestures, apply the following two essential principles. First, the gesture must match the words, the message, and your character. If, for example, you're discussing the shrinking work force, don't open your arms wide. Second, the gesture must look natural and not posed. In *Body Politics*, Nancy Henley says, "Nonverbal gestures carry the most influence when they are natural and not affected, when they enhance and harmonize with the verbal message."

One of our students adds her observation that the closed body is the nonverbal equivalent of the *I* statement: it says, "this is about me and not about you or about us." So, whether learning a resting position or adding powerful gestures, be skeptical, use common sense, and take a critical look at yourself on a silent video.

Ten Gestures That Usually Fail

1. Standing rigid with your arms at your sides
2. Clutching your chest with both arms
3. Gripping the podium or projector with white knuckles showing
4. Playing with hair, clothing, or face
5. Clasping hands behind you
6. Mismatching gestures and words
7. Shrugging when making assertions
8. Shrugging immediately after the talk
9. Tugging at clothing
10. Moving extraneously in any way

Seven Gestures That Usually Work

1. Resting arms comfortably
2. Opening arms and palms (if the words match)
3. Enumerating with the hand (don't make this your only gesture and never do it more than once in a presentation)
4. Tenting the fingers
5. Sweeping arm from one side to the other to show movement or progress
6. Chopping from top to bottom or side to side to match a parallel series
7. Avoiding extraneous movement

1. Watch an admired female newscaster or politician or an actress playing a positive, strong role.
2. Mimic the gestures you admire.
3. Watch yourself on video with no sound. Omit or add one gesture at a time.
4. Work with an associate who attends your presentations. Ask her to observe your eye contact and report back to you.

THE FEET FORM THE FOUNDATION

A magazine photo shows two famous newscasters facing each other. He's standing in the traditional male power position: comfortably clad feet 12 inches apart and flat on the ground. She's clad in high heels, standing in the female flamingo position: one foot flat and one bent back at the knee. He's solid. She'd fall over in an instant. Those postures we learned as little girls and cheerleaders don't just fade away.

Your feet and legs show even when you're behind a podium. Tightly folded knees or ankle knots and unnecessary movements show anxiety. Keep your feet flat on the ground about 12 inches apart and facing forward so they give you firm support. And wear comfortable shoes!

Beyond the Body: Your Voice Speaks Volumes

LET'S WHISPER ABOUT VOICE

> *The devil hath not, in his quiver's choice,*
> *An arrow for the heart like a sweet voice.*

Lord Byron might have referred to Charlotte's voice. What was it like? Was it a booming bass, a proud alto? No, it was not a man's voice: it was "small, sweet, musical, rather thin but pleasant." Charlotte's was a typically *female* voice, but it was not the voice of submission. When Charlotte spoke, everyone listened. Yet in our business culture, it's still the male voice that's held up as the ideal: deep, mellow, sonorous.

What should you do about your voice? Nothing at all, if it's not squeaky or shrill. If your voice is pitched too high, it weakens you; work to lower it and seek speech therapy if necessary. Listen to the voices of women in the news and try to mirror them as they speak. Although it is true that successful women have relatively deep voices, we have rarely found a woman whose voice pitch is so high or squeaky that it damages her credibility. If the language is strong, the pace is appropriate, and the statements are confident, the *sweet, musical, thin, small* voice shall be heeded.

Action Plan

Have you ever really listened to your voice? You can do so in two ways. Either turn the picture off your videotape or prepare an audio cassette of a talk. Then ask caring associates what they think about your voice and decide whether it hurts your career. It's expensive and difficult to change voice pitch (although speech therapy is usually covered by health insurance). Of the thousands of women I've worked with, perhaps three had voices that were troublesome enough to warrant therapy. If your voice is a serious drawback, seek out a speech therapist who specializes in voice. If not, embrace your voice and move on.

"I Come from Atlanta?"

Voice involves more than just pitch: it also involves intonation. Young women, in particular, often make their statements sound like questions. Two young executives were on a conference call with my office. The person in New York asked the other, "What city are you in?" She replied, "Atlanta?" Despite her sure knowledge of where she was, she said it like a question. If your voice ends every statement as if it were a question, then no one will listen to you. Why ask instead of tell? The woman in Atlanta, ambitious for a career in public relations, determined to stop asking instead of telling. She and a friend agreed to stop each other every time they did it. It took about a week for them to end this damaging habit. If your intonation turns every sentence into a question, you're sending a clear message: "I don't know what I'm talking about. Don't listen to me!"

Action Plan

Copy the Atlanta public relations woman. Find a collaborator who works with you every day. Each time one of you ends a sentence as if it were a question, wink or pinch or make a funny noise. If necessary, keep a record of how often you do it. This is a learned behavior. It fails. It's easy to unlearn. Get rid of it.

Faster than the Speed of Sound

Superman may have traveled faster than the speed of sound, but Superwoman never talked that fast. Why do some women talk too fast? They've told me time and again: when they feel listeners slipping away, they try to hold the floor by talking faster (sometimes louder), *and it always fails.* Now that you've learned to use a script with an accurate word count, you can easily check your speed. Aim for an average delivery of about 100 to 125 words a minute. That allows time for pauses and emphasis.

Action Plan

Invest in a stopwatch with a large digital readout. Monitor your time or have an associate clock practice presentations. When you speak at about 100 to 125 words a minute, you've mastered your timing and added to your professionalism. When you actually present, always stay within time limits. If the agenda doesn't show your schedule, let the audience know how long you'll speak right at the start: "During the next fifteen minutes . . ."

STAMP OUT WIMPY NOISES

Wimpy noises such as um . . . uh . . . show up on the video or audio-tape. When you hear them scuttling your presentation, you'll appreciate the need to stamp them out. Simply replace all your wimpy noises with silence. Women are so terrified they'll be interrupted (research shows that they're right) that they fear losing the floor if they stand silent for an instant. Yet those instants give you time to compose powerful words. At our workshops, women eliminate "ums" and "uhs" in a day or two of practice and a couple of videotape sessions. You will too.

USE SILENCE

Like smiles, silence can signify weakness or power, deference or control. When I speak of silence here, I don't mean the silence of being afraid to speak or of not getting your turn. I mean the controlled silence you choose to bring your message home.

Fine speakers know the value of well-placed silences. Look at Charlotte. "Day after day the spider waited, head-down, for an idea to come to her. Hour by hour she sat motionless, deep in thought." Jeff Scott Cook writes, "Speakers who phrase well and pause judiciously are universally regarded as more credible and knowledgeable than those who dash straight to the end." A professional speaker tells of a way she reminds herself about silence (yes, even professional speakers get nervous and forget to pause). When she comes to an important break between ideas, she stops and sips a bit of water. These sips are written into her script. Other speakers leave blank spaces to remind them to pause.

Pauses emphasize better than shouts. They give you and your listeners time to think, bridge between one idea and the next, and heighten anticipation. Yet unskilled speakers are so uneasy that they fill every instant with some kind of noise or weak language. There's no sure recipe, but here are tips about effective use of silence.

When to Use Silence

Before you speak, to get everyone's attention

Every time you would have said, "Um . . ."

Before and to drive home a critical point

Between strong parallels ("of the people . . . by the people . . . for the people")

When a new transparency appears on the screen, to give people time to read it

To think about the subject of a sentence and avoid saying *I*

Between phrases

To look quietly at a rude person or group with the aim of silencing them

During applause or laughter (smile!)

When someone else speaks

To give people time to take notes before you begin again

After you speak, before rushing off the platform

After someone asks you a question, to think or make a note about the answer

After you finish speaking, to allow time for questions or comments before moving on to the next speaker

Whenever you've inserted a pause marker in your script

Action Plan

Turn up the sound and note your silences. If you fill every instant with sound, practice the pauses noted here.

Transforming Nervous Nellie:
Sure-Fire Confidence Builders

"I lack self-confidence"; "I'm afraid to look stupid in front of people"; "I get so nervous I lose my train of thought"; "I'll prepare the boss's talk, but don't ask me to get up." When it comes to speaking in public, Roosevelt was right: "The only thing we have to fear is fear itself." The women who made the preceding comments all share one trait: they speak perfectly well sitting down or standing before a small group, but they dread public exposure so much that they freeze. Others fear it so much that they resort to self-defeating gestures. One woman walked out of a speaking workshop to avoid being videotaped.

Yet promotions go to those who present. While you're cowering in the corner, the guy next to you is volunteering to deliver the presentation. He gives it, makes mistakes, learns from them, and volunteers to give the next presentation. All while you, who did the critical work, cower.

Why? History has not been kind to women who speak out. Kathleen Hall Jamieson, in *Beyond the Double Bind*, describes one of the binds as Silence/Shame. Going back to biblical texts, she shows that women who spoke in public were subject to ridicule, condemnation, even death. So it's not surprising that women shy away from public presentation. Yet, as Jamieson notes and we've all observed, women confined to the home learned powerful forms of expression. Those powerful forms should remain with you as you take your place on the public podium.

For example, mothers of babies have learned how to slow and simplify their speech, play games that exploit the rhythmical patterns of parallelism, use large gestures, smile, touch, give clear instructions, read aloud with clarity and expression, tell stories. You've already seen that great communicators empower their public discourse in the same ways.

Still, women dread anxiety. We perceive stress as menacing. We fear public exposure of our defects. Some men do, too, of course, but no man ever walked out of one of my speaking workshops. Despite the powerful language we learned at home, women's life experiences have prepared us inadequately for the complex issues the presenter faces. We know how to enable, support, aid, serve as "the power behind the throne." We haven't envisioned ourselves sitting on the throne itself. We're scared. Yet, in Eleanor Roosevelt's words, "You gain strength, courage, and confidence by every experience in which you really stop to look fear in the face. . . . You must do the thing which you think you cannot do." She echoes Emerson's words, "Always do what you are afraid to do."

So, let's tackle the issue of self-confidence. My mail brings flyers every month for "self-confidence" seminars, and I laugh. You can't take a course in self-confidence. It's not a skill you can study and practice. People gain self-confidence in only two sure ways: they meet success and they learn new skills. When you know how to do something you couldn't do before, you grow self-confident. When you've succeed at something, you gain self-confidence.

Amelia Earhart quipped, "Hamlet would have been a bad aviator. He worried too much." Some people, even as children, seem self-assured, while others, like Hamlet, worry too much. Is it innate, or is it related to their experiences or how they were raised? We don't know and, for you as a businesswoman, it doesn't matter. What does matter is that you over-come your fear and gain the courage to face the world. That courage shows in your gestures. Ossie Borosh, a concert pianist, tells how her teachers emphasized powerful-looking gestures. They understood that, since the pianist is seen on stage, her performance must *look* powerful as well as sound beautiful. However, Ossie reports that her application of those lessons depends on how secure she feels about the music. Your gestures reflect your attitude as well as influence it.

How, then, can you overcome those years of diffidence training? First, have the courage to welcome nervousness, anxiety, and stress and make them your handmaidens. I, for one, like to feel anxious and stressed: stress spurs my creativity (as long as it doesn't magnify into terror). And other successful women tell me they like it too. It's exciting. Your body sends stress signals because it aims for peak performance. If you've ever been bored by a totally relaxed presenter, you'll realize that that's not how you want to present. So how can you prepare yourself to follow Martina Navratilova's advice: "Just go out there and do what you've got to do"?

Confidence Builder 1: Weigh the Consequences

Ask yourself, what are the consequences of failure? If I fail at this presentation, what will happen? List all the consequences. Will you lose your job? Will you miss the next promotion? Will the customer laugh at you? Will you feel bad? You'll be relieved to discover that the consequences of failure aren't so scary as they seem. You could lose your job even if your talk succeeds; you could be passed over for the next promotion anyway; few customers ever laugh at salespeople; and you feel bad already since you're afraid to give the talk. If the consequence of failure is death or illness, then you may decide not to do the talk at all, but that's highly unlikely. Few offices own guillotines.

This technique has served my clients well, not only in gaining courage to fail but in gaining courage to venture out into the world in other ways. The fear of failure is worse than the failure itself.

Confidence Builder 2: Laugh at Yourself

Laugh at yourself. People who laugh at themselves greatly ease their performance anxiety. Most of the problems you may have on the podium are funny. You trip. Your stocking runs. You forget the punch line. Your script is in another city. Your disk is incompatible with the equipment. You show up in the wrong place. Appreciating the humor in these not-quite-so-tragic-as-they-look situations relaxes you and enables you to do your best. You'll warm your audience if you don't act like a scared rabbit waiting for the kill. As Dame Margot Fonteyn said, "Take your work seriously but not yourself."

In my years as a public speaker, I've experienced every speaking disaster listed here, and some others that are too embarrassing to mention. Once, I was invited to work with a group of graduate students. Because they weren't out in the world of work yet, I stressed the centrality of professionalism in manner, in language, and in dress. The room was stuffy, so I removed my suit jacket. In the powder room during the break, I discovered that my pocketed sweater was on backward. This little joke on myself was funny, not tragic—and it showed my humanity.

CONFIDENCE BUILDER 3: TAKE A DEEP BREATH

Breathe deeply. When we get nervous, we tend to breathe shallowly. This deprives us of oxygen and intensifies the fear. If you concentrate on breathing deeply, you'll get that much-needed air and forestall panic. If you don't know how to deep breathe, take a yoga class or ask to sit in on a natural childbirth class. Yoga, meditation, and natural childbirth classes all teach deep-breathing techniques.

CONFIDENCE BUILDER 4: FORGET PERFECTION

Perfection is overrated. Much performance anxiety stems from the impossible goal of perfection. The sculptor Louise Nevelson wrote, "I never want perfection—I hate the word. I think that it's arrogant." Those who accept nothing less than perfection are those who accomplish little in the world. Worst of all, some use perfectionism as an excuse for not trying. *It's okay to fail.* Failure is a great teacher. Any successful woman will tell you a long list of her failures and what she learned from each one. You're not absolved from doing less than your best; just don't strive for perfection. Forget about perfection, prepare and rehearse fully, then do the best you can.

Sit Down and Look Strong

Till now we've looked primarily at nonverbal aspects of stand-up presentations, but everything we've said applies equally well to those sit-down talks that you do all day, and to meetings. Sit-down performances tend to be more relaxed because women aren't so nervous about them, but they also tend to be sloppier because we don't appreciate their importance. That videotape of your meeting revealed what you look like when you don't realize you're on stage. Do you slouch, attend to your doodling rather than to the speaker, talk to your table partner? Or do you sit straight, leaning forward slightly, arms in a comfortable resting position or pencil in hand, and offer the gift of attention to the speaker? When it's your turn, have you prepared a few words or a sentence? Do you show respect to the speaker who precedes you by acknowledging his or her contribution? If you do, maybe others will do the same for you. Civility can be modeled, especially by women in leadership positions. Pay close attention to yourself when you're sitting.

A strong repertoire of expressive language skills—planning, writing, speaking, and body language—plays a crucial role in your success. But a successful presence involves style as well. The next chapter takes a look at your costume for success.

Quick Tips

Learn postures of power.

Make first impressions count.

Stride to the podium.

Hold your head high.

Maintain eye contact.

Smile strongly.

Acquire a resting position.

Pick up gracious gestures.

Stop asking, start telling.

Keep track of time.

Savor silence.

Stamp out wimpy noises.

Imagine failure.

Laugh.

Breathe deeply.

Let go of perfection.

Sit down and look strong.

8

Success Has Its Style:
Play Your Role with Panache

The only coherent fashion statement I can recall from the entire movement was the suggestion that Mrs. Cleaver, Beaver's mom, would on the whole have been a happier woman had she not persisted in vacuuming while wearing high heels.

MOLLY IVINS

This is a book about language, power, and success. What does that have to do with style? After all, Naomi Wolf hit the mark when she said, "I spent two years locked in the library collecting the 600 footnotes in my book. I didn't write it with my hair." And, in response to newly issued "professional" Barbie dolls, the historian Joan Jacobs Brumberg, noted, "Until such time as we can make professional women unglamorous or low upkeep, where their power doesn't depend on their hairdo or their high heels, . . . we are sending the wrong message." Even today, many low-upkeep, unglamorous professional women succeed. At a recent international women's conference, I observed hundreds of senior executives: some dressed in the height of fashion and others dressed like bag ladies.

Still, anyone immersed in the world of work knows that style is language just as gesture is, and that there are styles of failure and success just as there are languages of weakness and power. And those styles of failure and success change with your changing position in the world. One of the side bars of the notorious Simpson murder case is the "remaking" of Marcia Clark, an attorney for the prosecution. A *New York Times* story describes how her presence was orchestrated. "The first signs of the remake were physical: shorter, better-kempt hair that framed her face, warmer and lighter-colored dresses with softer fabrics, more jewelry."

Yet style is more nebulous and harder to get a hold on than any other topic in this book. Nevertheless, since yours can drive you to success or shove you toward failure, we'll review the issues and suggest an approach to style.

The thesis here echoes and expands Molly Ivins's epigraph to this chapter. I urge you, as you consider your approach to style, to avoid trying to "vacuum while wearing high heels." Contrary to the dictates of "dress for success," you can adapt an interesting personal style as long as you stay within the constraints of good taste and practicality. Furthermore, the more talented, capable, secure, and powerful you are, the more freely you can flout or simply ignore the "rules."

Work Is Theater: How to Dress the Part

To make sense of all this, think of the workplace as a kind of theater, in which the role dictates your costume. Jane Alexander understands that she'd dress one way to play Lady Macbeth and a different way to play chairperson of the National Endowment for the Arts. This doesn't make her a slave to fashion, just a skilled actor who chooses costumes that work.

Renee Fleur is another skilled actor who has two jobs that require vastly different costumes. By day this Yale-educated linguist teaches English to Japanese executives. By night, she belly dances in a restaurant and at private parties. Although she crosses wider divides in her two jobs than most of us do, the demands on her style illustrate the importance of costuming oneself to fit the job. Imagine Renee showing up at the Japanese corporate headquarters in the scant, sequined, vividly colored outfit in which she dances (in bare feet)!

Given, then, that work is a kind of theater, what kinds of costumes help us play our roles successfully? And how far must we conform? Books on style help us less than common sense, a careful eye, and a friend, associate, or salesperson who understands the scene. My company is lucky enough to employ Marlene Maggio, a personal image consultant who helps working women create the styles that work best for them. Marlene structures her consultations from head to toe, from hair to shoes. She's turned many business ducklings into swans. She tapped her experiences to contribute practical ideas to this chapter.

Hair

"Hair should be transparent. If people don't notice your hair, the style works. Hair should be so integral to your appearance that it matches everything else about you," says Paul Lyons, a stylist who fashions the hair of career women in my city. He is so right. Successful hair is transparent; it should blend so perfectly with your style that no one notices it. If you're a high-fashion type, your hair looks like *Vogue* and changes often; if you're conservative, your hair is simple and consistent from year to year. Hair that works is clean, neat, and natural-looking. It demands as little of your time and attention as possible: busy women don't want to be slaves to the hairdresser. Like everything else in your style, it should look controlled; hair that demands tossing of the head to stay out of your eyes gives a lame message about you. So does hair that you must constantly touch or comb to keep in place. Avoid hair that is brightly colored, too long or bushy, unkempt, or smelly.

Within these general guidelines, however, you're free to emphasize your ethnic or racial identity. Professional women can look great—and powerful—in well-groomed Afros, cornrows, long, straight styles, and boyish cuts. Long or short, straight or curled, up or down, pick the style that fits you comfortably and demands the least of your time.

These rules, of course, apply only if you're on the way up. Once you get to the top, you can do pretty much as you please.

SMELL

Smell is a powerful, unspoken element of style. It can be sexy, subtle, neutral, or offensive. Yet no one talks about it. I work in a corporate setting and have only once met someone who smelled (and looked) dirty. Yet that doesn't mean every woman smells good. In private consultations, my staff and I are often repelled, not by the smell of dirt, but by other overwhelmingly strong odors that result from a mix of cosmetic products. If you look at the array of cosmetics, soaps, and shampoos in any drugstore, you'll see why. One woman can wear simultaneously an "apple blossom" shampoo, "floral" dusting powder, "powder fresh" deodorant, and three or four kinds of makeup with different odors. Or the woman can eat a diet that differs enough from standard fare that she emanates a distinctive odor, not unpleasant in itself but unpleasant to her peers. Or she may come from another country in which the American fetishes aren't pervasive; for example, she may not shave under her arms, wear deodorant, shower daily, or wash her clothes after each wearing.

Is there a common-sense approach to the problem of smell? Yes, in that some tips seem to work for everyone. First, try not to smell vastly different from the people with whom you work. Second, seek products that are odor free. Third, if you want some kind of perfume, wear only one odor at a time. Finally, if you come from another culture, ask a true friend if your odor is noticeable (no one volunteers that information).

FIGURE

In a lecture at Geneseo College, Naomi Wolf mentioned that glossy magazines will not carry photographs of a woman over size 14, no matter how important she is. The images you see on television and in magazines don't look anything like you or your colleagues. In my working and executive women's seminars, we see a cross-section of real women who work: they're short and tall, thin and fat, narrow and wide, striking and simple-looking. Within limits, there's only the most nebulous relationship between size and success. Justice Ginsburg is short and narrow, while Attorney General Janet Reno is tall and wide. As in most of the matters we've looked at, your size matters only if it's not transparent, only if it's so extreme that it draws attention to itself, and only if you dress in a manner that emphasizes your size and shape.

FACE

To make up or not to make up: that is the question. The decision to avoid makeup is perfectly legitimate. Men aren't expected to wear makeup, so women shouldn't be expected to either. If you choose to avoid cosmetics and let your natural beauty show, you'll emulate some of the handsomest women of our time. Don't be fooled by the magazines: many successful executives, doctors, lawyers, engineers, and secretaries don't wear makeup. Indeed, it's better to wear no makeup than to wear it badly.

If, however, you choose to use cosmetics, beware of the pitfalls. Think of women who use makeup unwisely. What do they do wrong? They wear too much. The worst makeup error is excess. Like successful hair, successful makeup is transparent—no one notices it.

Yet makeup can emphasize your best features and cover or minimize your worst. For example, some women have dark circles under their eyes or broken blood vessels on their noses. A little cover-up camouflages these and avoids costly treatments or surgery. A moisturizer base can keep the skin clean and prevent chapping, while a light liquid foundation gives skin a uniform look. If you have pale skin, you may want to add a bit of color on your cheeks. If you have beautiful eyes, consider a soft shadow or a touch of eyeliner to highlight them.

Don't get suckered by cosmetic salespeople. A friend with a good eye and a few samplers can save you from wasting money on cosmetics you won't wear. If makeup technique baffles you, seek out a consultant who can suggest which colors flatter you and how to apply them quickly.

CLOTHING

Although you're free to use or avoid makeup, you must choose clothing (unless you wear a uniform), and you must do so wisely. Here's where it's costly to follow fashion's dictates, but it's also costly to ignore them. The days are long gone when women, like lemmings, followed each year's fashions whether or not they worked. The dollars wasted on hot pants, short skirts, garish polyesters, high-platform shoes, and colors of the season could have bought small classic wardrobes that look good for years. Still, trendy clothes can be fun; just don't overdose or invest much money in them. Marlene Maggio says, "Keeping up with the times is fine in moderation. Keeping up with the classics is timeless."

Five years ago, an entrepreneur consulted with me about marketing her computer-instruction services to corporations. Within a few minutes, it was obvious that she was headed for failure. Although she aimed for a corporate audience, she still wore the clothes in which she'd been an underling. Her light blue, poorly tailored polyester suit and blouse, her five-and-dime earrings, her white, spiked-heel shoes with dark-tan stockings all sent the wrong message. Before she presented her product, we instructed her to go to the best department store in town and ask the personal shopper to find a dark, well-tailored wool suit and three white or ivory silk blouses, a pair of low-heeled pumps, and stockings in a shade to match. She had borrowed a hundred thousand dollars to buy equipment but hadn't seen her wardrobe as part of the investment in her business.

Of course, you can go too far the other way as well. A client of mine, a young women brought in to lead a high-tech team of older men, was accused of intimidating those who worked for her. We arranged to meet at her office in a small midwestern city. The day I met her happened to be "casual" day, so the men around the office wore chinos and tee shirts. She, however, looked exquisite in her designer leather pants, costly cashmere sweater, and gold earrings. It turned out that she traveled to Paris to outfit herself. No wonder she intimidated people!

An executive recruiter, who usually recommends that job-seekers err on the side of dressing a little better than those they expect to meet, agrees strongly with the idea of transparency. She tells of the senior financial woman whose clothes looked so expensive that they were the main topic of conversation after the interview. She warned that you should dress well, but not too well. Here's an example of the Goldilocks principle: it's no good if you dress too poorly, but it's no good if you dress too extravagantly. Style should be just right.

Does everyone have to find a personal shopper or a stylist? Of course not. Some women have a intuitive sense of style and can get their wardrobes together by shopping at discount stores and sales. But if you haven't figured it out for yourself, you need professional help.

Cindy Singer also needed professional help. She started out as a file clerk and rose through the ranks to become executive secretary to the vice president. Yet her clothing hadn't kept up with her career changes. She came to work in high-heeled mules, mesh stockings, and tank tops. Her long bleached-blonde hair looked stringy. Luckily for her, the vice president believed in mentoring younger women, so, instead of a frivolous gift, she bought Cindy a tailored pants suit for a holiday gift. The vice president then helped Cindy match her work costume to her job.

Marybeth Tolliver also learned that her costume must change with her changing role. As an engineer working in a "skunk works," a high-tech research center, she happily wore sweatsuits to work every day. But her talent won her promotion to ever more responsible positions in the skunk works. Finally, she moved into an executive job that required travel abroad. She asked Marlene to shop with her. Here's the travel wardrobe Marlene helped her select:

A Basic Professional Wardrobe

1 black dress—lightweight wool crepe or silk blend

1 black suit—lightweight wool crepe or silk; avoid man-tailored, so it can go from day to evening.

1 blazer—camel or tweed in black and caramel or black and red

1 pair black pants—well-tailored, loose legs, lightweight wool crepe

1 cardigan sweater—burgundy, red, or deep green, black trim

1 narrow black belt

Blouses:

1 light cranberry—silk or blend

1 cream—silk or blend

1 white classic cotton or silk shirt

2 suit sweaters—black and cream

1 camisole—black silk (to go under black suit jacket for evening)

Jewelry:

2 pairs of earrings—tailored, 1 gold, 1 pearl

2 pins—tailored, but good-sized

2 silk scarves—same color family as above

2 necklaces—1 long gold, 1 two-strand pearl

1 lightweight fur or classic raincoat in neutral color, depending on the climate

1 soft-leather shoulder-strap briefcase in black

1 small black-suede handbag for evening

Shoes:

1 pair of black suede or patent-leather low-heeled pumps or flat boots

1 pair of black-leather or leather-and-suede or patent flats

Businesswomen who travel know the vagaries of climate and weather. One day you're in New York in 33-degree biting cold; the next day you're in Washington and it's 40 with light snow. Then it's off to Dallas, where it's 60 degrees. Marlene suggests you deal with these radical changes by investing in "tropical weight" wools, wool blends, and silks. With changes in accessories, such fabrics span seasons and climates.

Accessories

Fine accessories represent a wise investment: they last, they stay in style longer than clothing does, they offer the chance to exercise your individuality. Pam Mason uses scarves and shawls as her trademark. Over the past decades, she's invested in silk or wool pieces unified in one way: they work with black or white or they have black or white in them. When she travels, she carries one or two dark suits or dresses and neutral silk blouses, along with a sampling of her collection. The scarves and shawls don't wrinkle or soil easily, they take up little luggage space, and they vary her look enough so that no one notices that she wears similar clothes every day. They also give her a distinctive, elegant look. Pam evaluates her accessory investment in what she calls "price per wearing." For example, the Liberty of London shawl she bought at Harrods in 1986 cost $100. She's worn it more than ten times a year since then, making the price per wearing under a dollar: a good investment indeed! And a far better deal than a polyester blouse that pills after one or two washes.

Consider investing in one quality, neutral-color briefcase, preferably one with a shoulder strap so your hands are free to carry luggage when you travel. A well-made briefcase lasts almost indefinitely, so it's a good investment candidate. So are dark handbags and wallets.

As far as jewelry is concerned, one pair of gold earrings takes you nearly everywhere, at a very low price per wearing. Depending upon your job, you may choose to wear some of the attractive, colorful costume jewelry now available. Beware of jewelry that is too big, hangs too low, looks cheap, or makes noise. Ethnic jewelry reveals pride in your origins; just be sure to stay within the bounds of good taste. One of our heroes, Orit Gadiesh, loves and wears big, clunky earrings and pins, which she designs herself.

Judi Green is an interior designer. In her travels all over the world, she's collected masses of singular ethnic earrings, beads, and bracelets. As a designer, she's sensitive to what's appropriate in what setting. When she decorates private homes, she wears a different style of earring in each ear, five or six multicolored bracelets, and a variety of antique-beaded neck-laces. But when she designed the American offices of a London law firm, she wore small, simple gold earrings with a tailored suit. She knows about costume.

SHOES

Shoes and feet have long been used to enslave women. Elderly women in China hobble on feet destroyed by brutal binding. Young women in America teeter on high spiked heels that restrict their move-ment today and threaten their future health. Why? Because high heels and pointy toes emphasize the slenderness of the foot and the leg. The woman who really dresses for success understands that freedom and comfort, not artificial standards of beauty, dictate the style of her shoes. Here again, quality counts. Since you need only a few basic colors, it pays to invest in superior leather shoes with leather linings, with heels low enough for you to walk comfortably, and with rounded or square rather than pointed toe boxes. If you want shoes with pizzazz, look for inter-esting heel shapes, unusual tie arrangements, and textures. Dark shoes look good longer than do light, smooth leathers longer than do suede, lined shoes longer than do unlined. Shoes that tie or have high vamps are more comfortable for walking than are untied or low-cut styles. Shoe manufacturers have gotten the message: it's easier than ever to find classy shoes that feel good.

Business Casual?

American businesses and law firms have bought into the idea of "business casual all the time." Whatever the benefits of business casual, it causes anxiety for women. If your company has a business casual policy, you could fill in this space with your story of the young executive coming to work in very short cut-off shorts or some other variation of inappropriate apparel. Or of the young professional whose informal clothes emphasize her youth and detract from her professionalism.

That's not to mention the cross-cultural problems of business casual. Dr. Frederique Segond, who works at a research center in France, tells the story of an American executive's visit. "The poor woman had no idea about the fact that there are different cultures. She sent us a note saying that the dress code would be business casual. Well, in France, it does not mean anything. So we tried to tell her that it was like an Indonesian instructor requiring the audience to wear their kabayas."

Marlene Maggio recommends a set of guidelines to solve the puzzle of business casual. First, remember that business casual does not mean dressing for gardening, playing tennis, or washing the floor. You're a businesswoman, and your business costume must fit your job. She suggests you have a casual section in your closet. Include blazers, cardigan sweaters, turtle and mock-turtleneck sweaters, denim and cotton shirts, slacks, split skirts, and walking shoes or boots (not running shoes). Sporty scarves, pins, and jewelry work well with dress-down clothes. Whether dressing down or dressing up, retain your presence and keep your dignity.

When it comes to matters of style, success, and confidence, you have more freedom than fashion magazines admit, provided you dress in a way that's comfortable for you and that costumes you appropriately to get the job done. Just remember not to vacuum in high heels.

Action Plan

Take full-length photos of yourself in work outfits. If you have a good eye, do your own critical evaluation; if not, find a friend or a professional stylist who can help you decide if your look exudes confidence and success. If it doesn't, make prudent investments in clothes, shoes, hairstyle, and makeup that match the job you want to have.

Copy the Models of Excellence

Like artists and those who learn language, we copy someone else's style until we find our own. Choose a woman at work whom you admire and whose style and presence you'd like to emulate. Ideally, your model should be a woman in your own field or in your company, a woman you see often. Pay close attention to her hairstyle, clothing, fingernails, and jewelry and adapt that style to your personality, age, and job. After you develop a sense of your own personal style, continue to sample outstanding qualities from a variety of women.

Quick Tips

Learn the rules before you flout them.

Think of work as theater—match the costume to the job.

Wear hair that's transparent.

Smell like your associates.

Dress to suit your size.

Wear classics.

Dress down in style.

Copy an admired model.

9

Writing the Language of Success: Use the Mighty Pen

Power is often the product of persuasiveness.
People who can use linguistic skills to win others
over to a point of view and get them to act . . .
are likely to achieve power.

ROBIN TOLMACH LAKOFF

Any delusion that the computer reduces writing demands has long passed. We all write more than ever, and new technology increases our writing volume even as it eases our tasks. As we advance in power and success, our writing demands grow, and we accept the primacy of written language. Although Charlotte spoke clearly and well, she, too, understood the primacy of written language. When Wilbur protests that he's not really "terrific," Charlotte insists that it doesn't matter: "People believe almost anything they see in print." And, of course, Charlotte wove the original Web site. Writing and the logic required by the written language will ultimately free you from the bonds of weakness, from what the philosopher Nietzsche called "the prison house of language."

Women too often find themselves imprisoned by their inability to write clearly, logically, and persuasively. Whether you wish to be an effective administrative aide, engineer, scientist, or leader, if you wish to give voice to your ideas and ideals, you must write well. While you moved up

179

the ladder, often in jobs that tapped technical, nonverbal skills, you could camouflage writing weaknesses under other strengths. But the higher the level you attain, the more you communicate, much of the time in writing. Professor Kathleen Reardon wrote a *Harvard Business Review* piece that describes the dilemma of a woman manager who has written a memo to the company's president and can't decide whether to send it or not. The memo details her view of the treatment of women at the firm. The woman, Elizabeth Ames, keeps the memo in her desk and seeks advice on whether or not to send it.

Weak Words from a Top Manager

The *Harvard Business Review* editors asked several experts to advise Liz on the question, Should Liz send the memo? Only one of them, Gloria Steinem, commented on the writing and tone of the memo, which actually are of central importance. Here are the memo and my response to Liz. As you read the memo, note the weak language forms and their consequences and consider whether your writing looks like this.[*]

The Harvard Memo

To: Mr. John Clark, CEO

From: Elizabeth C. Ames, Director of Consumer Marketing

Date: March 8, 1993

I've been working in the marketing department at Vision Software for more than ten years, where I've had my share of challenges and successes. I've enjoyed being part of an interesting and exciting company. Despite

---

[*]Reprinted by permission of *Harvard Business Review*. "A Memo Every Woman Keeps in Her Desk" by Kathleen Reardon, March/April 1993, p. 17. Copyright ©1993 by President and Fellows of Harvard College; all rights reserved.

my general enthusiasm about the company and my job, however, I was taken aback when I received your memo announcing the resignations of Mariam Blackwell and Susan French, Vision's two most senior women. This is not the first time Vision has lost its highest ranking women. Just nine months ago, Kathryn Hobbs resigned, and a year before that, it was Suzanne LaHaise. The reasons are surprisingly similar: they wanted to "spend more time with their families" or "explore new career directions."

I can't help but detect a disturbing pattern. Why do such capable, conscientious women who have demonstrated intense commitment to their careers suddenly want to change course or spend more time at home? It's a question I've thought long and hard about.

Despite Vision's policies to hire and promote women and your own efforts to recognize and reward women's contributions, the overall atmosphere in this company is one that slowly erodes a woman's sense of worth and place. I believe that top-level women are leaving Vision Software not because they are drawn to other pursuits but because they are tired of struggling against a climate of female failure. Little things that happen daily—things many men don't even notice and women can't help but notice—send subtle messages that women are less important, less talented, less likely to make a difference than their male peers.

Let me try to describe what I mean. I'll start with meetings, which are a way of life at Vision and one of the most devaluing experiences for women. Women are often talked over and interrupted; their ideas never seem to be heard. Last week, I attended a meeting with ten men and one other woman. As soon as the woman started her presentation, several side conversations began. Her presentation skills were excellent, but she couldn't seem to get people's attention. When it was time to take questions, one man said dismissively, "We did something like this a couple of years ago, and it didn't work." She explained how her ideas differed, but the explanation fell on deaf ears. When I tried to give her support by expressing interest, I was interrupted.

But it's not just meetings. There are many things that make women feel unwelcome or unimportant. One department holds its biannual retreats at a country club with a "men only" bar. At the end of the sessions, the men typically hang around at the bar and talk, while the women quietly disappear. Needless to say, important information is often shared during those casual conversations.

Almost every formal meeting is followed by a series of informal ones behind closed doors. Women are rarely invited. Nor are they privy to the discussions before the formal meetings. As a result, they are often less likely to know what the boss has on his mind and therefore less prepared to react.

My female colleagues and I are also subjected to a daily barrage of seemingly innocent comments that belittle women. A coworker of mine recently boasted about how much he respects women by saying, "My wife is the wind beneath my wings. In fact, some people call me Mr. Karen Snyder." The men chuckled; the women didn't. And just last week, a male colleague stood up at 5:30 and jokingly informed a group of us that he would be leaving early: "I have to play mom tonight." Women play mom every night, and it never gets a laugh. In fact, most women try to appear devoid of concern about their families.

Any one of these incidents on its own is a small thing. But together and in repetition, they are quite powerful. The women at Vision fight to get their ideas heard and to crack the informal channels of information. Their energy goes into keeping up, not getting ahead, until they just don't have any more to give.

I can assure you that my observations are shared by many women in the company. I can only speculate that they were shared by Mariam Blackwell and Susan French.

Vision needs men and women if it is to become the preeminent educational software company. We need to send stronger, clearer signals that men are not the only people who matter. That's why I'm writing to you. If I can help, please let me know.

A Response to "A Memo Every Woman Keeps in Her Desk"

To: Elizabeth Ames

From: Phyllis Mindell, Ed.D.

Subject: Hold the Memo. Learn the Language of Success.

Your memo in the *Harvard Business Review* article titled "A Memo Every Woman Keeps in Her Desk" reveals that, despite your rise to director of consumer marketing, you have retained the language of weakness. Whether you decide ultimately to meet with CEO John Clark, to get a group together, or to submit the memo, first get rid of women's traditional language of weakness and acquire the language of power. This memo reviews the details that sap the strength of your memo and suggests how to rewrite your piece so it works. Wherever possible, your own words are used (in bold). Words I suggest are in italics.

Elements of Weakness

Weak writing results from a critical mass of puny elements. Defects of structure and logic, grammar, and vocabulary strip your memo of its power. Let's examine each of these elements and see how you can transform it from puny to powerful.

Strong memos and letters work because they follow the structural conventions of modern business writing. Your piece lacks a keystone structure—a thesis statement—that should appear either at the beginning or at the end, or in both places. Although none is stated, an implied thesis is "**The subtle discrimination against women** *at Vision has cost us six of our* **highest-ranking women.** *Our future growth and prosperity require that both company policy and company practice change to stop this costly loss of talent.*"

In addition to its failure to state a thesis, your memo suffers from a weak lead that's unlikely to engage its reader. A strong opening might review the statistics on retention of male versus female executives at Vision or a dramatic prediction of the cost to Vision if it loses its best women.

Still another missing element is a clear call to action at the end; you never tell John precisely what he should do. You probably want more than just **stronger, clearer signals that men are not the only people who matter.**

Furthermore, the memo's flavor of meditation or stream of consciousness makes it seem illogical and renders it impotent as a business document. The reader senses that you are adding information as you recall it rather than organizing and grouping the ideas for greatest impact. The argument will gain energy if you group ideas and assign them to a hierarchy of importance. For example, the **"men only" bar** at the resort is offensive and possibly illegal. In contrast, some of the **small things** seem trivial and whiny. For example, the seventh paragraph sounds like one written by a whiny child who adds every possible naughty act she can imagine to her litany of complaints: an executive whose energy is drained because a man said he was going home early to **"play mom tonight"** is thin-skinned indeed!

The memo suffers not only from structural defects but from weak grammatical forms as well. It hedges. Hedges hide behind language without making assertions. They add length but not information; they are a hallmark of weak language. Here are a few of the hedges in your memo: **I can't help but . . . I believe . . . Needless to say . . . There are many things that make women feel . . . I can assure you . . . I can only speculate.** Although hedges play a role in ordinary spoken discourse and occasionally in writing, masses of them make you look tentative and insecure.

Another grammatical issue that dogs your writing is the tendency to start sentences and phrases with the word *I* (15 *I* sentences and phrases), even though you're not the subject of the memo. *I* sentences draw attention away from the actual subject to the writer instead. For example, your opening tarries so long on you that the issue of the two resignations has to wait six lines. Readers generally attend to sentences that begin with actual subjects or issues. Start your memo with the words *"Your memo announcing the resignations of . . ."* and add a verb that tells what the memo did (*disturbed, concerned, demonstrated, brings to light, points up*).

Other dangers of *I* sentences are that they make the writer seem adolescent, and lead to weak verbs rather than to strong action verbs (**have been, have had, was taken, can't help but, believe, feel, can assure you, can be of help**). The ability to discuss subjects and issues without reference to oneself signals maturity and suggests that what you say matters.

Substantial writers choose substantial words as well. Mark Twain said, "The right word is to the almost right word as lightning is to the lightning bug." Your word choices tend to be lightning bugs rather than lightning words. They are vague and emotional: **general, long and hard, never seem to be, couldn't seem to get, many, feel, often less likely, a small thing, quite powerful, was taken aback, devaluing experiences.** Like rivulets of water that erode a rock, your weak word choices erode the message . . . and its credibility.

How to Recast the Memo

Here's a systematic way to plan and write your memo, based upon the Organization System.

1. *Think about your reader.* You've worked with John for a long time. You tell him **of his own efforts to recognize and reward women's contributions.** The reader believes this, but wonders why you address the memo to him as **Mr.** while referring to yourself with first and last name only. Think about John and your relationship to him. Is he a leader whom people will follow? Is his behavior toward women a model for others? Is it his style to put ideas on paper or to talk them over? Is he easily intimated? Is he delegating so much that he loses control of personnel issues? The better you understand John, the more precisely you can target your memo to convince him.

Your understanding of John helps you decide whether the memo will work. Because they're written documents, memos and letters stay around for a while. This longevity enables you to document the issues fully and at leisure in a way you can't do orally at a meeting. Decide whether this memo is the best approach to reach John Clark.

2. *Determine the purpose(s)*. Written documents aim to *do* something. What precisely do you want to accomplish in this memo? It can *persuade, document, detail, review, suggest action,* or *request a meeting.* Your memo fails because it has no clear purpose, no anticipated outcome.

Now you're ready to create a preliminary thesis statement. At this early stage, you need only a working thesis; you'll refine it as the details and structure emerge. A possible thesis: *The* **subtle** *discrimination against women at Vision has brought about the loss of* **its highest ranking women** *and threatens to impoverish its future. To stop the talent drain, we should reevaluate all the elements of our corporate culture to align them with our* **policies to hire and promote women.**

3. *Brainstorm all the relevant details.* Jot each down, in a few words or a phrase, on a small sticky note. Lay the sticky notes out on a table so you can see them all. If you have a hypercard program in your computer, you can do this step on-screen. Your sticky notes might look like this:

resignation *of xx strong managers in two years*

reasons similar

pattern of committed women departing

overall atmosphere that erodes women's sense of worth

climate of female failure

subtle messages that women are less important, less talented, etc.

women talked over and interrupted at meetings *rude behavior*

side conversations

"men only" bar at retreat *illegal?*

informal discussions exclude women

Mr. Karen Snyder

have to play mom

tired of struggling against a climate of female failure

little things that happen daily

men hang around bar while women quietly disappear

Now evaluate the details. Are they all equally important? Should some be eliminated? Do you need more facts and figures to bolster your thesis? Add details as needed and remove the trivial or irrelevant ones.

4. *Group the details.* When you see the details all at once, you may find that they group themselves in ways you hadn't considered. For example, all the information about the women who left might be more persuasive if kept together. Or it may work to group the offenses company policy can prevent.

5. *Order the details within each group.*

6. *Affix the groups of sticky notes onto large index cards or sheets of paper.* Give tentative titles to each group. Such titles as *Possible Legal Issues, Formal and Informal Meetings, Exclusion from Critical Events* might be appropriate.

7. *Order the index cards in a way that best supports the thesis.* Consider the primacy and recency effects: the first and last items are most likely to be remembered.

8. *Cast the thesis in its final form.*

9. *Decide how to lead and end the memo.* The lead sets the tone and engages the reader. The end sums up and calls to action. Write the call to action with special care. John must understand exactly what he should do. Instead of plopping the problem on his desk, suggest specific solutions and actions. These could include:

- Review departures to see if they could have been prevented.
- Discuss issues with men who demean, letting them know that their behavior is unbusinesslike, unacceptable, and possibly illegal.
- Model behavior other men can emulate.
- Avoid restricted conference locations.
- Make sure that concerned women attend relevant meetings.
- Deal with casual remarks as they occur.

10. *Set up the paragraphs and write the topic sentences and transitions.* Build logic into the memo. Each paragraph must flow from the one

before it, and all must support the thesis and lead inexorably to your call to action at the end.

11. *Write the memo in the language of success.* Avoid weak words, hedges, and vague modifiers. Avoid the "touchy-feely" language of emotions. Do not inject opinion. Use "I" only when you're the legitimate subject. Write objectively about issues, facts, events, and policies. Use the active voice primarily, but accuse in the passive voice to avoid looking hostile (as you did when you wrote, **Women are rarely invited**). And use the rhetorical techniques of parallelism, enumeration, questions, and so on.

12. *Edit by reading aloud.* Ask trusted associates to read the memo for tone as well as for content.

13. *Proofread.* Elizabeth, history and tradition have taught women the language of weakness, as revealed in your memo. As we take our places as leaders, we must shed that language and acquire the language of power. Your memo offers a fine beginning

Now decide what to do with your piece. Even if it remains in your desk, you'll have thought through a difficult issue and prepared yourself to confront it in the future.

Writing in the Twenty-first Century: How the Language of Success Empowers You

The computer lets you write poorly for the same reasons it lets you write well. On the one hand, your word processor frees you to revise easily, format effectively, and benefit from the wonders of spell and grammar checkers. On the other hand, it lulls you into the sense that the computer writes. Computers don't write. Women write. If the woman writes well, the computer delivers the message; if the woman writes garbage, the computer only pretties it up. Whatever you do, don't write like a man. Girls start life with stronger writing skills than boys. If you haven't fallen too deeply into the Alice-in-Wonderland of corporate writing, you're probably still in touch with that childhood advantage. Make the most of it: write clearly, write often, write in the language of success. Written work stays around; it's seen by people at all levels in and outside the office. Clear writing allows your ideas to shine, complete and uninterrupted, and keeps the credit where it is due. It is a skill that translates into success in any field. Research shows that, other skills being equal, clear writing enhances even technical careers. The skills covered so far in this book promise to transform you into a powerful writer. Think of weak language as a gag that imprisons good ideas in your brain—clear writing removes the gag and frees those ideas.

Beyond the issues of weakness and power that we've already covered, and the general writing issues everyone faces, women's writing tends to be too breezy, in a friendly rather than a business style. Just as you dress up for your children's weddings because the photos will stay around, dress up your formal writing because it, too, stays around. As a general principle, the more formal the medium, the more distant the writing should be (academic and research pieces, letters, proposals, reports); the less formal the medium, the less formal the writing can be (memos, E-mail).

Still, choose your writing battles. Women often report that they'll edit a minor piece six times. The language of success requires efficiency: invest time in pieces that go out and travel up and down the chain of command, such as letters, proposals, and reports. Stint on memos and computer communications, but remember that they, too, stay around and can return to haunt you. E-mails are legal documents and they remain forever. Avoid writing that could embarrass or get you into trouble.

TECHNOLOGY CHANGES, PRINCIPLES REMAIN THE SAME

From Charlotte's spinnerets to printing presses to electronic networks, technology transforms writing. We tailor our writing styles to the media. For example, I've never received e-mail with the salutation "Dear Dr. Mindell"; while even strangers often greet me with "Hi" (a salutation that never appeared on a business letter). The networks have and will transform both our language and our literature. We see new metaphors: *surf, tunnel, flame, digital suburbia, hackers;* acronyms; new words coined and new uses for old words. When I wrote the first edition of this book, Amazon was just a river and Ebay didn't exist. Some innovations come and go: does anyone still use those strange acronyms such as AFAIK (as far as I know), IMHO (in my humble opinion), BBS (bulletin board service), IC (I see), TNX (thanks); or emoticons like (:-(for frowning)? Apparently, they do, but only a few obvious ones (when you read Kira Marchenese's notes that follow, it'll be clear that use of emoticons and other shortcuts is age-related).

The applications change, but the writing principles of the language of success—clarity, brevity, power, logic, and civility— empower you as long as people read and write.

E-mail Peeves and Tips

Pet peeves on e-mails arrive daily on my screen. They're unreadable; they're too long; they're annoying; they scream; they should never have come to me. The world's impression of you arrives on the screen every time you transmit an e-mail. When you rush a sloppy e-mail to save a couple of minutes, you could waste hundreds or even thousands of minutes while readers struggle to decode the message. The skills and principles we've covered so far lend themselves nicely to e-mail writing.

Kira Marchenese, whom you met as a young assistant, is Senior Program Manager at AOL, where she stands at the forefront of e-writing. Here are her comments on successful e-mail:

> So much office communication is done electronically that it needs the full range of moods and levels of formality that we have in spoken interactions. Electronic information is exchanged that is the equivalent of stopping someone in the hallway or calling over the cubicle wall, and the strict standards of Standard Written English are out of place in that level of electronic chatter, just as formal presentation techniques would be out of place.

However, always remember that e-mail is stored forever. Thoughtless remarks or poorly chosen words can easily be misinterpreted and will come back to haunt you.

For anything formal, definitely use caps and punctuation. No caps conveys a certain comfort level and casualness . . . it's fine if it's appropriate to the situation. No caps equals calling out over the cube wall. If you have to schedule a meeting through someone's assistant, use caps.

Instant messages and short e-mails are easy to read with no caps, but don't write large blocks of text in all-lower. Even in informal typing, keep punctuation.

As far as emoticons go, they're not used in formal documents . . . memos, proposals, and so on, even if those things are sent in e-mail. But in the less formal correspondence, they're perfectly acceptable. They are best used where the words alone come across as stiff, stern, or mean. Don't overuse and don't use fancy ones (strings of seven symbols that no one can interpret). The three basics that everyone knows are:

:) (smile), :((frown), and ;-) (wink). I'll also occasionally use :-\ (what can you do?) because most people can figure it out. For acronyms . . . BTW, FYI, all okay, but not in anything formal.

One last note . . . in e-mail messages to a group of people, clearly call out anything that needs to be brought to one person's specific attention. For example, I'll send out a summary of meeting notes and will call out action items or questions using bold, color, line breaks, or bullets. That way, people's names jump right out at them and don't get lost in the fuzziness of group mail. AOL is wonderfully flexible because you can use color. In an e-mail conversation where we're replying to each other in the body of the note, we each type in a different color so no one is confused over who said what.

E-mail tips:

Select Recipients—don't circulate every e-mail to everyone on every circulation list.

Apply the rudiments of the Organization System—a few sticky notes save time and money.

Open with the thesis—even for informal notes.

Predict the thesis in the subject line (don't just copy the original).

Give precise, concise, legal information.

Maintain a professional tone (polite, pleasant, professional).

Use correct grammar and punctuation unless it's a line or two for a close associate.

Omit unnecessary words.

Follow the principles of the language of success.

Avoid sloppy and touchy-feely words.

Respect privacy.

Set and follow conventions for your group to follow (for example, encourage everyone to predict the thesis in the subject line and open with the thesis) and agree on which acronyms and emoticons you'll use.

Mark the priority level.

Edit aloud once, unless it's very casual.

WOMEN AND THE WEB

You write more than ever, you write to more people in more places all over the world. The Web offers women a singular opportunity for gender-free writing. The reader can't tell if you're tall or short, married or single, young or old, pregnant or not. Without paper, letterheads, or job titles, the Net permits your writing to shine and saves you from traditional gender biases. Thus, the electronic media offer women a historic opportunity to overcome traditional barriers of age, of gender, of race, of appearance. Charlotte's web continues to weave its magic—through the written word.

Action Plan

Synthesize the lessons of the language of success in a piece of writing, preferably a difficult one (a letter of complaint, an employee evaluation, a discussion of a serious problem at work, or a language issue you face). Follow the organization system. Shun (or delete) the grammar of weakness. Use the grammar and words of power. Send it to me for critique and suggestions: pmindell@well-read.com.

In the next chapter you'll learn how effective reading drives success.

Quick Tips

Write to take your seat at the policy table.

Follow the conventions.

Include a clear thesis statement.

Call for action—if you want it.

Write the grammar of power.

Talk about the subject, not about yourself.

Follow the principles: What is it not about? What is it about? What does it do?

Organize.

Edit and rewrite.

Proofread.

Write the language of success on-line.

Adjust formality and conventions for e-mail.

Surf the Net.

10

Why Can't a Woman Read More Like a Man? Empowerment Through Reading

All books are either dreams or swords. You can cut or you can drug with words.

AMY LOWELL

After spending nearly two hundred pages urging you not to communicate like a man, am I about to tell you to read like a man? Well, only if you don't already.

My doctor knew that I was writing a book about reading so, as part of his professional patter, he said, "My wife says I don't read enough novels." I thought, I don't read many novels either . . . because I read so much work-related stuff. Does that mean I read like a man? That question led to discussions with business and professional men and women and to the observation that successful women read like men (and, of course, like other successful women).

Not that men read better than women do: they read differently. They read instrumentally. We'll define *instrumental reading* as reading that serves as a means, a tool, or an implement toward an accomplishment. Contrast instrumental reading to reading for pleasure or escape. When you curl up in your easy chair with your favorite murder mystery or romance, you're reading for pleasure or escape. When, however, you're plowing through *The New England Journal of Medicine* or *The Law Review*, you're probably reading instrumentally. Of course, this isn't always true: my novelist friends read murder mysteries to analyze their structures, and my business-school administrator friend reads medical journals for fun. By the time you finish this chapter, you'll have fun reading instrumentally.

This chapter lays the groundwork for instrumental reading skills and attitudes that equip you for reading and managing on paper, on-line, on e-books (or whatever the medium turns out to be), efficiently and effectively. You'll see how the idea of structure that helps compose talks and written communications also helps craft efficient reading strategies. After exposure to *power reading*, you'll learn how to attack texts like a fencer instead of a good girl and how to adapt the speed and deep reading skills to tomorrow's media.

Reading and Success: What (and How) You Read Does Make a Difference

We can adapt this chapter's epigraph, *All books are either dreams or swords. You can cut or you can drug with words*, to say that women read to dream, but we must also read to cut. In March 1993, the writer Naomi Wolf spoke at Geneseo College. One of the young women in the audience noted that "the romances we read reinforce the notion that success lies in winning the right man and having him take care of you." That young woman had learned a style of reading that reinforces weakness, timidity, and dependence, a style that once helped literate women escape the boredom of their lives but hinders us today at work. Puny reading is a problem both of substance and of style. It involves not only what you read but how you read.

WHAT DO YOU READ?

If your answer is "journals," "research," "business and professional books," in addition to novels, poetry, and magazines, then you're reading instrumentally already, and seeking speed and efficiency to help empty your in-basket. If your answer is romance novels, *People* magazine, spy stories, murder mysteries, that's all right. Reading will always relax and entertain us. But, if your answer ends there, learn power reading.

Reading: Path to power

A glimpse at the history of reading and writing reveals different traditions for men and women. Writing and reading began as business tools. The earliest writings probably kept inventories and genealogies. So, from the start, literacy helped merchants and businessmen do their jobs more efficiently and rely less on memory. Those business readers were men; most women remained illiterate. In the middle ages, a nobleman warned, "It is not appropriate for girls to learn to read. . . ." When advancing technology brought books to the marketplace, in the nineteenth century, the men in power remained suspicious of reading for women, fearing that newspapers would harm and even addict women. One expert even cautioned against travel books because there's no merit in accumulating a "superficial selection of facts." Another urged that "healthy substances be substituted for the ingestion of unsuitable print." When upper-class women finally acquired literacy, they were primarily housebound; for them reading offered an escape, not a tool of success. Think of your favorite fictional literate women: *Madame Bovary, Mrs. Dalloway*, Jo from *Little Women* . . . they all read to escape. And the novels written for women, in Martha Nusbaum's words, ". . . have narrowed our sense of the possible" by implying that women must choose between autonomy and love.

Tolstoy's Anna Karenina is one great fictional heroine who understood both the romantic and the instrumental value of reading. Here's what Tolstoy said about Anna's reading in both the romantic and the instrumental modes:

Anna Arkadyevna read and understood; but it was distasteful to her to read, that is, to follow the reflection of other people's lives. She had too great a desire to live herself. If she read that the heroine of the novel was nursing a sick man, she longed to move with noiseless steps about the room of a sick man; if she read of a member of Parliament making a speech, she longed to be delivering the speech; if she read of how Lady Mary had ridden after the hounds, and had provoked her sister-in-law, and had surprised everyone by her boldness, she too wished to be doing the same. But there was no chance of doing anything; and twisting the smooth paper-knife in her little hands, she forced herself to read.

. . . she did a great deal of reading. . . . Moreover, every subject that was of interest to Vronsky, she studied in books and special journals, so that he often went straight to her with questions relating to agriculture or architecture, sometimes even with questions relating to horse-breeding or sport. He was amazed at her knowledge, her memory, and at first was disposed to doubt it, to ask for confirmation of her facts. . . .

Anna Karenina, then, read both like a woman and like a man. Virginia Phelan suggests that, had Anna lived in a world in which she had the opportunity to work and use her talents productively, she might not have ended up under the wheels of a train. If she lived today, Anna would spend time surfing the Web to expand her knowledge: she wouldn't need to live vicariously but could build her own rich life. Whatever your attitude about autonomy and love, you demand success at work—and instrumental reading fosters that success.

How Do You Read?

An incident at an executive reading workshop illustrates the differences between men's and women's reading styles and hints at an explanation of those differences. Three women and two men were practicing an advanced reading skill in which they had to find a critical item in an article. The information they sought was divided between the beginning and the end of the piece. When instructed to find the required sentences, the two men read quickly and marked their responses. All three women seemed to read as fast, but they reread the segments a few times before they underlined portions. When they described their notations, the two men and two of the women had found one but not both of the crucial pieces of information.

The third woman hesitated to tell what she'd underlined at all; finally, she indicated one of the required segments as well. After it was revealed that the two segments should have been underlined, the hesitant woman said, "I underlined both, but I was afraid to say so and be the only one." She was the first to master the skill and the only one *afraid* to tell her response. She later said that she saw herself as a poor reader despite having had the highest score in her university reading class.

For this woman, the reading "deficit" was not about reading but about courage. Reading demands skill and courage. To find information, to filter effectively, to work efficiently, to grasp, to resist, to synthesize: for these, we arm ourselves with courage. We also learn the skills.

Reading: The Heart of Communication

Slave owners and tyrants have always known that reading offers a path to power; that's why it was a crime to teach slaves to read. When Malcolm X arrived in jail, he was illiterate. He learned to read there and wrote in his autobiography, ". . . as my word-base broadened, I could for the first time pick up a book and read and now begin to understand what the book was saying. Anyone who has read a great deal can imagine the new world that opened . . . I never had been so truly free in my life." In prison he came to see illiteracy as a second, inner jail that could confine him forever. If you can read but don't, you join the millions of aliterates who lock themselves in that same inner jail. And the computer won't unlock that jail but imprison you even more deeply. What do we do on the computer? We read and write. We shop, too, but if your time is restricted to shopping, the language of power has eluded you.

Empowerment grows from the written word, your reactions to it, and your use of it to make wise work decisions. Reading is not just a communication skill; it's *the fundamental* communication skill. The written word, whether in print or on the computer screen, brings ideas and information faster and more efficiently than any other medium. Efficient reading is the mother of language power.

Ambitious women must learn a lot and learn it fast. Dr. Sylvia Ruiz tells her own story of power reading: "I found out that a new division of my company was to be formed, and I had a shot at a top job. The division's work, however, was related to but different from what I do, so I had to learn a whole new field in less than three months. I had to plow through 50 books and over 300 professional articles, distill what would be relevant to the new division, understand the advanced technologies, and envision my place in the scheme. I refined the flagging and marginalia applications to a color-coded system. For example, I coded theoretical information differently from applied information. I mastered the subject and landed the job. There was no way I could have done it without power reading."

How to Read for Power

Power reading consists of the techniques I designed to help businesspeople get through their in-baskets efficiently by managing, filtering, and adjusting reading speed. In my reading workshops, however, educated women who were otherwise able readers had a hard time applying some of the subskills. For example, they hesitated to mark texts and add margin notes (were they taught not to dirty their books?). Worse, they shied away from the critical skills of disagreeing with the author, of questioning ideas in print, and of synthesizing reading with their everyday work lives. Yet these very skills foster success. Women's traditional ways of reading actually cheated them of success. To read powerfully, gain a repertoire of advanced reading skills and have the courage to apply them aggressively to the articles, books, letters, search engines, Web sites, even advertisements that fill your in-basket and computer screen.

As noted in earlier chapters, skills, power, and self-confidence enmesh so tightly that it's hard to tell where one ends and the others begin. In reading, they're virtually interchangeable. Power reading involves the confident and selective application of four essential skills: *scanning, skimming, pre-reading*, and *deep reading*. The power reader zips through her in-basket and screen, filtering ever more finely for the items worth careful reading. I've detailed the system in another book and will briefly review it here, dwelling on high-level skills and the future of reading.

The very rapid filters

First, learn to navigate the sea of information that floods your desk and computer screen. Do that with the aid of the computer and the very rapid reading filters: scanning and skimming.

Scanning. Scanning is the rapid search for a particular item. It's the only truly visual reading skill and doesn't engage much brain power; therefore you scan very fast, shrinking your in-basket sea to a pool in record time. Scanning proves your best weapon against information overload. Whenever someone says she "reads" *The Wall Street Journal* or *The New York Times* every day, you can bet she's scanning the headlines and filtering out all but the relevant articles.

Because scanning requires little brain power, the computer can do much of it for you. Learn how to use and manage the various search engines, information-seeking, and clipping programs. For example, a program is available that will scan all your bookmarks to find those that have been updated since your last visit and to scan for and highlight critical key words. At a recent *Power Reading* seminar, stock analysts learned how to analyze the structures of financial reports, determine the key words that preceded data they sought, and tailor their search engines to cut through the verbiage and find precisely what they require. The computer brings an avalanche of information: efficient scanning saves time and serves you well.

Skimming. The second rapid-reading filter is skimming, which you will find more rewarding when you do it efficiently. Skimming exploits the structures and conventions of written language. Reading builds on those structures and conventions to speed through any written form. To skim, scroll through or look over the article or book hastily without going into depth. Look for and evaluate the structures that contain vital information: author and title, date of publication, publisher, contents, index, reference list, appendices. Next, flip the pages or scroll from front to back to pick up visual information and judge whether to invest more time. You can skim most books in two minutes or less, covering up to 100,000 words a minute.

Can you skim digitally? You can, if you scroll the item in question and familiarize yourself with the conventions and structures in the publication. Skimming works best if you can check the end material to judge reference lists and other structures, such as appendices, glossaries, and indices. Because so many Web sites exist and they follow such varied organizational patterns, skimming on the computer remains problematic. Still, I predict that Web sites will gradually grow more structured and will develop more universal conventions, making it easier to skim in the future than it is today.

Next time you search the Web, think about how you search and read on the screen and how to gain efficiency.

Kathleen Barry Albertini, an efficient Web investigator, tracked her application of the power reading filters during a Web search. She varied scanning and skimming to suit the different structures on the Web. She notes, "I use the power reading techniques automatically when I scan long journal articles. While the searching software may highlight the words I requested, I also grab structures such as leads, subtitles, headings during the skimming phase."

Of course, there's a hitch with the very rapid filters. Woody Allen quipped, "I learned to read very fast by running my finger down the middle of the page and I was able to read *War and Peace* in twenty minutes. It's about Russia." The scanning and skimming filters show what's in a book or Web site but yield virtually no comprehension. The power reader demands understanding, which you gain in the next phase: prereading.

Prereading: Three ideas and four steps

Prereading filters the material that has survived scanning and skimming. It's the reciprocal of the organization system: the reader digs for the structures the writer built into the piece. When prereading, exploit your knowledge of writing conventions to quickly find the central structures, the thesis statement, and the topic sentences. When you've finished prereading the piece, you've covered it quickly by carefully reading only selected portions. Your skill yields extraordinary understanding because the thesis offers the key to comprehension. Knowing the thesis and the topics enables you to decide whether to read every word deeply and carefully.

Prereading builds on three fundamental ideas and consists of four steps. Simple but not simplistic, the prereading technique speeds you through just about every article, book, study, newspaper, and magazine that crosses your desk, computer screen, e-book, or reading device of the future. But you must adjust it to the material and the medium.

1. *Read with your mind.* Prereading is an active process that engages your mind. Reading happens in the brain, not in the hand, not in the eyes, not on the screen. The eyes serve only to carry information to the mind. The hand turns the pages or clicks the mouse. The screen is just another reading medium, one you adjust to as you adjusted from hardcover to paperback books. If you have any doubt about that, watch a blind person read Braille. That's why traditional "speed reading" always fails: it assumes that eye training will improve reading.

2. *Read precisely and rigorously.* Precision reading is a central tenet of power reading. In prereading, for example, you never try to paraphrase (as you were taught to do in school). Rather, you seek to find what the author says, *in the author's own words.* So, for example, if you wanted to cite the thesis statement, you would copy, flag, or underline rather than paraphrase it. Paraphrasing costs too much time, wastes intellectual energy, and fails to attain the efficiency required for success and leadership.

3. *Tailor prereading to your requirements.* Once you understand the principles and steps of prereading, tailor the technique to the structures and mediums in your in-basket. For example, if you manage an engineering team, you may choose to preread all the pieces relevant to the specialties on the team and pass each article on to the person who should deep read it. That keeps you abreast of new developments without bogging you down in details.

The four steps of prereading add efficiency and power to your tool kit.

1. *Look at the structure.* For short pieces, step 1 is merely a quick glance to see how long the piece is and whether the title or subtitle states the thesis. For long articles and whole books, skimming yields a good idea of the structure, order, relevance, and timeliness of the piece. When you visit a new Web site, check the site map or home page to see the structures.

2. *Find the thesis statement.* By convention, writers place thesis statements where they're easy to find: in the title or subtitle or near the beginning or end. In books, the thesis is often found in the preface or introduction. If you know the structures of items in your in-basket, they lead you to the places where you're likely to find the thesis quickly. Articles on the Web usually show the thesis in the title or subtitle. Underline, flag, or otherwise mark the thesis if you can: it's the heart of understanding, and you don't want to search for it again later.

3. *Find the topics.* Seek the topics only, not the details. The writing convention that guides you here is that of the paragraph. Usually, the first sentence tells its topic, and later sentences flesh out the details. Simply find and mark (if you can) the topics of the paragraphs. In books, the first and/or last paragraphs of the chapters often tell their topics. Ignore the details for now.

4. *Decide whether to deep read.* At this point, you know a good deal about the piece: you know its structure, its thesis, and its topics. You also know whether it's well-written and well-organized and whether it contains information vital to your work. Is it essential to read every word? Here's where women seem uneasy about letting go. They often report that they feel compelled to read every word of every piece, and they do so even after deciding it's not essential, not well-written, or not new material. Accepting the risk of not reading every word demands courage and confidence in your judgment. Because deep reading represents a huge investment of your limited human capital, use the highest standard to filter for deep reading. If the book or long piece doesn't promise to change your life, decide *not* to deep read it. Prereading yields so much useful information that only about 10 percent of your in-basket will reach deep reading.

   If reading on the screen, print the pieces you choose to deep read. As of today, it's just too hard to deep read on the screen, with its jiggly letters and poor resolution. However, clear screens and text-marking devices will soon be readily available for deep reading on the screen. Laura Miller, an editor at *Salon* magazine notes, "When I find something I can use, I save it . . . and print it out later or keep it on my desktop when I'm writing the article I'm working on." I do the same: I preread the piece on the screen without marking it, then print and file it for later deep reading. Will technological innovation change these practices as it gets easier to mark and store information for easy access? It might, but power readers will be ready—because reading will always take place in the brain.

Practice prereading a few times before you move up to deep reading. Try any magazine, editorial, or research piece. If the periodicals you read are available both electronically and in print, find two pieces of similar length and try prereading one on the screen and the other in hard copy. Compare the amount of time each takes and the outcome. See the model file card. Try filling in a card for each piece, setting it aside, and returning in six months to see whether you retained more from on-line or from paper reading. If prereading helps, use the same format to record book notes on your word processor.

Well-Read (wel´-red´) **www.well-read.com**	**Preread for Precise Understanding** 1. Look at the structure. 2. Find, mark the thesis statement (read beginning <u>and</u> ending). 3. Note the topics. 4. Decide. "What of it?" "Does it warrant deep reading?"

Author_____

Title_____

Publication:_____   Date:_____   Pg:_____

Thesis_____

_____

_____

_____

Topics:_____

_____

_____

Comments:_____

_____

© 2000 Well-Read (wel´-red´)

After you've tried a few short pieces, preread this or any other non-fiction book. In just a few minutes, you'll have superb understanding and the freedom to mine the rich interior details, or to move on.

Deep reading as an instrument of success

Once you've decided to invest in deep reading, whether on- or off-screen, attend carefully to every word, every nuance, every idea. Keep a dictionary handy: not a single word should escape you. Have a pencil and a pad of small sticky notes or flags, or the marking function of your program, and mark anything you want to comment on, retain, or use at work. Mark the items you've always marked: important details, data to recall, notes on the logical flow, and so on. You probably have a shorthand of your own. But go beyond analysis to the higher levels of synthesis and critical reading, which we'll discuss in detail.

Synthesis—the ultimate success strategy

Synthesis is more than a reading skill: it's the management ability that drives success. The dictionary definition of synthesis is "the combination of separate elements . . . to form a coherent whole." The word joins the elements *syn*, meaning "together" and *tithenai*, meaning "to place," so synthesis literally means "putting things together." The difference between power readers and merely competent ones is that power readers create or envision relationships between what they read and what they do at work. Learn synthesis reading because it's thought provoking, practical, and efficient: it makes you not only a more effective reader, but a more creative thinker and worker as well.

How to Synthesize. You've preread the book or article and decided to deep read every word. You know the thesis and the topics covered and you aim to go beyond, to make it work for you in business. In addition to reading precisely, you're mentally asking, how can I use this information? Synthesis takes you beyond the text. As the poet Helen Vendler writes, "Through the text the reader becomes a writer, producing new meaning." Synthesis transports you through and beyond the text into your own work life, enabling you to produce new meaning.

Action Plan

Here are two paragraphs from a piece about listening excerpted elsewhere in this book. If you're reading for synthesis, you're asking questions like these: Are you like the women described in these paragraphs? Do you suffer from being too nice? Do you play by a different set of rules from those of the men in your group? Could the solutions suggested work for you? None of these questions is about the text. Add marginal notes or *marginalia* as you read and respond to these paragraphs. Then form the habit of adding marginalia that go beyond the words of other pieces you read deeply.

> Niceness is a powerful trap. One of the most frustrating realities women face at the conference table is the fact that they won't get attention by smiling and waiting their turn. Tannen says that men aren't interested in the concept; they simply don't value the idea of taking turns. "Many women do want to listen, but they expect it to be reciprocal," she explains. "I listen to you now; you listen to me later. They become frustrated when they do the listening now and now and now, and later never comes."

> When I participate in a seminar or meeting, I have my own personal rule: Be one of the first to speak. Get an idea out on the table quickly and you become a presence up front. The alternative, I discovered long ago, is to feel like the new kid on the block, awkward and unsure of exactly where to cut in as the discussion moves on. Plagued with the hesitancy of niceness, for which there is no reward, I would sometimes be left out of the discussion totally because someone else had presented my ideas before I'd opened my mouth. Now I speak up early to make a point that will weave itself into the fabric of the discussion. Only then can I relax and take part unself-consciously.

READ LIKE A FENCER: NO MORE MS. NICE GIRL

Don't be a passive reader. To encourage aggressive reading, deep read provocative pieces that you're sure to take issue with. Men seem comfortable disagreeing and debating with texts, but many women are uneasy doing so. When they come to an idea they abhor, they write marginal notes such as, "I don't really agree" or "I don't like the idea." They use the grammar of weakness to reflect their fear of asserting themselves. If they strongly agree, they write, "I like this." They've absorbed the lesson that good girls don't attack or resist. The dark side of this is that "good girls" lack creativity and conviction.

Aggressive reading also tests your language of power. It gives you the chance to hone your resistive and argumentative language in a safe and private environment. No one can fire you because of marginalia: aggressive reading is your razor-sharp foil of empowerment. Those critical skills will then transfer into your spoken and written language.

=== *Action Plan*

Reread the two extract paragraphs. This time, instead of synthesizing, or sympathizing, fence with the author. Defy her. Use marginalia to parry and thrust, even if you agree. Force yourself to play devil's advocate. Cast your arguments in the grammar of power. If you disagree, tell precisely why. If the author gives spurious arguments, note the error. *En garde!*

INFILTRATE THE ENEMY CAMP: READ WHAT YOU ABHOR

Women often say they deep read a piece because they "like" it. Consider the opposite option. Deep read books that are wrong, writers with whom you disagree, consultants whose policies threaten your company. When you read to cut and not just to dream, you'll find it more useful to probe opposing arguments than those with which you agree. Next time you scan the daily paper, seek out the columnists who are wrong on every point. Argue with them. It's a sure way to hone your critical—and power-reading skills.

Rebel! Read Aloud

When was the last time you read aloud? If you have young children, perhaps you did so last night. If not, you probably haven't read orally for many years. That's a shame, because oral reading is another thread in your web of language. Oral reading empowers you in several ways: it aids memory, it exposes you to good writing, and it enhances your presentations if it's well done. In the chapter on presentations, I urged you to write a script to ensure the quality and timing of your talk. Now consider reading all or parts of that script when you give the talk. Conventional wisdom says, "Never read your talk." And the way most people read, conventional wisdom is absolutely right! Yet public speaking worries melt away if you learn to read well orally.

It turns out that oral reading poses no special problems for women. Don't you read to your children or in church? Oral reading is one home-honed skill that serves you well at work. Take advantage of it. Extend the text-marking skills covered in this chapter, pick up the formatting and performance tips given here, exploit your hours of practice in reading to kids, watch yourself on video, and *voila!*: you're a professional oral reader.

How to Prepare a Text for Oral Reading

1. Count words in the text as a whole and in each paragraph or segment.
2. Choose a large enough, easily readable type face.
3. Set narrow top and side margins; set the bottom margin at 5.5". Prepare a header with the name of the talk, page number, and date in the upper right corner.
4. Read the text aloud, marking pauses and points to emphasize. Craft a shorthand you recognize and use it consistently. Here are a few suggestions:

/ /	Pause
bold 〰〰	Emphasize
☺	Remember to smile
{xx xxx xx}	Read these words together as a phrase
/ /	Leave room for a sticky note that refers to a particular person or audience
① ② ③	Reminder to enumerate or deliver in parallel
(stop and drink water)	Any gesture you want to remember

5. After you've practiced and placed the markings where you want them, print the talk on card stock. Card stock doesn't make noise, it's easier to handle, and it lasts longer than paper. Determine the location of the page breaks; for example, just before a new idea begins as a reminder to pause. Print the word count on each page. Finally, drill a hole in the upper left corner and hold the pages together with a loose-leaf ring.

TIPS ON READING A TALK

Pace yourself

Cover about 100 to 120 words a minute, including time for pauses and asides. Practice till you've nearly memorized the text. Actually memorize the first and last 15 seconds. When you do, you'll feel confident enough to maintain eye contact.

Success in oral reading rests on eye contact. Never look down while you speak. Each time you glance at the page, take in a full phrase or sentence. Then look up while you speak it. Remember the inviolable rule: speak only to people, not to slides, scripts, walls, or anything else.

What if you lose your place?

Try holding the place with your finger or a blank card held just below the line you're reading. If you still get lost, don't get flustered, simply pause for an instant while you find the lost place. If you follow an outline or list, check off each item as you cover it. Or try using a larger type face (16 or 18 points) or skipping lines.

Videotape yourself

If you decide to read most of your text, request a podium—it hides the loose sheets, the page turning, and the efforts to hold your place. If you show slides or transparencies in a darkened room, make sure your script is well lit.

If you follow all these tips and practice several times and still can't get the knack of it, you may want to avoid reading aloud. However, I've never worked with a woman who couldn't master oral reading. Indeed, it's a piece of cake for most of us.

As your career advances, you'll speak in ever more formal settings, ultimately reading speeches on TelePrompTers. Oral reading skills you hone now will take their place among your "spinnerets" as you grow increasingly adept at weaving your web of language.

Action Plan

Videotape yourself as you practice oral reading.

Consider forming a community of readers with your peers. Your reading group will aim to discuss relevant books and articles. You may also practice oral reading skills on portions of the books and articles.

Quick Tips

Gain power through reading.

Read instrumentally.

Learn power reading.

Scan.

Skim.

Preread.

Deep read.

Read precisely.

Synthesize.

Read like a fencer.

Infiltrate the enemy camp.

Brandish the pencil as a tool of power.

Apply power reading on-line.

Rebel! Read aloud.

11

"But I Thought You Said ...": Precise Listening Prevents Problems

Her most notable quality, colleagues say, is her ability to listen and process what she hears. "And you have to love to learn and really listen to what the client says."

GLENN RIFKIN

You're not listening! It's well documented that men don't listen to women. In contrast, studies show time and again how well women listen, how sympathetic, how empathic we are. We even "listen" better to non-verbal cues: Judy Hall reports that "women become more adept at judging nonverbal expressions and recognizing faces." Why, then, should a book like this devote a chapter to listening? Well, lots of other studies show that most adults are poor listeners. In *Charlotte's Web*, for example, Dr. Dorian, the psychiatrist, notes, "It is quite possible that an animal has spoken civilly to me and that I didn't catch the remark because I wasn't paying attention. Children pay better attention than grownups."

Listening: A Top Leadership Skill

When women discuss their communication aims, listening emerges as a recurring theme and as a high priority. Women sign up for my listening workshops because their bosses or staff tell them they're poor listeners. Highly educated managers and coaches ask me to design listening workshops for them because they perceive their inadequacies. In fact, studies show that people spend most of their listening time planning responses or thinking about subjects like sex or the grocery list. And, although listening ranks near the top of any list of leadership qualities at work, the single most frequent communications complaint at our workshops is that others don't listen.

Here are some quotations from a top-level coaching group: "As coaches, we need to become effective listeners"; "My primary objective is coaching, my primary tool of learning is listening"; "The people I coach tell me I'm a poor listener." These represent what women who work say about their own listening skills and those of their associates.

WHAT IS LISTENING?

Listen is an old, unambiguous word. Its definition is "to give attention with the ear, attend closely with the purpose of hearing"; "give ear." Contrast listening to hearing: we hear all kinds of sounds all day, yet we don't listen to them. Close your eyes for a moment. What do you hear? The air conditioner, the street noises, people talking in other spaces, a radio playing, the whir of the computer. . . . You *hear* all of these but you do not *listen* to them: you're able to filter them out. So listening is always mindful. We listen or don't because we choose to. Listening problems arise when we choose to hear when we should have chosen to listen.

Impediments to Listening

FILTERING

We've read about how men filter women out. But we all do it. We decide, consciously or not, to filter people because of gender, age, country of origin, race, gestures, appearance, even smell. These traits trigger something in us that says, "This person isn't worth listening to." We then either don't attend or are so distracted by the filter that we attend to the trait instead of the message. As victims of such exclusion and belittlement, we should be sensitive to our own filters, yet we rarely think about them.

Juanita Suarez comes from Brazil; her native language is Portuguese. She manages a customer-support group that works primarily on the phone. People filter her because of her accent; they assume that anyone with a heavy accent can't hold a responsible position. So they ask for her manager . . . and she must explain each time that she is the manager. If you filter people out or are distracted on the basis of accent, chances are you're doing what Juanita's callers do.

Action Plan

Here's a list of filters that distract people or make them decide not to listen. Check those items that prevent you from listening at work. Jot down the names of people you've filtered out because they had any of these traits. Jot down the names of people whose traits distract you from their messages. Target those people for listening practice.

Filters That Block Listening

- ❏ Gender
- ❏ Age
- ❏ Size
- ❏ Invasions of body space
- ❏ Foul language
- ❏ Lack of education
- ❏ Aggressiveness and hostility
- ❏ Timidity
- ❏ Bad grammar
- ❏ Poor enunciation

❏ Body odor

❏ Poor table manners

❏ Rudeness

❏ Laziness

❏ Inappropriate clothing

IMPRECISION

A second cause of failed listening is imprecision. Dr. Monica Gray cites an example of imprecise listening at work. She asked her administrative aide to set up a computer spread sheet on which she'd enter new research data. The secretary seemed to be listening but she not only set up the spread sheet (which took an hour) but added existing research data (which took ten hours). Monica's aide didn't filter her out; she just didn't listen precisely.

INATTENTION

Another culprit of failed listening is a vagabond mind. An executive requested that I prepare a listening program for her. She said, "I sit at meetings all day, and when I leave I can't for the life of me remember anything that happened." Her wandering mind filtered the meetings out and the distractions in. Minds wander for a variety of reasons. Check those that apply to you.

Why Minds Wander

❏ Anxiety

❏ Boredom

❏ Variations in speed (Your mind works faster or slower than the speaker's.)

❏ Other priorities

MISMATCHES

Mismatching also leads to failed listening. Research reveals that failed conversations can result from mismatched language and assumptions. If you're more or less educated, literate, specialized, or informed than the person with whom you're conversing, one or both of you is likely to use vocabulary, grammatical forms, or concepts that escape the other. The same is true if you come from different countries or regions, are of vastly different ages, or have different assumptions about the subject. One story of a mismatch comes from a young professional woman who met a man from another culture at a conference. Their lively conversation on professional issues resulted in an exchange of business cards. A day later the man called for a date. The woman was taken aback and said, "Didn't I mention that I'm married?" The man said he knew, but he'd like a date anyway. A mismatch of cultural assumptions led to a mutual failure to communicate.

We can mismatch on what we take for granted. One such mismatch occurred between Dr. Jacqueline Braverman and me. She leads some of our listening courses, to which we bring fresh bagels from the Bruegger's Bagel Bakery. Jackie and I live in the same suburban town, but the workshops met downtown. One morning she volunteered to pick up the bagels and, assuming that they came from the bakery in our suburban town, she went there to pick them up. Unfortunately, we'd ordered the bagels from the downtown shop. I assumed she knew that; she assumed she knew where to go for the bagels. This wasn't a serious mismatch; we donated the downtown bagels to people who'd enjoy them and laughed at our failed conversation. But it reminded two communication specialists how vulnerable we all are to mismatches.

Mismatch failures cut both ways: the speaker fails to match, the listener fails to grasp and responds inappropriately, the speaker fails to match, and so on. It takes two to fail at a conversation.

As you know if you live with teenagers, age differences lead to vocabulary mismatches. A client in her twenties asked Marlene Maggio how to tailor her long hair into a twist. Marlene suggested she use a *rat*. The shocked client needed a quick clarification of *rat*. Marlene explained that a rat is a cone-shaped insert, stiffened somewhat like *buckram*. The client asked what buckram is. And so on.

Think about your mismatches. If you're a manager or a supervisor, do you speak the same language as those whom you direct? If you read widely and they don't, it's likely that you suffer both content and grammar mismatches, or vice versa. For example, people who don't read much find it hard to understand complicated sentence forms because they appear primarily in print. That means that they'll have trouble understanding long, complex sentences such as, "Please note that the vat at the far end of the room, the one with the blue lid and four dots on the outside, which was filled with soup early this morning, is about to boil over."

Do you listen accurately to what you're told? Do you compensate for differences in background, education, and assumptions? Check the sources of mismatches when you listen at work:

- ❏ Vocabulary
- ❏ Grammar
- ❏ Conceptual differences
- ❏ Information known to one party and not the other
- ❏ Failure to understand power structure
- ❏ Different aims

INFLEXIBILITY

A final cause of failed listening is inflexibility, trying to deal with every listening situation in the same way. One manager noted, "Because I'm so empathetic, I plumb forget to communicate." Women are famous for being good, empathetic listeners. We report to researchers that we're more empathetic and less aggressive than men. Indeed, perhaps we've been so busy with "womanly" empathetic and sympathetic listening that we've overlooked the other business applications of listening. Perhaps empathy is not the prime listening tool for working women, however well it may work at home. Empathy should take its rightful place as only one among the listening skills for women who work.

Quiet: I'm Listening

Think about it. When you listen, you don't talk. That's the hallmark of listening. Yes, in some cultures, we show we're listening by interrupting, but before we start interrupting, we remain silent. Therefore, listening is fundamentally a silent activity. Although you'll soon learn specific things to say after listening, remember not to speak while you listen.

What do you do? How do you let the speaker know you're attending? How can your behavior send attentive, professional signals while helping you to grasp the message? And how can your behavior send signals that say, "I'm a professional," "I care," "I understand," or "You are a valuable person—what you say matters to me."

As a woman, you've been in situations where someone who should have listened showed that he or she was not, even without talking. What did the person do? Was it the style of sitting? The eyes? The head? The hands? The legs? A prop?

Action Plan

Check items on the following list that suggest poor listening. Double-check items that reflect your behaviors. Add other negative listening behaviors.

- ❏ Lays head on table and closes eyes
- ❏ Makes eye contact with speaker
- ❏ Seems to doze
- ❏ Holds pencil and appears to take notes
- ❏ Whispers or writes notes to table partner
- ❏ Gazes at the wall or ceiling
- ❏ Slams the pencil down and crosses arms

- ❏ Glares at the speaker
- ❏ Works on laptop
- ❏ Smiles and nods
- ❏ Sits up with head high and arms open
- ❏ Uses cellular phone
- ❏ Clicks pen up and down, taps on desk
- ❏ Walks out

Everyone agrees on the meanings of these silent behaviors. It turns out that positive messages don't just look good to the speaker, they also help you concentrate on the message. The person who works on her laptop while someone else speaks doesn't just look rude, she's preventing herself from listening. The person who closes the body and eyes doesn't just look bored, she's preventing herself from listening. In contrast, the person who takes careful notes, makes eye contact, responds with nods and smiles doesn't just seem to be listening; she actually listens!

So, follow the nonverbal aspects of powerful listening: ensure that you can see, open the body, hold the head up, make frequent eye contact, nod, smile, and be prepared to take notes. Now we'll move on to specific listening responses.

Seven Listening Techniques That Work

Just as instrumental reading uses reading as a means to succeed, so instrumental listening uses listening as a means to succeed. Just as the reader flexibly applies a variety of skills, the listener flexibly applies a variety of techniques. Success as a listener depends on your ability to match the strategies to the situation. The sections to follow describe listening strategies, followed by descriptions of real work situations with words you might say if you apply the techniques. Once you understand and practice each approach, you're free to mix 'n' match strategies to situations. The watchword here, as always, is control.

TECHNIQUE 1. "LISTEN" TO BODY LANGUAGE AND OTHER NONVERBAL CUES

Here's where we have an advantage: studies show time and again that women read body language signals more accurately than men do. Also, since body language conveys part of the message (except when you're on the phone), learn to observe carefully. Gestures and voice quality supplement and even supplant the words in a message. Watch for congruence: if the gestures and the words fit together naturally you can have confidence in the words. If, however, someone tells you how successful the project was while sweating and wringing her hands, try probing more deeply.

Because different cultures ascribe different meanings to the same gesture, be wary when reading the body language of people whose backgrounds vary from yours. For example, the American/European "V" for victory sign has a foul and vulgar meaning to Koreans. And the unspoken rules about personal space vary from country to country: if a man from another country seems to crowd you, he may just be following a different set of guidelines for personal space. Chapter 7 and your increasing awareness heighten your perception of physical cues.

TECHNIQUE 2. LISTEN PRECISELY

Precision listening grows from precision reading. After noting the serious shortcomings of paraphrasing versus the rich rewards of precision reading, I investigated whether these rewards might also accrue to the precision listener. They do. In precision listening, you avoid paraphrasing the message and seek instead to preserve and record the speaker's *exact words*. How? Just keep a pad or sticky notes on hand and record what you hear, as much as possible, as accurately as possible. You can't write as fast as you can hear, so you must leave some words out, but time and experience enable you to get enough of the exact words to retain a substantial and precise record of the event.

To demonstrate the advantages of precision listening, I run an informal experiment at my workshops. Participants present brief self-introductions.

Listeners are instructed to pay close attention to half of the speakers and to listen precisely with notes to the other half. They're asked to record as many exact words as possible. After putting the notes away for three days, they retell what they remember. The results astound. People retain both the content of the recorded messages and the flavor of each individual's language. When they listen carefully without precise notes, they remember only generalizations, no details (or inaccurate ones), and few direct quotations or exact words.

Precise listening makes a precise woman, fostering exactitude, rationality, and clarity. It generates other benefits as well.

Benefits of precision listening

1. *Prevents filtering.* Copying exact words helps cure you of filtering for appearance, race, gender, powerlessness, or the other blocks to listening. One manager describes her interview with an employee she disliked. "Forcing myself to record his words made me get his message. In this case, he was right and I would have rejected his argument outright had I not attended to his words. He was also a little more civil because he saw me taking notes."

2. *Ensures accuracy.* In the precision-listening experiments described earlier, those who took notes agreed on all the particulars of what they heard: how many years the person has worked at the company, the job title, the precise goals, and so on. If you take precise minutes, people won't question their accuracy. In our office, when potential clients call to inquire about our workshops, my staff and I record their words and our responses. These responses may include pricing information, dates of availability, and details about how to tailor a program. When we prepare the formal proposal, sometimes months or even years later, we lift the clients' words from the notes, thus saving us labor and impressing the client with our professionalism.

3. *Fosters civility.* When someone sees you writing her words, she's less likely to curse or insult another person. She also receives the message that you actually care what she says.

4. *Retains flavor of individual language.* Here are some comments recorded at a workshop. June described how she has to "capture new ideas quickly in reading"; Nancy must deal with "100 percent irate customers screaming and hating [her] company"; Stephanie complains that she's "caught in a circle of endless revision." If Stephanie calls for a follow-up, I can ask her if she's broken the "circle of endless revision."

5. *Increases vocabulary.* I added June's colorful metaphor of "capturing" meaning in reading to my vocabulary. Now June's metaphor enlivens my conversations, as do many other words spoken by colleagues and associates.

6. *Enhances retention.* We discussed the limits of memory earlier. If we can hold only seven words in short-term memory, imagine how little we retain in long-term memory. Precision-listening notes trigger recollection of words we'd forgotten in addition to the words we noted. For example, two colleagues attended a lecture together a year ago. One listened carefully; the other listened precisely and recorded exact words on her pad of sticky notes. Months later the topic came up again. The woman who took notes found hers and reconstructed the lecture; the associate looked on in awe and decided to do precise listening in the future.

7. *Provides permanent records.* Women are seen as flighty, forgetful, ditzy. Your precision-listening notes erase that impression. Lori Sturdevant is an executive secretary. Her busy boss doesn't always remember what he requested or when and accuses her of not completing work on time. On March 15, he asked why the report he'd requested wasn't ready. She checked her notes and indicated that he'd requested the report for March 16, and it would be ready on time. Events like this one changed his perception of her ability and efficiency.

8. *Focuses attention.* You're busy. You're pressured. Your mind wanders when you should listen. But note-taking calls home the wandering mind. Precision listening focuses attention where it belongs, on the message.

9. *Helps follow structure.* If the speaker organized her talk and states a thesis, a structure, or an enumerated sequence, your notes mirror that information and ease the task of following it. For example, if the speaker says, "I'll describe seven benefits of this factory site," you list 1–7, with spaces for words.

10. *Assists selling.* In *Thriving on Chaos*, Tom Peters urges business leaders to "become obsessed with listening." Salespeople know that the higher the proportion of time they invest in listening, the better chance they have to sell their product. There's a good reason for this. If you listen precisely, you understand the customer's requirements and priorities. More important, by repeating the customer's own words, you show that you and he (or she) are, literally speaking the same language. A client called our office to inquire about a presentation skills class. He'd taken one and thought he'd gotten the material "under my belt." His phrase, "under my belt," showed up in the follow-up letter he received. I don't usually use the term "under my belt," but my willingness to echo his words showed him that we speak the same language, literally.

11. *Clarifies directions.* The women with whom I work report that about one in four of their failed language encounters involve giving, receiving, or following directions. Secretaries and administrative assistants report bosses' vague directions. Managers report aides' inability to follow their directions accurately. Precision listening prevents these costly failures. If the directions lack clarity, you'll know as soon as you try to copy them.

12. *Ensures permanent phone records.* If your business is like most others, phone conversations can take place years before business comes to fruition. Precision listening ensures that you'll be ready.

13. *Enhances your professional stature.* When research began for my six-year odyssey on the language of success for women, no book was planned. But, because we value precise listening, my workshop assistants and I recorded women's stories in their own words. Since publication of the 1995 edition, women have e-mailed or called to ask

how I knew what they said. I knew what they said because of precision listening. If the stories and words in this book ring true, it's because they are.

Technique 3. Repeat or Paraphrase

To be sure you got the message straight, repeat the exact words or paraphrase. Repetition clarifies, shows the listener you're paying attention, and lets you "rehearse" the message to help you remember it. Hearing her own words may also remind the speaker to be more clear. To avoid distortion, favor precise repetition of at least the key words, the verbs and nouns. Paraphrasing can help if the message is cast in unfamiliar language, is especially inarticulate, or is offensive and not repeatable. Here are phrases that help when you seek to repeat or paraphrase.

Crib Sheet

Ways to Begin Repetitions and Paraphrases

Repetition: Let me repeat exactly what you said

This will help us serve you better. You said . . .

You seem to have said . . .

Paraphrase: If I understand you correctly,

You seem to be saying,

In other words,

My interpretation is,

Let me test my understanding,

Yours: _____

_____

Technique 4. Empathize

Empathy means *identification with and understanding of another's situation*. When listening empathetically, you don't judge, advise, or instruct, but reflect sympathetically on what the person said (and to the body language). Empathetic listening has its roots in psychoanalysis and focuses on the feelings of the speaker. Research suggests that women are superior empathetic listeners. In business, there are moments when empathetic listening works. For example, if an employee sits before you weeping, he or she doesn't seek precision listening, guidance, or powerful leadership but rather sympathy and empathy.

Crib Sheet

Words That Empathize

Oh, my.

That must have upset you.

You seem so distressed.

What a frustration.

Yours: _____

_____

Do not say, "You are upset," only what you "seem." Also avoid such terms as, "I know how you feel."

Technique 5. Clarify

Clarify when you're not sure you understand. Clarification questions go beyond repetition. They seek expansion of the message heard.

Crib Sheet

Words That Seek Clarification

Please explain . . .

What does empowerment mean?

Please clarify the concept of the flat corporation.

This use of the term *productivity* needs explanation.

Yours: _____

_____

Technique 6. Probe

Probe for additional information. Here's a list of probes that business people find helpful. Add others relevant to your job. The best probe questions seek specific, open-ended information. Probes direct the questions without suggesting the answers.

Crib Sheet

Words That Probe

Please give me the details.

What exactly happened?

What happened next?

What was the problem?

Who was involved?

Where and when did this happen?

What solution might work?

Yours: _____

_____

TECHNIQUE 7. LISTEN INSTRUCTIONALLY

I coined this term to describe what the trainer, manager, or meeting participant does when trying to teach or lead people. *Instructional listening* engages the other listening skills but responds to direct the discussion while validating the comment. Coaching and teaching fall short when the instructor or leader neglects the listening part of her job or handles it as a problem of empathetic rather than instructional listening.

An example: an instructor was running her first class. She had full mastery of the subject matter and spoke interestingly and clearly. Yet, responses seemed flat. As the day wore on, fewer people spoke out or asked questions. After reviewing the class videotape, we linked the problem to the lack of instructional listening. Here's an example of her response to a question.

A dialogue that failed

Instructor:	We've reviewed the steps in the Quality Program. Any comments or questions?
SAM:	My group had trouble with the idea of empowerment. No one seemed to understand what it is.
Instructor:	(Smiles and nods to questioner) Yes. Now we'll see how to implement each step.

The instructor preferred lecture mode, so she'd ask a question or elicit information, which she then ignored as she returned to the class content. It appeared that the instructor's lack of response dampened future contributions. Had the instructor used class responses, she could have answered appropriately, validated the questions, and used them to enrich the learning. The contrast was clear in the videotapes of another class, in which audience response grew as the day progressed. The difference lay in the fact that this time the instructor responded to the specific content of the questions and wove them into the next segment of her presentation. Here's how she changed her response.

A dialogue that succeeded

Instructor:	We've reviewed the steps in the Quality Program. Any comments or questions?
SAM:	My group had trouble with the idea of empowerment. No one seemed to understand it.
Instructor:	Thank you for raising the issue of empowerment. Its definition has plagued nearly every user. We'll look at it more closely in the next section on implementation.

The instructor's response in the first script neither confirms nor denies the value of the question: it just ignores it. If you respond that way as a leader or instructor, you'll get fewer questions and less engagement by the audience. The second script occurred after the instructor had analyzed her tape and thought more about the value of instructional listening. This time she responded specifically to the content of the question—she didn't stop to answer, but she validated the speaker and the question and then guided everyone to the next step. She could also have answered the question if it were relevant to the topic at hand or if it related to a topic coming up soon.

FIT THE TECHNIQUE TO THE CIRCUMSTANCE

Healthy doses of common sense and respect for the Janus Principles steer you toward success and flexibility in listening. If you've had trouble in the past, pay careful attention, especially to encounters that fail, take precise notes, and review later what you said, what he said, and how an alternative approach might have produced a happier outcome. And keep the options open; you've seen that powerful listening engages a repertoire of skills. Carol Millet, a human resources manager, told of an incident where a listener decided that empathetic listening was not the style of choice. An overly committed high school student had found herself late with a school project and was crying. Her father happened by, looked at her weeping, decided to be an instructional rather than an empathetic listener and said, "Crying won't solve this problem." So she dried her tears and finished the project.

Now you've shed the language of weakness and acquired the recipes for the language of success. Does that mean your language troubles are over? Well, some are, but new strains will appear, because the world is a complex place, with many influences and many forces at play.

Quick Tips

Avoid filters that distract or interfere.

Pay attention.

Be alert to mismatches.

Keep quiet.

Use powerful body language.

Acquire a repertoire of instrumental listening skills.

Listen precisely.

Gain the benefits of precise listening.

Listen to body language.

Repeat.

Paraphrase.

Empathize.

Clarify.

Probe.

Instruct.

Match listening technique to the situation.

12

Running the World—
Onward and Upward

---

*What distinguishes leaders . . . is that they find a voice that allows
them to articulate the common dream. Uncommon eloquence
marks . . . every one . . .*

WARREN BENNIS

You've come a long way, shedding the grammar, words, gestures, and styles of weakness; learning the grammar, words, gestures, and styles of power. Weak language no longer blocks your success. Newfound confidence encourages you to experiment. You've transformed your life by transforming your language. Now consider leadership.

Think of a leader in any sphere that you'd like to emulate. Did you choose a political leader? A military leader? A business leader? A personal or family leader? A medical or scientific leader? What about a fictional character? Charlotte, the spider? Nancy Drew? Another character? In preparing for this chapter, I reviewed much of the writing about leadership and found too many studies that still use the male model. Yet many of you do or will lead, whether you run a program with no staff, coordinate a small team, manage a family, or run a major global organization. It's worthwhile to learn, practice, and refine your own language of leadership.

Language doesn't just ease your way; it gives voice to your highest ideals. The language of success says that women can succeed and lead without compromising their integrity or veering from their moral compass.

This chapter introduces a developmental view of leadership, offers guideposts to evaluate your skills, and makes practical suggestions to enhance your own leadership and the way you'll nurture future leaders.

Let's start with the big picture. Leadership has many elements, but language always lies at its heart. Study after study has shown that the one tie that binds all leaders is the ability to communicate effectively. Consider also that leadership is not a thing like a building but rather a fluid, emerging series of challenges and issues that follows a predictable developmental pattern. Leaders reach stages at varying levels of proficiency with a number of skills. You probably know managers who perform at a high level in one aspect of leadership but not in another. For example, a manager may understand the economics of a work situation while seeming incapable of listening to the ideas of her staff. You yourself may excel at one aspect of your work while lacking in another.

The Four Levels of Leadership

Consider the view that leadership follows a staged developmental pattern, that its nature varies with one's level, that we can consider four levels. Using the metaphor of the journey, let's call them *novice, apprentice, master*, and *mentor*.

The notion of levels of leadership links to Howard Gardner's studies of leaders in his superb book, *Leading Minds*. Gardner selected eleven men and women from different countries and backgrounds who led in various disciplines, government, and business. He studied their lives in detail and sought common threads. The most prominent of these turns out to be language: all the leaders had exemplary communication ability.

The developmental levels, as implied in Gardner's studies, inspired the discussion in this chapter.

Given Gardner's ideas as backdrop, let's link the language of leadership to the principles and practical skills you've learned from this book.

As you've seen, the principles form three questions: First, what is it not about? It's not about you! For leaders, that holds true as it does for women in the factory or the classroom. Leaders understand themselves well enough and their egos are strong enough that they know that leadership is about those whom you lead and the subject matter, not about you. Leaders do not rise and fall on their strategic decisions or mistakes only; they rise and fall on their application of this fundamental principle.

On the day I write these words, the CEO of one of the world's largest firms was fired, in part because morale had fallen low: he had failed to share a vision. His strategic direction went unchallenged, but he neglected the first principle. On the day the company's stock suffered a sharp decline, he complained to *The New York Times* about the decline in his own net worth. On the day he was fired, he was quoted as saying, ". . . I'm a very big shareholder, and a lot of my future net worth is dependent on how well [his successors] do." Public obsession with one's own net worth prefigures failure of leadership.

Had this leader understood the first principle, he might have said, "Our company is going through a difficult time, but we have the finest employees on the globe and the best products in the world. We'll return, stronger than ever." Instead, he chose to talk about his own net worth. He was stuck in his area of expertise (finance) rather than on making the necessary transition to leadership, and his language reflected that failure to grow.

The second question asks, What is it about? What is the subject? Had that CEO talked about the products, the staff, the future, or even chosen the pronoun "we" instead of talking about his net worth, he might have succeeded in sharing a vision.

The third question, What does it do?, calls for the action verbs—
"We'll return," for example—that we've detailed in earlier chapters.

This book has prepared you well for the language of leadership: simply refine the structural, rhetorical, and body-language ideas you've
already encountered. Of course, leadership taps other skills as well, but
language lies at its core.

With the principles of the language of success in mind, let's define
the developmental levels of leadership and link them to their language
foundations.

THE NOVICE

To start, I have sketched an emerging level, in which the potential
leader shows promise but is as yet unformed as a leader; let's call this
potential leader the *novice*. This stage is not necessarily age-related; if
you've toiled in a research lab for 30 years and suddenly find yourself leading the department, you may be a novice at leadership despite your
acknowledged high level of expertise in your field.

Who is the novice? The novice earns her name: leadership is new to
her; she's green; she doesn't know the ropes; she hasn't figured out the difference between doing a good job independently and spurring others to
do a good job. The novice shows these early traits, as noted by Gardner:

- ❏ Speaks skillfully
- ❏ Shows keen interest in other people
- ❏ Has general energy and resourcefulness
- ❏ Is willing to confront people in authority (not necessarily hostile)
- ❏ Takes risks
- ❏ Shows early concern with moral issues
- ❏ Is competitive

❏ Enjoys achieving a position of control

❏ Seek(s) power in order to attain certain goals

If you checked several items on this list, you may be a novice, starting your journey to leadership.

The novice leader asks: How shall I craft myself? What shall I make of myself, my life, my leadership promise? And leadership promise isn't restricted to MBAs and "fast track" junior executives. A young woman who attended our seminar for secretaries sensed potential for leadership in herself. She perceived injustice in the way other secretaries treated each other and sought to change the atmosphere of her department to make it more humane. With no special training and no formal education, she saw promise in herself as a novice leader. Are you a novice starting on the journey of leadership? What communication skills must you learn and refine?

Communication Skills to Develop While You're a Novice

- Start building an excellent reference library.

- Read widely.

- Gain experience speaking in small and informal settings.

- Listen intently.

- Move toward writing proficiency (remember Charlotte!).

- Gain the courage to act on moral impulses.

- Seek competitive situations.

- Speak out about injustice, unfairness.

- Seek appropriate external support, mentoring, and education.

- Take advantage of company learning opportunities.

- Offer to organize and lead small groups and meetings.

- Start acquiring the skills in the Leadership Evaluation.

- Inform human resource people and managers that you seek leadership opportunities.

THE APPRENTICE

Let's now explore a second level, which we'll call the *apprentice*. The dictionary defines apprentice as "one who is learning a trade or occupation." Perhaps the best way to discriminate the apprentice from the novice is our acknowledgment that the apprentice is on her way; she is learning how to lead rather than simply showing promise. She might lead a small group, start a neighborhood organization, organize friends for social activities, or may have just won a promotion. The young tenured professor, the engineering team leader, the president of the parents' association may all be apprentice leaders.

The apprentice must be prepared for the cycle of success, failure, and renewal that is the lot of all leaders. If the apprentice chooses to learn how to lead, she must broaden her sphere and communicate with larger groups. As you progress through the apprentice stage, continue to enhance the skills you started as a novice, and add advanced language and leadership techniques listed here.

Skills to Develop While You're an Apprentice

- Use advanced Web reading resources.

- Gain independence in finding reading, and retaining articles and books on leadership.

- Write clearly, not only for professionals but for a widening audience.

- Volunteer for challenging presentation opportunities.

- Learn and practice the principles of persuasion and rhetoric.

- Cultivate oratorical skills, addressing larger audiences.
- Bear yourself in a way that earns authority.
- Continue to seek and work with mentors.
- Start or continue a lifelong habit of risk-taking.
- Follow Emerson's dictate, "Always do what you are afraid to do."
- "Walk the talk." Model ideals through your behavior.
- Continue to build the skills in the Leadership Evaluation.

THE MASTER

If we see the novice and apprentice as "emerging" leaders, we see the *master* as a "seasoned" leader. The master has known real success and is accepted as a leader by peers and followers. The job title might be director, vice president, manager. As a master, you possess a well-formed sense of yourself.

Leadership poses large issues for masters: they must make the opportunity for reflection, must perceive the big picture. The seasoned leader moves onto ever larger stages. Talks are no longer for small groups but for large, perhaps international, meetings. Audiences are no longer peers alone but professionals from other disciplines and the public. Persuasion is no longer based in your area of expertise, but is political as well: sharing a vision, encouraging others, rewarding success, nurturing young leaders. Reading is no longer the professional journal in your own field but books and articles about the wider world and about leadership itself. Writing goes beyond data and research findings to plain-language descriptions that reach out to touch varied audiences. You may appear on TV; you respond to interviews; you give voice to the ideas and preferences of the group. Warren Bennis notes, "What distinguishes leaders . . . is that they find a voice that allows them to articulate the common dream." Thus, language and communications always advance the leadership agenda.

Gardner talks of the seasoned leader's "charisma, flexibility, capacity to adjust stories to changing circumstances while remaining an individual of conviction." And, always, you grapple with the risk of failure. You have grown tough, robust, energized by setbacks, and you return to the fray with a new vigor, construing every defeat as an opportunity.

As a master, you already have strong communication and leadership skills: continue to develop and refine them. Respond to staff and customer evaluations of your communications. Many leaders think they communicate effectively until they discover what others say about them. Ask peers, reports, and managers to evaluate your skills on the Leadership Evaluation.

As a master, you know how to apply your communication skills to run successful meetings, manage others, work with customers, lead growing organizations, and balance the Janus paradoxes.

THE MENTOR

Yet a higher level of leadership beckons. A few seasoned leaders continue to stretch and grow, beyond the career, beyond the area of expertise, beyond the personal. Let's call this level the mature leader, the *mentor*. The mature leader no longer concerns herself with career, earnings, gaining followers: she has moved beyond daily, small, local issues to play her role on a larger stage. She may earn national leadership, often beyond her professional specialty.

Mentorship can be seen in the lives of two women leaders who are moving or have moved beyond the categories I've laid out here. One example is Dr. Diane Wara. While continuing her leadership role in pediatric immunology, she now also serves as associate dean of Minority and Women's Affairs at the University of California at San Francisco Medical School. Dr. Wara travels the world to convince governments to adopt policies that will reduce the AIDS rate. Another example is Dr. Lynne Reid, Wolbach Professor of Pathology at Harvard Medical School. In her 70s,

Dr. Reid strives to educate women and young faculty in medicine, to ease their paths to the leadership she has attained. You can probably add some mature leaders to this list as well.

With it all, the mentor continues to grapple with the recurring communication issues: how to inspire a shared vision; how to get people to rise above their narrow interests; how to refine the already strong voice; how to craft a "story" that conveys the message ever farther from the intimate circle.

Evaluate Your Leadership Skills

In sum, the language of leadership never sits static. Just as leadership constantly renews itself, so its language constantly renews and refreshes itself. We never finish learning how to lead; we never finish learning the language of leadership. And, for women, sometimes leadership and power form a second language, one that differs from what we learned as little girls.

You've begun to see yourself at one of the four levels of leadership, or more likely, at all of the levels. Perhaps you have mastered the skills of public speaking, but act like a novice when leading meetings. The old reaction would have been, "I'm just not a very good leader," but you should move beyond that kind of thinking.

Leadership doesn't lend itself well to quantification, yet we all think we recognize it when we see it and when we don't. Efforts to measure leadership use personality measures in which people are judged by their own, their staffs', and their superiors' views of their attributes. If the right questions are asked and if the responses are in the right spirit, they aid leaders immeasurably in seeing themselves as others see them. However, these measures share shortcomings that can limit their value in helping people learn how to lead. They tend to push people into a few categories, despite our knowledge that each of us is a mix of many and often conflicting characteristics (the Janus Principles in action).

I designed the Leadership Evaluation by reviewing corporations' lists of leadership attributes and converting them to behaviors if possible. Next, I listed behaviors cited in research as well as those displayed by my clients as they transformed themselves from novices to masters, from fearful to confident, from managers to leaders. Finally, I grouped them under the general categories of Managing Self, Managing Others, Managing Meetings, Leading Teams, Leading Organizations, Reading, Listening, Writing, and Speaking. As you work with the items, you'll find inevitable redundancies: for example, the skill of knowing persuasive language techniques overlaps with the skill of commanding rhetorical techniques. These overlaps reflect the integrated nature of language: grow in one aspect and you grow in others as well. If you learn to filter successfully in reading, you'll know how to filter effectively at meetings. (The lists exclude behaviors that appear unrelated to communications, such as analyzing spread sheets, setting strategic direction, and so on.) Evaluate yourself, ask associates to evaluate you, check yourself from time to time to be sure you continue to develop.

How to Use the Leadership Evaluation

First, make sure you understand each item. Most of them extend ideas covered in this book. Next, survey your skills as you see them. Finally, if you wish, duplicate the form and ask others to evaluate your skills. See if your assessments match those of others. (Remember, self-awareness is a critical attribute of emotional intelligence.) Decide which of your novice or apprentice skills you want to work on, and learn them. It's as simple as that.

Leadership Evaluation

Name: _____

Relationship to person being evaluated   Self _____   Superior _____   Peer _____

Here is a list of general attributes of successful leaders—Managing Self, Managing Others, Managing Meetings, Leading Teams, Leading Organizations, Reading, Listening, Writing, Speaking—along with specific behaviors that support these attributes.

We've categorized these behaviors as:

1. Novice   This behavior is new to the leader and does not appear in her repertoire.
2. Apprentice   The leader appears to have learned the rudiments of this behavior and shows it sometimes but without mastery.
3. Master   This behavior appears consistently and the leader appears to have mastered it.
4. Mentor   The leader knows this behavior so well that he or she can mentor others in its acquisition.

SPECIFIC BEHAVIOR

	Novice	Apprentice	Master	Mentor
Managing Self				
Welcomes risk				
Seeks and works well with mentors				
Understands and expresses the "stories" of peers				
Uses logical skills of analysis and synthesis to make sound, timely decisions				
Determines when to decide, when to seek consensus, and when to let others decide				
Seeks critique from a variety of perspectives				
Meets or exceeds others' expectations				
Solicits information and views of others				
Expresses agreement and disagreement without emotion or rancor				
Documents change objectively				
Gains self-confidence through experience				
Accepts and manages the "recurrent cycle of failure and renewal"				
Learns from mistakes				
Avoids distractions of daily events, attends to large issues				

	Novice	Apprentice	Master	Mentor
Exercises strong hold over widening audiences				
Crafts charismatic presence				
Managing Others				
Communicates, in writing, speech, and gesture, a clear and inspiring vision				
Creates an environment that welcomes diverse opinions and nurtures cooperation				
Defines objectives clearly and concisely				
Encourages open, direct communication through:				
Precision listening				
Neutral language				
Distancing techniques				
Eye contact				
Gestures of acceptance				
Appropriate choices of sentence forms				
Avoidance of harassment and intimidation				
Serves as a role model and mentor				
Uses appropriate sentence forms and word choices to develop subordinates' confidence				
Leads through personal strength; maturity; clear, civil communications				
Recognizes the impact of behavior on others				
Reads and responds appropriately to the relevant moods and motivations of others				
Encourages effective behavior through active listening, feedback, and persuasion				
Knows effective persuasive language techniques				
Managing Meetings				
Meets only and for as long as necessary to advance specific goals				
Models appropriate meeting behaviors				
Starts and ends on time, arrives prepared, adheres to agenda, keeps precise records				
Encourages and enforces civil argument				
Prevents both "groupthink" and divisive discord				
Builds consensus when appropriate				

	Novice	Apprentice	Master	Mentor
Leading Teams				
Uses appropriate sentence forms and word choices to integrate team				
Instills a sense of ownership and pride				
Allocates authority and necessary resources				
Builds and molds teams, fosters open communication				
Maintains and documents working relationships across groups				
Attains synergy within and among teams				
Encourages quiet members to contribute, controls aggressive members				
Leading Organizations				
Translates strategic intent into concrete plans through written and spoken language				
Maintains consistency between words and actions				
Adheres to corporate values				
Expresses values clearly to others				
Keeps up to date on the broad-based requirements of running an organization				
Stays abreast of developments in the larger business, political, and social arena				
Reading				
Reads to glean vital information, strategic data, new ideas				
Uses on-line and print resources efficiently				
Invests reading time wisely through filtering				
Manages reading process				
Participates in and leads communities of readers				
Analyzes and synthesizes incoming information and ideas				
Reads critically				
Listening				
Listens strategically				
Uses appropriate body language				
Manages listening modes: precision listening, clarifying, probing, empathizing and instructing				

	Novice	Apprentice	Master	Mentor
Writing				
Understands primacy of written language				
Avoids verbiage, passive voice constructions, inappropriate jargon, excessive "I" statements				
Strives for clarity, brevity				
Models clear writing				
Prefers active voice, action verbs				
Maintains appropriate tone				
Speaking				
Conveys clear vision				
Prepares fully				
Analyzes audiences				
Speaks powerfully at small and large meetings				
Uses nonverbal language of power				
Manages media: computer, television, projection, others				
Matches style to leadership role				
Integrates visual and verbal				
Respects time constraints				
Commands rhetorical techniques				
Reaches growing audience				
Reads formal and informal scripts effectively				
Retains eye contact with varied audience members				

©2001 Phyllis Mindell

13

The Executive Suite:
How to Lead with
the Language of Success

Some people really have almost a distaste for that word [power].
They feel it is alien to conscience. Power for power's sake, no.
But the positive use of power for positive purposes is very
important. You have to understand that. You've got to have a
seat at the policy table if you want to make a difference.

ELIZABETH DOLE

You've pondered your leadership level, assessed communication skills on the Leadership Evaluation, and broadened and deepened your language repertoire. In this chapter, we explore issues that continue to dog women as our careers advance.

What do leaders do all day? As you progress up the ladder, you invest ever greater portions of the day communicating. The Harvard Case Studies track CEO days. The schedule for a typical leader apportions her day as follows: 20 percent reading, 20 percent writing (dictating and word processing), 40 percent formal presentations (she's also listening and speaking informally during these presentations), 30 percent in informal meetings (at which she speaks and listens while sitting). These figures add up to more than 100 percent because the communications overlap. She spends **all** her travel time communicating: speaking on the cellular or airphone; reading books, proposals, and periodicals; and dictating or writing on her notebook computer.

And a typical job description for the senior vice president for Strategy and New Business Development for a Fortune 500 firm requires 25 percent functional skill and 75 percent communication of the strategic plan, internally and externally. Leadership demands superior communications.

Yet, despite the progress of the past two decades, many women have yet to generate a language that works in the executive suite. Whatever your management style, whether you're a dictator, an enabler, a mentor, a drill sergeant, or a coach (or all, depending on the situation), the language of success delivers the message. All the powerful language forms we've covered in this book work well at every level and with any management philosophy. In this chapter, we'll look at specific issues women leaders address and see how you can apply the language of success to prevent, manage, or resolve them—not as a man but as a powerful woman. As it happens, Charlotte faced and handled many of the same issues. We'll see once again how Charlotte managed and how we can emulate her.

Manager and Mentor: What Charlotte Teaches Us

Charlotte could have written the book on management for women. Despite her size ("about the size of a gumdrop"), her eight hairy legs, her refusal to "dress for success," and her pedestrian ethnic origins ("just a common grey spider"), she supervised all the animals in the barn, led the formation of an empowered work group, mentored the runt pig, and managed to be a true friend at the same time, all through powerful language. You can, too.

Nine Ways to Lead People Through Language . . . and Inspire Them to Follow

If you manage people, you know that some resist solely because you're a woman. Charlotte also met and overcame resistance to her leadership.

After the descriptions of Charlotte's approaches, you'll find other stories about leadership and discussions of ways to expand and tailor each to your management situation. You'll also find "crib sheets" of language suggestions.

1. BE VERSATILE

When asked what *versatile* means, Charlotte replies, "Versatile means I can turn with ease from one thing to another. It means I don't have to limit my activities to spinning and trapping and stunts like that." The woman who controls her language is also versatile. She applies the Janus Principles to adjust to each situation. She controls grammar and vocabulary to adjust to each audience and each situation. For example, your informal language may be filled with "I think . . ." and "I feel . . ." because you won't take the time to monitor each word, whereas your formal talks should avoid many references to yourself and should certainly avoid "I think" and "I feel." The language of success also gives you the versatility to adjust to the level of anger or hostility in the audience. In general, the higher the hostility, the more you should distance yourself and the more carefully you should control the language. Likewise, the stronger the emotions, the more distant you should be. Your judgment and knowledge of the audience counts, too. Comments to the CEO about new personnel policies will be cast in quite different words and grammar from comments to factory workers.

In the *Harvard Business Review*, Daniel Goleman cites studies of six distinctive leadership styles: coercive ("Do what I tell you."), authoritative ("Come with me."), affiliative ("People come first."), democratic ("What do you think?"), pacesetting ("Do as I do, now."), and coaching ("Try this."). Instead of simplistically saying one or the other is best, he suggests that successful leaders read situations and use the style that works. This reinforces the Janus Principles: it's not authoritative *or* democratic; it's authoritative *and* democratic. Successful leaders, like Charlotte, are versatile.

The Versatile Woman Controls Her Language

Adjust words, grammar, and distance to:

the audience	business executives	"These are five impediments to listening."
	nursing home aides	"Five things stop you from listening."
the formality	formal	"How, then, can women extract what's useful from the research?"
	informal	"So what should you do tomorrow?"
the level of hostility	low	"That's garbage."
	high	"That seems like an unworkable solution." *or* "A better solution should be found."
your power	low	"It might be helpful if you . . ."
	high	"Please . . ."

2. ACCEPT CREDIT FOR ACCOMPLISHMENT MODESTLY BUT STRONGLY

Charlotte never explained away her accomplishments by crediting others for them: "The message I wrote in my web, praising Wilbur, has been received . . . I dare say my trick will work and Wilbur's life can be saved." Note that she switched to passive voice when she spoke of what had to be done—she wanted to enlist the aid of the work group, yet she acknowledged her own leadership. Women managers often are so self-effacing that they say things like, "It's not my achievement; it's theirs." Male managers, on the other hand, accept the credit for what they've done. The language of success gives you ways to accept credit for your attainments without either downplaying or bragging about them.

How Not to Accept Credit

It was really nothing.

I got lucky.

It wasn't me; it was the team.

I worked hard.

I tried.

I don't know if it was really only luck or not, but I was the only woman who took the supervisor exam and the only one who passed.

Despite the incompetence of the team, I pulled the show together on my own.

Crib Sheet

How to Accept Credit

Thank you.

Under my leadership, the employees at Zuckerman's Barn succeeded in a joint effort to save the life of the runt of the litter.

This task could not have been accomplished without your cooperation and support.

I could not have accomplished this task without your cooperation and support.

We could not have accomplished this task without everyone's cooperation and support

Your cooperation and support contributed so much to my (our) success.

I was the only woman who took the supervisor exam and the only one who passed.

3. Persuade in the Language of Power

The sum total of the language of weakness and deferral and the inclination not to listen to women is that women leaders report that they're not as persuasive in the executive suite or the board room as they should be. Top executives describe themselves in such terms as "a blithering idiot," "like a total jerk," or "unconvincing."

Yet Mr. Zuckerman, the unimaginative executive type (and you certainly come across people just like him!), was convinced by Charlotte's printed words. "You know . . . I've thought all along that that pig of ours was an extra good one. He's a solid pig. That pig is as solid as they come. You notice how solid he is around the shoulders . . . ?" Charlotte wove the web of suggestion. By labeling Wilbur *some pig*, *terrific*, and *radiant*, she persuaded the humans that he really was.

Your web of words can also suggest. Pam Mason, a business owner, told of her difficult negotiations with a vendor. The vendor's product had declined while his price increased, but he was still the best and cheapest source of a particular item. She aimed to keep him as vendor, persuade him to cut the price increase, and get him to restore the quality. She could have approached him by complaining and threatening to go to another source, but good business dictated that she continue buying his product. She used the language of success to win him over: "You've supplied the preferred product and it's helped our business grow. We're eager to continue working with you. We understand that prices go up. Can we work out a way to continue our productive relationship, bring the product quality back, and keep an affordable price?" The vendor was disarmed by the supportive yet powerful words and yielded a better deal than Pam had anticipated.

If you control grammar, words, and rhetoric, you can persuade as well.

4. Say No Powerfully, but Kindly

About 25 percent of the problems reported by women in my workshops involve the inability to say no to those above and below in the hierarchy and to peers as well. Power brings the ability to say no without seeming hostile or negative.

Charlotte was a girl who *could* say no, and explain why not. When the animals were choosing words for Charlotte's web, one came up with "Pig Supreme." Charlotte didn't hedge: "No good . . . it sounds like a rich dessert." Later, the rat brought in a PRE-SHRUNK label from an old shirt. Charlotte countered, "Pre-shrunk is out of the question. We want Zuckerman to think Wilbur is nicely filled out, not all shrunk up." You, too, can say no without intimidating or insulting. The solution here is to control distance; avoid *I* and *you* and talk about the subject, or switch into the passive voice.

Crib Sheet

Ten Ways to Say No Powerfully

1. Perhaps a better solution is available.
2. That solution doesn't promise success.
3. That solution doesn't sound practical.
4. This solution promises to be more economical.
5. Time won't permit this meeting to continue.
6. This problem deserves attention; let's set up an appointment to do it justice.
7. Company policy prohibits gifts from vendors, but thank you.
8. Rather, consider this alternative.
9. The data don't support this conclusion.
10. This conclusion seems to be based on inadequate data.

5. LEAD MEETINGS THAT WORK

Charlotte ran her animal work group in a straightforward, no-nonsense way. She started with a roll call, showing that she was and would remain in charge: "I shall begin by calling the roll." She did not say, "I never really have called a meeting before, and I'm so grateful you gave me the opportunity to do so." Charlotte also exercised her leadership by setting a clear agenda: "Now I called this meeting in order to get suggestions. I need new ideas for the web." She did not say, "Now how does everyone feel about the prospect of having Wilbur killed off?" She also tapped the wisdom of senior staff. The oldest sheep was the one who threatened Templeton the rat if he didn't help find words for the web.

Meetings tests your leadership mettle. Meetings bring groups together or tear them apart, build morale or destroy it, result in action plans or end in deadlock, inspire shared effort or drive destructive competition, test new ideas or quash them. Think about meetings you've run. Did they foster the positive ends—or deteriorate in acrimony and inaction? At our team communications seminars, delayed and disorganized meetings top the list of complaints.

One leader whose meetings work is Sister Edwardine Weaver, who presides over board meetings for a professional group at a university. Sr. Edwardine lacks budget monies to entice people. If food is served at all, it's coffee and cookies. She lacks the power that you have if you manage a work group; her group consists of volunteers, busy people who give valuable time to attend her meetings. Yet Sr. Edwardine gets everyone to come, to contribute, to volunteer more time, and to be pleased that they did. I walked through a typical meeting Sr. Edwardine runs and listed the language elements that make it work, from planning to completion (note that her language techniques are similar to Charlotte's). They're listed here—you can use them as a meeting crib sheet.

Meetings That Succeed, Step-by-Step

1. Set the date at the prior meeting.
2. Send reminder notices that arrive ten days before the meeting, telling people of date, beginning and ending time, place, purpose, and preliminary agenda.

3. Start promptly.

4. Welcome people individually; thank them for contributions.

5. Respond to every comment in a favorable way, even when disagreeing. Comments may be neutrally favorable ("You think it's too late to invite people?"), negatively favorable ("It's too late to change that item, but thank you for suggesting it."), or positively favorable ("We should be able to do that. Thank you.").

6. Encourage creative, civil argument.

7. Require civility and courtesy.

8. Follow the agenda.

9. Repeat the consensus, if one exists. If not, determine follow-up. This tactic fosters interchange without stalling the agenda.

10. Record assignments and action steps. Circulate if appropriate.

11. Cover all agenda items.

12. Clear the next meeting date.

13. Thank each person for his or her specific contribution or for coming.

Note the central role of language, both in Sr. Edwardine's meetings and in Charlotte's. Without strong language, both spoken and written, there simply can be no leadership. Sr. Edwardine and Charlotte have philosophies that drive their language; they each act on the belief that success emerges from organization, structure, planning, civility, courtesy, and respect for individual dignity. They each tap the talents and ideas of widely varied players. Unlike what happens at some corporate meetings, no curses are ever spoken, no hostile body language is ever displayed, no rudeness has ever been seen. If you apply the language of success, these ugly moments won't mar your meetings, either. Guaranteed.

Prevent Meeting Failures with the Language of Success

Rule	Response
Quash incivility.	Cursing is both intolerable and illegal.
Nip rude behavior in the bud.	Side conversations disturb both the speakers and the meeting. (If that doesn't work: we'll wait till we have your attention.)
Set rules; brook no violations.	At these meetings, everyone attends to the speaker. If you have other work to do, kindly do it back at your office.
Prevent interruptions.	Sue hasn't finished. Please hold the comments.
Stop hostile time-waste.	A lengthy discussion of a topic that's not on the agenda will blow us off course. This issue might be better explored later, in private.

Run Meetings That Work with the Language of Success

Rule	Response
Model civil language.	Thanks for that suggestion. It won't work (may not work; doesn't look promising; may not have possibilities) for this project, but may be great for xxx.
	A great deal of effort went into this proposal. It deserves a fair hearing.
Show courtesy.	Thank you for xxx.
	Please xxx.
Recognize contributions.	Sally's project has come in ahead of schedule. Thanks.
	Melanie's idea about redesigning this machine could save us money.
Prevent groupthink.	Before we all go along with this, does anyone see a problem?

Encourage reticent speakers.	Jill, you're an expert at this. Will it work?
Thank people.	Thanks for an interesting idea.
	Thanks for coming on time.
	Thanks for your courtesy.

Action Plan

Are you satisfied with the results of your meetings? If not, view a tape recording of a meeting and note which of the steps you missed. If your meetings require different steps, jot them down. Also observe the verbal and body language. Joint viewing of a tape can act as an wake-up call to the uncooperative or timid.

6. Praise Others' Accomplishments When Appropriate

Charlotte didn't hog the credit. When the goslings were born, she said: "Every one of us here will be gratified to learn that after four weeks of unremitting effort and patience on the part of our friend the goose, she now has something to show for it. The goslings have arrived. May I offer my sincere congratulations!"

Morale soars when accomplishments gain recognition. And it sinks when accomplishments are overlooked. Public recognition not only bolsters morale but teaches as well. The surest way to get people to repeat positive actions is to let them know they're appreciated. I'm not talking about dishonest or trivial recognition, but about precise words praising specific attainments or efforts. Thanks for accomplishments goes up and down the ladder: administrative aides thank bosses; managers thank workers; leaders thank followers; team members thank each other. It's the best way to ensure that positive behavior will continue. Here are do's and don'ts to tailor to your work environment. They all follow the principles of the language of success.

Do's and Don'ts of Recognition

Weak Praise	Powerful Praise
I love the job you did on that report.	That report came in on time. It's clear. It's specific. It's a sound job all around. Thank you.
You did a terrific job.	Your ability to engineer a sound project has grown.
	This project reflects all the ideas management wanted.
This was a good meeting. You're great.	You got the meeting organized and managed every detail, from the coffee to the transportation. I've put a note about it in your personnel file.
I like to work for you.	Those directions were clear and specific. Thanks.
You're a good xxx	The work always arrives on time and correct. Thanks.

Action Plan

List five behaviors that people should get thanks for. Follow the language of success principles to construct your sentences: What is it not about (you)? What is it about (subject of the sentence)? What does it do (prefer an action verb)?

7. Overcome Hostility, Win Cooperation

At one point in *Charlotte's Web*, Charlotte needs the cooperation of Templeton the rat. After his hostile rejection, she appeals to the old sheep for advice. The old sheep suggests, "I'll appeal to his baser instincts, of which he has plenty." She then threatens Templeton: "Wilbur's food is your food; therefore Wilbur's destiny and your destiny are closely linked. If Wilbur is killed and the trough stands empty day after day, you'll grow so thin we can look right through your stomach and see objects on the other side." Even this threat comes in straightforward language: no emotional words, no overt hostility, nothing personal.

We may be stretching a point here; you probably have never worked with a human like Templeton: "The rat had no morals, no conscience, no scruples, no consideration, no decency, no milk of rodent kindness, no compunctions, no higher feeling, no friendliness, no anything." Charlotte and the old sheep do not try to make the rat a good guy; rather, they trade on his greed and vanity to get him to support their management goals. Do you have any rats in your group? Can you use the language of power to manipulate them to accomplish your goals?

What about dissenters who aren't rats? You can win their cooperation through language as well. Judy B. Rosener's study of women leaders in the *Harvard Business Review* quotes one who says, "When I know ahead of time that someone disagrees with a decision, I can work especially closely with that person to try to get his or her support." Civility and compromise, persuasion, and cooperation give you an edge that coercion does not (most of the time). Abraham Lincoln wrote, "When the conduct of men is designed to be influenced, persuasion, kind, unassuming persuasion, should ever be adopted. It is an old and true maxim that 'a drop of honey catches more flies than a gallon of gall.' . . . On the contrary, . . . dictate to his judgment . . . or mark him as one to be shunned and despised, and he will retreat within himself, close all the avenues to his head and his heart and you shall not be able to reach him."

You have the language skills to do what Lincoln suggested. Even if you can't persuade the dissenter, you can assuage her and keep her goodwill for the future. Craft sentences like, "We'll have to agree to disagree on this one," "The final decision here is mine. In this case, your ideas won't be used," or "The consensus went against you this time; perhaps next time we'll be persuaded to adopt your proposal. Thanks for the suggestion." Not in the heat of argument but in the quiet of your office, set up statements that communicate effectively with your dissenters.

Action Plan

Jot down the initials of the Templeton in your organization. List ways you might appeal to her baser instincts and coerce her into cooperating. Next, jot down the names of dissenters whose cooperation you seek. Compose sentences that enable you to win them over.

8. Mentor the Inexperienced

Despite her natural requirement that she stay behind in the barn to produce her egg sac, Charlotte went to the fair to protect Wilbur. When you've made it into power, you're sometimes obligated to put your own interests second to lend a hand to the younger and the weaker. We can't consider ourselves to be at the highest levels of language till we've learned to mentor others. Are you willing to go out of your way to nurture and protect the vulnerable members of your team? You should be. Mentoring is a womanly task. The word *mentor* comes from the name of the wise old man who aided Odysseus's son in *The Odyssey*. But the Mentor who nurtured wasn't really an old man: "he" was a "she," the goddess Athena taking human form to help the young and vulnerable, just as you'll do when you mentor.

In addition to Athena, the archetype of the successful mentor is the parent. A good mentor does just what a good parent does, except that mentors get to pick their mentees. Good parents protect the young while fostering their independence and creativity. Good parents teach as much as the young can absorb. Good parents praise accomplishments, criticize shortcomings, and set new goals. Finally, good parents know when to let go and encourage the young to leave the nest.

All mentoring responsibilities engage the language of success. Here's a crib sheet to get you started.

Crib Sheet

The Language of the Mentor

> You've shown promise as an engineer. This advanced design presents a challenge, but I'll help you.
>
> Jim will try to interrupt your presentation—I'll stop him.
>
> Your idea sounds far out, but give it a try. I'll support it with some budget funds.
>
> Thank you for challenging that proposal. Your argument overlooks the politics, but it's on the right track.

Why don't you take that management program at the community college?

The use of 'like' to break sentences shows weakness and makes you look less smart than you are. We'll work to end it.

Now that you know how to design a simple contraption, try moving on to a more complex one.

You've grown into and beyond this job. Much as I don't want to lose you, it's time to look for a better position.

Action Plan

Successful mentoring engages all the topics in the language of success. Identify a promising young person and learn to mentor him or her.

9. Transform Weak Players by Showing Confidence in Them

"When Charlotte's web said *SOME PIG*, Wilbur had tried hard to look like some pig. When Charlotte's Web said *TERRIFIC*, Wilbur had tried to look terrific. And now that the web said *RADIANT*, he did everything possible to make himself glow." Ever since the spider had befriended him, Wilbur had done his best to live up to his reputation. Think about the "runt" of your team. Is she a potential prize-winner who needs your affirmation and guidance so she, too, can be radiant? Can you prepare scripts that enable you to affirm and guide without compromising your integrity?

Crib Sheet

Words Can Transform the Weak

Your on-time record has improved steadily this month. It should be near-perfect by the end of the next month.

When you started, you missed nearly every benchmark. Now you've missed fewer than half. This progress shows your promise.

Thank you for helping with the reception. It's not part of your job description, but it shows your willingness to support our group.

The first time you got up to speak, your hands shook and you fidgeted. Now you assume a powerful posture and hold it. The next goal is to organize so the talk itself is clear.

These comments show effort on your part; however, the goal was not to proofread but to edit for accuracy. Please try it again, and ask for help if it's not clear.

Everyone at the office enjoys your pleasant personality, but it's inappropriate to visit with friends on the phone during the business day.

If you want your career to advance, learn how to repair the copy machine without calling for help.

The crib sheets and examples in this chapter reveal that the principles of the language of success remain the same even as the settings change.

Quick Tips

Take management lessons from Charlotte.

Be versatile.

Accept credit for your accomplishments.

Persuade in the language of power.

Say no kindly.

Run meetings that work.

Praise others' attainments.

Mentor the inexperienced.

Transform weak players through language.

14

Issues and Answers: Putting It All Together in a Complex World

If you don't like the way the world is, you change it. You have an obligation to change it. You just do it one step at a time.

MARIAN WRIGHT EDELMAN

We've constructed the web of strong language, thread by thread, step by step. Despite your understanding of all the separate elements, when you arrive at work each morning you put all the pieces together in complex settings. You must synthesize all the elements of the language of success. The person demeaning you may be your supervisor, the CEO, a factory worker. He or she may be responding to a weak comment you've made, a body-language blooper, or to some internal motivation. A listening situation may require both empathy and probing, then veer toward instructional listening. Other elements may intervene. This chapter shows how to consider varied elements of a scenario as you weigh your language responses in a world where the Janus Principles prevail.

Issue 1: Slurs, Slights, and Put-Downs

Stories of slurs, slights, and put-downs fill my files. The offenders cross boundaries of age, education, race, and job title. In most cases, they meant no harm: they learned these terms as children, and no one ever confronted them. Although we've covered possible responses, both oral and written, in other chapters, this problem runs deep and wide enough to warrant a section of its own. Here are some ways to respond.

A. IGNORE IT

Avoid thin skin. If you want to play in the big leagues, you can't act like a rookie. If it doesn't happen often, if you'll never see the person again, if no damage was done, make a mental note and let it be. It'll make a funny story when you meet your network group.

B. GIVE ONE BACK

This solution works only for the quick-witted and confident. When Dr. Sylvia Ruiz was told, "Come on up here, honey, and tell them what you did," she had the moxie to say, "It's Dr. Honey to you, honey."

Most of us couldn't think of such quick responses and might not give them if we could. Still, if it works for you, do it.

C. RESPOND IN PUBLIC BUT NOT IN KIND

A female entrepreneur took a college course for businesspeople. The professor prided himself on encouraging women entrepreneurs. One of the male students asked, "What if your spouse doesn't support your going into business?" The professor said, "Some people say this joke is sexist, but it's not. A bigamist has one wife too many. So does a monogamist." The entrepreneur retorted, "It is sexist. And it's irrelevant." (Note that she didn't say, "I feel that it's . . .") The professor approached her after class, apologized, said she was right, and that he'd never use that "joke" again. And one suspects that he weighed his words more carefully in the future.

When, as a young consultant to a steel firm, Orit Gadiesh was told, "Women are considered to be bad luck in steel companies," she replied, "Well, then, you should make sure I go to every single one of your competitors."

Justice Sandra Day O'Connor was the first woman on the Supreme Court. An attorney addressing the court said, "I would like to remind you gentlemen of a legal point." Justice O'Connor quipped, "Would you like to remind me, too?"

If you have the courage and quick wit to speak out publicly in a way that doesn't meet insult with insult, you can both model and teach civility, in the language of power.

D. Respond in Private

If the remarks are repeated, if your image suffers, or if you find the slurs too hurtful to ignore, you may choose to respond in private. That gives you time to review the grammar of power and to jot down a crib sheet. Don't just walk into his office. Ask for an appointment and tell how many minutes you require—this won't take long. Write your own crib sheet or copy this one. Choose the sentences that fit your personality and language style.

Crib Sheet

Foil Put-Downs

Your briefing was so helpful and we look forward to working with International Global, but it was marred when you said, "Back to the phones, girls." Just as men find it insulting to be called boys, women find it insulting to be called girls. Kindly call us women rather than girls. Thanks.

Thanks for inviting me to that meeting of key executives. Since I was the only woman, and it was my first meeting, it was important to establish my credibility. It might have been more helpful if, instead of praising my appearance, you praised my success with the last job.

Calling a woman *a trip, a thing, a dolly, a girl, a great-looking woman, a first name, honey, a gal, darling, a babe, Bubbly Betsy, pretty, Perky Peggy,* or a diminutive of her first name (*Ruthie, Kathy, Susie*) makes the woman look unprofessional and unimportant (puts her down). You'd get more respect, and so would I, if you told about my business qualities instead. You could say I'm a competent secretary, a successful marketer, a fine trainer, a respected writer, a careful editor, and so on.

E. RESPOND IN WRITING

If the comments verge on harassment, seriously damage your work or career, or profoundly hurt you or other women, consider writing to the perpetrator. Remember that writing stays around: the written complaint demands more time, effort, and consideration than the spoken comment. If you choose to write, review the grammar of power and choose the most distanced and formal voice. Before writing, keep precise notes on the exact words of the slurs; date them, and save them for compiling. For even a short note, follow the organization system. Don't make the same mistake Elizabeth Ames made in the Harvard memo: choose only the most serious incidents. If there is a solution, suggest it. Then, after you've written the complaint, hold it for a while so you can think about the consequences. It's a good idea to have someone else review it before it goes out. Never, ever send a piece whose only purpose was to vent your anger.

Here are two memos on the same topic. The first is written in the language of weakness; the second in the language of power.

Weak

I felt so awful when you introduced me as the "best-looking gal in town." Here I'd worked so hard to win that award and get to be vice president, and you blew it by getting everyone to eye my figure instead. I get so mad when you do that to me. You're always blowing your own horn and putting women down. It really hurts my feelings when you do that.

Powerful

Last Tuesday, you introduced me at the board meeting as "the best-look-ing gal in town." Compliments are fun to receive, but not in a setting like that. Since my title is Vice President of Customer Service and our audience consisted of our biggest customers, that introduction didn't do World Service any good. Companies devoted to service don't want to look as though they choose vice presidents on the basis of looks. It might be more helpful in the future if I were introduced as "the woman who won the international service award in 2000" or "the woman who built our marketing department into the biggest in the field." Thanks.

F. Ask a Mentor for Help

Managers should support their staffs. Just as the farmer chose Wilbur for death because he was the runt, so the bullies choose the young and the weak for harassment. If you're not in a position to choose the options just listed, find a caring senior person or group leader and ask for help. Don't whine. Document the slurs (date, place, and exact words) and ask for help in the language of power. Here's a sample.

A situation has gotten out of control, and it's making it hard for me and the other younger women to get our jobs done. I tried to talk to Mr. Brainless about it, but he laughs and says he's only joking. On January 12, he called me "Tootsie," on January 14, "My little gal," on January 15, "cutie pie," on January 16, he said he'd like to "eat me up," on January 17, he said, "Your blouse is pretty, but I bet what's in it is prettier." The early remarks irritated and demeaned, but now they harass. Other people hear these remarks and sometimes they repeat them. Is there a way you can prevent Mr. Brainless from saying things like this?

In sum, the language of success has given you a tool box of resources for handling slurs and put-downs. Decide which will work in any partic-ular situation. You'll emerge stronger, more confident, and less likely to be victimized again.

Issue 2: Apologies

Women apologize more than men do, and it has nothing to do with being sorry, or even having anything to apologize about. Linda Sylvester even observed that she apologizes every time she misses a shot in tennis, while the men with whom she plays never do. Another female tennis player apologizes when she hits a shot too powerful to return. Deborah Tannen suggests that women use "ritual apologies," while men do not. Ritual or not, if you say you're sorry when you're not, you may appear weak. Prepare a variety of options to fit the situations in which apologies are appropriate.

Crib Sheet

When you're actually sorry

> If you shove someone by accident or do something else wrong, it's entirely appropriate to be sorry and to say so. Truthfulness doesn't weaken you.

When you're sorry, but you didn't do it, and it's not clear who did

> It's regrettable that you were inconvenienced by the xxx.

> The xxx inconvenienced you (or whatever else happened). Is there a way the company can make it good (rectify it, make it up to you, cover the damage)?

When you did it, but don't want to take the blame

> Call up the handy, distanced, murky passive voice. The poet Andre Coudescru calls the passive voice "the ventriloquist's voice. Use it to throw blame." Sometimes you'll use it to throw blame from yourself. Witness the politicians' oft-used "Mistakes were made." The ventriloquist's use of the passive voice has come out of Washington during every administration for the last dozen years.

The mailing was sent late.

The check was made out to the wrong person.

The records were lost.

When you know who did it, but don't want to incriminate her

Apparently, there was a miscommunication.

The instructions don't seem to have been clear enough.

The billing error must be corrected.

Regrets serve useful purposes in civil language. "I'm sorry" has its place, but so does honesty. Save the apologies for times when they're appropriate.

Issue 3: Miscommunication— What to Do When the System Fails

We've addressed the "horror stories" of miscommunication and inappropriate language raised earlier in the book and in this section. Still, we have some scenarios filled with miscommunications at every level.

THE SCENARIO: DROWNING IN THE SECRETARIAL POOL

Jean manages a secretarial pool. Most of the people in it work well together, but one woman, Jezebel evades responsibilities and work. She arrives late, leaves early, and spends hours on the phone with family members, placing an unfair burden on the other secretaries. Jean's boss approached Yvette, one of the other pool secretaries, with a priority rush job, which Yvette couldn't accomplish. After Jean went to the boss's office and said, "Yvette can't get this job done on time," the boss said, "Okay, let Suzanne do it."

Suzanne was angry, Yvette was angry, Jean was angry. The boss was displeased because people seemed not only inefficient but eager to pass the work from one person to another.

The problems

When leaders use the language of weakness, not only they but the people who work for them and the people for whom they work suffer the consequences. Jean's weak language worked against her in three ways. First, she failed to control the work habits of the malingerer, Jezebel, allowing an unfair work burden to fall on the others. Second, she used a language form that blamed the victim (Yvette) rather than the real culprit. Third, she failed to prevent the injustice of burdening Suzanne with the work. We'll examine each of these issues and suggest solutions.

The solutions

a. *The malingerer.* Employees who don't carry their share of the load cheat everyone: their employers, their supervisors, their fellow workers, and themselves. Jean's responsibility was to manage the malingerer so that she couldn't evade her work. Here's where the passive voice gives you the grammar of power. Jean could have said, "Your work isn't being completed on time. Measures will have to be taken. A report has been filed in the main office."

Jean doesn't have to point a finger at the malingerer or accuse her outright. The passive voice keeps the hostility level down while clearly stating both the problem and the consequences.

Let's say Jean's approach works for a day or two. Now she shifts her language to reward the behaviors she wants: "Your work arrived on time this morning, and it was accurate. Thanks."

Note that she doesn't talk about her feelings, doesn't say, "I like this job." Nor does she exaggerate, with falsities such as, "This is great!" A simple, accurate statement of fact works for leaders as it works for everyone else.

b. *The complaint—blaming the victim.* Although Jean meant well, the way she framed her statement to the boss made it seem that Yvette was too slow or incompetent to accomplish the rush job, which, of course, wasn't the case at all. Yet history confirms that we blame our victims: ("I raped her because of the way she dressed," "Why didn't they act like the rest of us?"). Here are two solutions that would have worked for everyone.

Jean could have said to the boss, "An unproductive worker in our department has placed an undue burden on all the others: your job can't be completed on time." Or, if she didn't want to discuss the real cause of the problem, she could simply have used the passive voice once more and said, "The job can't be completed on time." This would protect Yvette from blame for a circumstance she hadn't created and would protect Suzanne from the unreasonable assignment.

The language of success enables you to tell the truth without rancor or hostility.

Issue 4: Giving Criticism

Criticism daunts us as we move into management. You want to be kind and nurturing, yet staff problems and shortcomings confront you. Can you offer helpful criticism to shape people to the standards you require? Life prepares us to be positive, to be sensitive, to be generous—but not to be critical. The language of success gives you the critical tools to build employee skills and morale in a truly helpful way. If you listen skillfully and control distance, grammar, and vocabulary, you can say whatever must be said clearly, simply, and successfully.

My company offers a three-day presentation skills workshop. Clients sometimes call it "the workshop from hell" because they see themselves on videotape and receive many critiques. Something wonderful takes place at these workshops. On the first morning a dozen nervous strangers face one another and the consultants. By the third afternoon, they're calling each other "family," laughing, and sometimes crying to see the dramatic gains they've made. The language of critique accounts for the workshop participants' powerful gains. Because they've learned how to give both positive and negative criticism, they serve as each other's advocates and teachers. Many report later that, though they've grown in speaking ability, their most vital gains involved the language of critique. And the ideas that drive it are so simple.

Here's the starter's crib sheet. Your knowledge of the grammars of weakness and power has prepared you to see the rationale behind each statement. Use these cribs for now—soon you'll craft your own successful critiques.

Crib Sheet

How to Give Criticism

- Avoid:

    I liked . . .

    I noticed . . .

    I felt . . .

    I want you to . . .

- Never start critique with "I."

- Start sentences with the subject:

    The memo states its points clearly and succinctly.

    The thesis statement didn't stand out enough.

    The design solved most but not all of the engineering problems.

- Use appropriate lingo:

    The tricolon about marketing brought your point home.

    The "journey" metaphor carried the audience right along.

    The "atom bomb" metaphor doesn't seem apt for a mayonnaise sales campaign.

    The transparency about reorganization isn't in parallel.

    The lead story about the lighthouse warmed the audience at the start.

- Distance for negative and positive remarks:

    An area for future growth is the walk to the podium.

    You may find that a smile at the end works better than a shrug and a sigh.

    You seemed to overcome the nervousness.

    The gesture made the idea easier to understand.

CAN YOU BE KIND AND LEAD? YES!

Mignon's worldwide supplier group is rehearsing for a presentation. The members, skilled financial analysts and engineers, haven't done many presentations, and they look to Mignon for leadership. Terrence knows his material, but his awkward mannerisms, poor organization, and tacky visuals hurt his presentation.

You can lead kindly if you speak the language of success. Mignon's old way was to listen to Terrence and say, "I really liked it, Terrence. Do you think you could fix up those slides?" Or "I felt you did a good job. I feel it would be better with good slides." But saying you like something or you feel something is useless. It reverts to that touchy-feely squishy thinking workplace in which women don't thrive. Eliminate words like *good*, *poor*, *like*, *great*, *feel*, *need*, and *I* when you fashion critiques. Instead, apply the principles of distance and focus on the subject instead of the person. Add precise verbs and you'll soon master the art of criticism—and the art of leadership.

We've explored several ways to distance language for greater power. The easiest and most potent, of course, is elimination of the *I* sentence. Stop, think about the subject you want to discuss (which is never yourself when you critique), start the sentence with the subject (the voice, the report, the slides, the gestures, or whatever), and pick the verb that says precisely what you mean. Here are examples Mignon (and you) might use when evaluating a presentation:

Weak	Powerful
I felt you did a good job. I feel it would be better with good slides.	Terrence, the talk has improved since you started it, but the slides cut your credibility. Professional-looking slides in color with clear captions will reflect well on you.
	or
	Terrence, that overall statement of the thesis worked well. Your subject matter knowledge will emerge more clearly if you start with an overview of topic and use clear slides. Less information on each and the use of color helps make slides more effective.
I loved the thesis statement.	The thesis statement works.
I thought the slides were good.	The slides were easy to read.
I felt you looked skilled.	Your expertise came through.
You felt confident.	You looked confident.
I didn't go for the clenched fist.	The open palm gesture looked friendly.
It made me uncomfortable when you pointed.	Pointing at the audience can appear hostile.
I felt you looked impressive.	You looked impressive when you strode to the podium.
You looked scared and disorganized. Can't you try to be more confident?	Jingling the coins in your pockets and staring at the ceiling was distracting and made you seem insecure. Working without an outline seemed to increase your nervous gestures.

Does all this mean that strong leaders never announce, "I loved it," or "It was terrific," or "Congratulations!"? Of course not—those options stand side by side with the critiques offered here. They just don't equip you to teach or to help, which is your job as leader. Learn to control all the forms, so you can speak the language of success to accentuate the positive and eliminate the negative.

Issue 5: Confronting Tough Personal Issues

Marlene Pendleton, a powerful manager, says, "It's easy for me to criticize any aspect of professional work in a straightforward way. But when someone has a personal habit that interferes with his or her career, such as body odor or poor table manners, I'm so uneasy that I don't talk about it. This is unfair to the person. It's poor management, and I don't know what to do about it."

Because mentoring puts you at the pinnacle of a skill, it acts as the crucible of your success as a leader. Mentors go beyond the easy topics; they care enough about those who work for them to handle even awkward topics.

Personal subjects like body odor, table manners, and work habits seem to discomfort managers most. Indeed, when I raise these issues, leaders say they face them at work and don't know how to handle them. If you learn to approach difficult questions such as these, however, you can approach any complex problem that crops up at work.

Human resource managers, executives, psychologists, and members of my leadership network agree that no flawless answer has emerged for personal problems. They plague managers every day, yet no one has worked out the answers with complete success. Most do exactly what Marlene does; they ignore the issue, thereby failing to fulfill the role of mentor. Because there's no ideal response, here are a number of flawed "answers." If you have successful solutions, please inform others about your methods.

Keep distant

One solution is to tell the truth in the most confidential, most distanced, most objective way you can. Try starting the private discussion with a general comment about the problem. Say that people, fairly or not, often judge others on personal characteristics. Ask if the person ever saw it as an issue. Then, try, "It might be a good idea to rethink your xxx. It's damaging your career."

Write

If the direct approach is unbearable to you, consider writing. The drawback of writing is that it remains forever. The advantage is that you have plenty of time to write carefully. Attempt this only if you're a strong writer and fully in control of perspective. Be sure the hurt to the reader won't erase the benefit.

Use the I statement

I reluctantly concede that this may be a time to violate the principle of "no *I* statements." You could open by admitting how difficult the topic is, saying something like, "Discussing personal characteristics is difficult, but when we all work together, each person's practices affect all of us. That's especially true in our enclosed area, where aromas become more noticeable . . ." One manager thinks the following might work: "I find your xxx unpleasant." Or "My allergies act up when the odor of (garlic, smoking, fabric softener, musk) is close by. Have others mentioned this to you? It's an awkward subject, but it would be much easier for me to work closely with you if that aroma weren't there."

Dr. Virginia Phelan suggests that admitting we don't know how to deal with this issue is an example of what women bring to leadership; men have been raised to believe that there must be a right answer. We know hard questions may have no sure answers, but we'll be stronger leaders if we ask them anyway.

The web, now complete, shimmers with success. It's time to look at where you've come and where you aim to go. Chapter 15 benchmarks your progress and prepares you for the pinnacle of achievement in the language of success—mentoring. Finally, we end this tale with success stories of women like you.

15

Our Heroes, Ourselves: Empower Yourself and Others

We never know how high we are
Till we are asked to rise
And then if we are true to plan
Our statures touch the skies—

The Heroism we recite
Would be a normal thing
Did not ourselves the Cubits warp
For fear to be a King—

EMILY DICKINSON

We've woven the web. You've encountered skills that you learned quickly, skills that will take years to master, and skills you'll want to pass on to others. Women aim high when high performance is demanded or when they demand it of themselves. As Emily Dickinson wrote, fear alone keeps us from being heroes; with courage, "our statures touch the skies." Powerful language gives us the tools to overcome fear so that we can indeed transform ourselves into heroes.

Toward Mastery and Mentoring

This book is about becoming a successful woman, and with success comes responsibility. As you master the skills of powerful language, you'll convey those skills to others. You'll reach the summit of accomplishment when you mentor, just as you've been mentored by the women in these pages. Mentors are more than just models to copy, however. A true mentor helps us to grow by showing her faith in us and teaching us to have faith in ourselves.

Christina A. Gold, the first woman to head Avon Products' United States, Canadian, and Puerto Rican operations, described how a mentor, Mun Lavigne, helped her to grow by challenging her fear of public speaking. Lavigne persuaded Gold to make a management presentation despite her anxiety. "I was afraid of the people who worked for me, so imagine how I felt about addressing management," Gold recalled.

Lavigne recognized her fear and helped her to prepare for the challenge. "I made her polish her speech, look people in the eye, vary her tone of voice. I worked her so hard that by the time we went to New York she wouldn't speak to me on the plane." He continued to challenge her with a series of increasingly difficult jobs. "I'd keep pushing her to try new things . . . we had a love-hate relationship, but we ended up with a lot of love and very little hate."

Just knowing that someone believes in you encourages growth. Becoming a mentor means believing in other women and teaching them to believe in themselves. It made the difference in Christina Gold's work, and it will make the difference in the work of those around you as you master the language of success and mentor others. With encouragement and teaching, all women can grow strong, and our shared strength will transform the business world into a place of success.

Track Your Progress

Mentor yourself by setting goals and tracking your progress. Use the four levels of achievement:

NOVICE	You strive to acquire this new skill.
APPRENTICE	You understand and apply this skill sometimes, but it hasn't entered your everyday repertoire.
MASTER	You understand and control when and how to use this skill.
MENTOR	You've risen beyond mastery to the highest level. You're nurturing this skill in younger or less confident people. You've joined the pantheon of mentors and models.

Decide which level you've attained on each. Track your progress as you grow more adept. Celebrate your successes, and don't let setbacks deter you from your goal.

	Novice	Apprentice	Master	Mentor
Grammar				
Controls *I* statements				
Avoids intimacies				
Trims hedges				
Trashes tags				
Shuns the *f* verb				
Dislikes *like*				
Controls passives				
Copies models				
Strives for correctness, not hypercorrectness				
Modifies accurately				

	Novice	Apprentice	Master	Mentor
Links ideas effectively				
Eliminates excess words				
Understands grammar lingo				
Prefers action verbs				
Matches distance to situation				
Controls passives for distance				
Becomes She Who Must Be Obeyed				
Says "no" when necessary				
Establishes relationships with parallels				
Words				
Pursues precise words				
Grasps connotation				
Hedges powerfully when necessary				
Uses jargon judiciously				
Learns Greek and Latin roots				
Broadens range of metaphors				
Takes advantage of dictionaries and other resources				
Organization				
Follows an organization system				
Speaking				
Scripts talks when appropriate				
Manages time with stop watch				
Eases listeners' memory burden				
Spins effective yarns				
Employs rhetorical techniques				
Displays powerful visuals				
Speaks strongly when seated				
Interviews effectively				

	Novice	Apprentice	Master	Mentor
Body Language				
Incorporates powerful body language				
Strides to the podium				
Controls gestures from head to toe				
Maintains eye contact				
Assumes a suitable resting position				
Manages voice, inflection, and speed				
Savors silence as a tool of power				
Uses confidence-builders				
Style				
Costumes for the role				
Seeks classics				
Dresses down in style				
Conquers tricky dress situations				
Writing				
Writes successfully with powerful forms				
Delivers efficient e-mail				
Follows conventions				
Adheres to the three principles				
Reading				
Reads instrumentally: scans, skims, prereads, deep-reads				
Masters the in-basket				
Reads deeply for analysis, synthesis, criticism, and resistance				
Applies power reading on-line				
Masters oral reading and uses it when appropriate				
Listening				
Listens instrumentally				
Employs a variety of listening skills				

	Novice	Apprentice	Master	Mentor
Recognizes filters that block and distract				
Maintains silence when appropriate				
Benefits from precision listening				
Matches the listening skill to the occasion				
"Listens" to body language				
Empathizes				
Paraphrases				
Clarifies				
Probes				
Listens instructionally				
Managing				
Evaluates leadership level				
Develops leadership skills				
Leads in the language of power				
Emulates Charlotte as mentor and manager				
Embraces versatility				
Accepts credit for accomplishments				
Refuses effectively				
Persuades competently				
Mentors the young				
Transforms weak players				
Managing Complexity				
Understands the Janus Principles				
Accepts and deals with complex situations				
Acknowledges that some problems defy solution				

Happy Endings: The Language of Success

This book started with true stories documenting the failure of the language of weakness at work. Let's end it with true success stories.

LANGUAGE TRANSFORMS A WEAKLING

Lavi Walton is an engineer. Young, bright, and capable, she anticipates a promising future. Yet when we met, she looked, talked, dressed, and walked like a frightened adolescent. She shuffled to the podium for her first talk, averted her eyes, shrunk into herself, and modeled the language of weakness. She spoke so softly we strained to hear her. She littered her sentences with *I* phrases, hedged at every opportunity, and seemed totally out of control. Yet after two days of specific instruction and several videotapes with class critiques, the powerful woman within her emerged. She delivered her course critique proudly, voice strong, head held high. By the time she finished speaking, tears welled in the eyes of several classmates, and the class gave her an ovation. She'd learned to stand up and speak like a woman. Here are excerpts:

> In order to impress upon you the relevance and appropriateness of the language of power, I will first inform you of a situation I encountered, and, second, explain to you how the ideas . . . literally opened my eyes to what had really occurred.

> I was at my weekly group meeting. The purpose . . . was to determine the format for presenting the costs of the Brand A and Brand B machines to customers. The cost for each machine was calculated by two different methods. Therefore, there were two different bottom-line costs for each machine. I commented, I quote:

> "I feel like the two numbers will be a cause of confusion for the customer; therefore I think the numbers should match or be given different titles."

> The group discussed my comment and decided to leave the presentation as it was. I can remember thinking, "Maybe the inconsistency of the numbers won't be a problem for the customer."

Before we presented this information to the customer, our group had to do a dry run for the department head. One of the points the department head made was, I quote:

"The difference in the numbers will be a point of confusion for the customer. The numbers must match or be titled differently."

. . . He had just validated what I thought all along. I even went to my manager and told him that the department head just repeated a comment that I had made earlier. My manager acknowledged this but could not explain why my comment was not accepted. At this point, I let the situation rest.

But not until I learned [the language of success] did I realize what really occurred. The department manager and I had not said the same thing. I said, "I *feel* like the two numbers will be a cause of confusion for the customer; therefore I *think* the numbers should match or be given different titles." He said, "The difference in the numbers *will* be a point of confusion for the customer. The numbers *must* match or be titled differently." It's so obvious now!

My youth is strike one against me. My gender is strike two against me. Strike three was the tentativeness and lack of confidence with which I spoke. But now, I realize there are specific things I can do to compensate for those strikes already against me. To keep from striking out, I must demand respect through powerful language and a powerful image.

Lavi couldn't change her age or her sex, but she could and did change her language. Language changes don't work only for the young. Here's a tale of an executive with a Ph.D.

LANGUAGE PROVIDES THE POWER TO LEAD

Dr. Laurette Black was hired to manage a project that looked beyond hope. It was far behind schedule, and she was expected to pull the project together on time. She was utterly overwhelmed; she'd moved to a new city, a new industry, and a new job, and her first project seemed doomed to fail. Her language reflected her distress and feeling of powerlessness. But as she acquired the language of success, she came to understand that her group could perform well if she could only pull it together.

When the group met to work out the schedule, staff members came in wringing their hands and saying, "I feel terrible about the schedule. It's not going to work," "I feel we've failed before we've begun," and so on. Dr. Black knew that a leader must target the subject, not the feelings. When she told the group, "We're here to work on the schedule, not our feelings," it was as if a light went on. Everyone focused on the schedule, and they met the deadline.

Our successes take different forms. In Chapter 5, you read about how Linda Rubin organized her fund-raising talk. Here's what happened to Linda after the talk she so dreaded.

LANGUAGE LEADS TO OPPORTUNITIES

Linda's extensive preparation enabled her to overcome her fear and show her true delightful and competent self. The talk was a great success, called "brilliant" by one of her colleagues. Eight weeks after the talk, an executive recruiter called Linda about a high-salary development job in a distant city. Linda wasn't looking for a new job, so she asked the recruiter how he'd gotten her name. He told her that he'd talked to development directors in three cities, and all had given her name; all had attended Linda's talk. Like a pebble dropped in a lake, Linda's powerful language had rippled far beyond the immediate circumstances.

Carol Millet faced an unusual communication problem that no man has ever had to deal with. Here's her story.

THE IMPORTANCE OF IMAGE

Carol Millet aimed for a top management job. Requesting a critique of her presentation style, she sent me a videotape of a symposium she'd presented at a national meeting. She was to explain how the research division had arrived at new procedures that everyone in the company had to follow.

The videotape proved a revelation about the problems unique to businesswomen. Carol's short stature and youthful appearance had led people to discount her despite her executive position. On the day of the symposium she was also in the seventh month of pregnancy. The organizers (male) of the meeting had determined that, though the dress code was business casual, the presenters would wear cotton tee shirts emblazoned with the company logo. In addition, microphones were strapped to the presenters' backs. Picture this small, young-looking woman with long blond hair in her seventh month wearing a tee shirt and a microphone pack giving orders to men in business shirt sleeves and women in business suits.

A few substantive weaknesses also prevented Carol's fine presentation from being an outstanding success. For example, she spent too much time introducing herself and mentioned her pregnancy (although it was obvious). Also, because she lacked a script, she slipped into weak language forms such as "I've spent a lot of time . . .," "I'm going to try . . .," ". . . we feel these are a critical few . . .," "I think from a visionary standpoint . . .," "What I need you to do is . . ." The conclusion was flat: she thanked everyone for their time.

Carol's situation revealed specific ways in which men's and women's communications differ. No petite, long-haired blond man in a tee shirt with a microphone strapped to his back has to give major presentations while pregnant. He also doesn't have to explain that he's pregnant. Whatever the appropriateness of the tee shirt may have been for this meeting, it failed as a costume for Carol.

As a result of her consultations, Carol changed one aspect of company policy and three aspects of her presentation. First, she convinced the organizing committee to let presenters decide on their own attire. Second, she resolved to script at least the opening and closing portions of important talks. Third, she learned about the grammar of weakness and shunned it. Finally, she met with a style consultant to improve her professional image.

A few months later Carol gave her next presentation. She shortened and groomed her hair, added enough makeup to avoid looking like a teenager, and attired herself suitably. She also wrote and timed the script for her talk. Preferring not to introduce herself, she arranged for a colleague to do so. He described her as the research team leader who had organized and run the project (no comments on how she looked or how cute she is!). Her introduction already taken care of, she opened and closed her talk with generous comments about audience members. The script kept her from slipping back to weak phrases. These small changes made the difference between an acceptable and a memorable presentation.

Finally, asked to discuss her own growth, Amy Yodanis, a young publishing executive, said, "What is it really about? It's really about management, leadership, and controlling yourself. In constantly evaluating your language, you are also evaluating other people and where they are, the people you have responsibility for. It is beyond the small 'speech' issue and is something much bigger." Amy is right: it really is about something much bigger.

We Can Be Both True Friends and Good Writers

Annette Olin Hill wrote, "A major issue for women . . . is whether they can succeed in traditionally male professions without adopting an exclusively masculine point of view." Your story, and the stories told in this book, affirm that we can. The success stories never tell of women becoming like men. They tell only of women using the language of success to become strong women.

Like the places in which you work, Charlotte's barn was a difficult and not necessarily humane environment, in which the profit motive prevailed. Still, Charlotte managed to lead, to grow, to nurture, to protect the weak, to generate new life, to foster the cooperation of others, and to save the life of her friend. Like Charlotte, women face the challenges of succeeding in the workplace without compromising our integrity, our femininity, or our moral compass. Language is a powerful tool of such success, if we choose to make it so. Like Charlotte, we can be both "true friends" and "good writers."

Bookshelf

Albertini, Kathleen Barry, 3/14/2000, unpublished e-mail.

Axtell, Roger, *Gestures: The Do's and Taboos of Body Language Around the World*. New York: Wiley, 1998.

Baker, Sheridan, *The Practical Stylist*, 2nd ed. New York: Crowell, 1969.

Buchanan, Constance, *Choosing to Lead*. Boston: Beacon Press, 1996.

Burgoon, Judee K, David B. Buller, W. Gill Woodall, *Nonverbal Communications: The Unspoken Dialogue*, New York: McGraw Hill, 1989.

Cho, Emily, *Looking Terrific: Express Yourself Through the Language of Clothing*. New York: Putnam, 1978.

Cook, Jeff Scott, *The Elements of Speechwriting and Public Speaking*. New York: Macmillan, 1989.

Deutsch, Claudia H., "Relighting the Fires at Avon Products." *The New York Times*, April 3, 1994.

Earhart, Amelia, *Last Flight*. New York: Orion Books, 1988.

Erikson, Erik H., *Childhood and Society*. New York: Norton, 1963.

Feierman, Joanne, *Action Grammar*. New York: Fireside, 1995.

Gadiesh, Orit, "True North." Excerpts from a speech, unpublished, July 19, 1992.

Flint, Kate, *The Woman Reader 1837–1914*. Oxford: Oxford University Press, 1993.

Gardner, Howard, *Leading Minds: An Anatomy of Leadership*. New York: Basic Books, 1995.

Goleman, Daniel, "What Makes a Leader?" *Harvard Business Review*, November–December 1998, pp. 92–102.

Goleman, Daniel, "Leadership That Gets Results," *Harvard Business Review*, March–April 2000, pp. 78–90.

Hall, Judy, *Nonverbal Sex Differences*. Baltimore: Johns Hopkins University Press, 1984.

Henley, Nancy, *Body Politics*. Englewood Cliffs, NJ: Prentice Hall, 1977.

Hills, Carla, "U.S. Trade Policy in 1994." Speech presented at the Commonwealth Club of California. Published in *The Commonwealth* (San Francisco), March 11, 1994.

Ivins, Molly, *Nothin' but Good Times Ahead*. New York: Random House, 1993.

Liddell, H. G., and R. Scott, *The Greek-English Lexicon*. New York: Oxford University Press, 1983.

Manguel, Alberto, *A History of Reading*. New York: Viking, 1996.

Marchenese, Kira, April 3, 2000, unpublished e-mail.

Margolic, David, "Remaking of the Simpson Prosecutor." *The New York Times*, October 3, 1994.

McGrory, Mary, "I Have an Attitude About the Information Superhighway." *Rochester Democrat & Chronicle*, March 5, 1994.

McPherson, James, "The Unheroic Hero," *New York Review of Books*, February 4, 1999.

Miller, Laura, "The Digital Reader," *Salon*, 3/31/2000.

Miller, Laura, April 2, 2000, unpublished e-mail.

Mindell, Phyllis, *Power Reading*. NY: Prentice Hall Custom Printing, 1998.

Mitchell, Richard, *Less Than Words Can Say*. Boston: Little Brown, 1979.

O'Brien, Maureen, "Publishing's Best-Kept Secret." *Publisher's Weekly*, April 25, 1994.

O'Connor, Colleen, "Finishing School," *Business 2.0*, April 2000, pp. 336–338.

Pearce, Carol Ann, *Career Chic*. New York: Putnam, the Perigee Group, 1990.

Penelope, Julia, *Speaking Freely*. White Plains, NY: Pergamon Press, 1990.

Radcliffe Public Policy Institute and The Boston Club, "Suiting Themselves: Women's Leadership Styles in Today's Workplace." Cambridge, MA: Radcliffe Public Policy Institute, 1999.

Rivkin, Glenn, "Don't Ever Judge This Consultant by Her Cover." *The New York Times*, May 1, 1994.

Rosener, Judy B., "Ways Women Lead." *Harvard Business Review*, November-December 1990.

Soukhanov, Anne H., *The American Heritage Dictionary*, 3rd ed. Boston: Houghton Mifflin, 1992.

Tannen, Deborah, *Talking from Nine to Five*. New York: William Morrow, 1994.

Tolstoy, Leo, *Anna Karenina*. New York: Penguin Books, 1961.

Tufte, Edward, *The Visual Display of Quantitative Information*. Cheshire, CT: Graphics Press, 1983.

White, E. B., *Charlotte's Web*. New York: Harper & Row, 1952.

About the Author

Dr. Phyllis Mindell is president of Well-Read (wel'-red'). She has published many articles, columns, and research papers on all aspects of language and communications. Her books have earned international attention: *Power Reading* (Prentice Hall) was selected one of the 30 best business books of the year. The first edition of *A Woman's Guide to the Language of Success: Communicating with Confidence and Power* was translated into German and has remained a best-seller for over five years. She and her books have been featured in *The New York Times*, the Gannett Newspapers, Bloomberg Business, and dozens of newspapers, magazines, and television programs in the United States and abroad.

A popular speaker, she keynotes and lectures at national and international conferences, including Association of American Medical Colleges, University of Michigan Medical School, The Chautauqua Institution, The University of Rochester Leadership Institute, Nuclear Regulatory Commission, State of Pennsylvania Leadership Institute, Financial Women International, Hispanic Association of Professionals, The Executive Center, and The Women's Network.

She holds a doctorate from the University of Rochester, a masters degree from the City University of New York, and a bachelors degree from Brooklyn College. Her postdoctoral studies include neurolinguistics, writing, and literature.

She and her husband live and work in Rochester, New York, and Boston, Massachusetts. Their children, Ossie Borosh, Joe, and David, and their grandchild, Arye, light up their lives.

About Well-Read (wel'-red')

Well-Read (wel'-red') designs and presents research-based professional and executive workshops on how to lead, read, write, speak, and listen effectively and efficiently. These are available as public seminars in Rochester, N.Y., and Boston, Mass., and as custom seminars anywhere in the world.

Well-Read's clients communicate clearly, concisely, and powerfully at Corning; McKinsey; Korn/Ferry; Harvard, University of California, Michigan, and Georgetown medical schools; The Metropolitan Opera; Paychex; PriceWaterhouseCoopers; Paine Webber; Eastman Kodak; Xerox; Fidelity; Motorola; National Association of Realtors; Mobil Chemical; Bausch & Lomb; Centocor; Blue Cross & Blue Shield; Xerox European Research Centre; and other large and small companies and nonprofit institutions worldwide.

In addition, an extensive series of women's programs has taught thousands to take their places at the leadership table, on the podium, and in the executive suite. Women's seminars include such titles as "A Woman's Guide to the Language of Success," "Language and Leadership Skills for Women," "Presentation Skills for Senior Level Women," and "Professional Language Skills for Support Staff."

Called "the world's experts on professional communications," the Well-Read family of experts includes specialists in all aspects of language, audiovisual production, film direction, team talk, and style.

Well-Read's Web site offers detailed program information as well as educational articles and recommended books.

You can reach Well-Read and Dr. Phyllis Mindell at:

Phone: 800-245-0806
E-mail: pmindell@well-read.com
Web site: www.well-read.com

Index